Cognitive Behavioral Treatment for Generalized Anxiety Disorder

The second edition of *Cognitive Behavioral Treatment for Generalized Anxiety Disorder* is an essential read for all clinicians, researchers, and anyone who wants to learn about how cognitive behavioral therapy (CBT) can be applied to treatment for generalized anxiety disorder.

Building on the idea that intolerance of uncertainty keeps people with generalized anxiety disorder (GAD) stuck in repeated cycles of excessive worry, anxiety, and avoidance, this revised and updated edition lays out the essentials of GAD assessment and diagnosis, step-by-step illustrations of CBT treatment, and questionnaires and monitoring forms that can be used in assessment, treatment, and research.

Readers will come away from the book with a clear sense of how to:

- design powerful, individualized behavioral experiments targeting the fear of uncertainty;
- help clients discover and re-evaluate their beliefs about the usefulness of worry;
- encourage clients to view worry-provoking problems as challenges to be met, rather than threats;
- use written exposure to help clients confront lingering worries and core fears.

Melisa Robichaud, PhD, is a clinical psychologist specializing in CBT for anxiety disorders, with an emphasis on worry and GAD. She holds clinical faculty positions at University of British Columbia and Simon Fraser University, and is a past President of the Canadian Association of Cognitive and Behavioral Therapies.

Naomi Koerner, PhD, is an associate professor in the Department of Psychology at Ryerson University. She has been conducting research on worry and GAD for over 15 years. Dr. Koerner also works as a clinical psychologist and maintains a private practice.

Michel J. Dugas, PhD, is a professor of clinical psychology at the Université du Québec en Outaouais. Dr. Dugas is a fellow of the Canadian Psychological Association and the Canadian Association of Cognitive and Behavioral Therapies.

"In this thoroughly updated book, Robichaud, Koerner, and Dugas provide *the* definitive, theoretically driven, evidence-based guide to assessing and treating individuals with generalized anxiety disorder (GAD). The six treatment modules provide core strategies for changing patterns of thinking and behaving that maintain anxiety and worry. The book is filled with clinical examples illustrating how the strategies are used, as well as many helpful worksheets and assessment tools. Anyone who works with clients with generalized anxiety disorder should read this book!"

—*Martin M. Antony, PhD, ABPP, Department of Psychology, Ryerson University and author of* The Anti-Anxiety Workbook

"*Cognitive Behavioral Treatment for Generalized Anxiety Disorder* draws upon recent research related to intolerance of ambiguity, misperceptions about the utility of worry and avoidance strategies to develop a comprehensive and progressive model of care. The treatment methods flow in a progressive and clear manner, with many clinical examples and practical tools to help clinician use the ideas. Rooted solidly in science, this book is also highly pragmatic and written in an engaging and easy manner. The three authors are all experts in the field and their knowledge is apparent throughout. This is a must read for anyone who works with patients who struggle with GAD."

—*Keith S. Dobson, PhD, professor of clinical psychology, University of Calgary and president, Canadian Association of Cognitive and Behavioural Therapies (2018–2019)*

"This book presents state-of-art conceptualization, assessment/diagnosis, and evidence-based treatment of GAD. Written by internationally-recognized experts, the second edition of *Cognitive Behavioral Treatment for Generalized Anxiety Disorder* masterfully outlines an efficacious and effective treatment protocol that targets the underlying cause of excessive worry—intolerance of uncertainty. Many excellent, clinically relevant examples are used to guide readers through the model and treatment protocols so they can flexibly apply the armamentarium of strategies to tailor treatment individually and effectively. This book is a must read for clinicians, students, and researchers interested in the optimal treatment GAD."

—*David J. A. Dozois, PhD, C. Psych, professor and director, Clinical Psychology Graduate Program, University of Western Ontario*

"Experts in researching and treating generalized anxiety disorder, Robichaud and colleagues offer sage guidance through current conceptualizations of chronic anxiety and worry as well as a cutting-edge treatment approach that is both novel and well established in cognitive-behavioral empirical foundations. The text is well written, informative, and useful. A worthy addition to the library of any clinician, researcher, or student interested in improving their knowledge of this debilitating condition."

—*Douglas Mennin, PhD, proessor of clinical psychology, Teachers College, Columbia University*

Cognitive Behavioral Treatment for Generalized Anxiety Disorder

From Science to Practice
Second Edition

Melisa Robichaud, Naomi Koerner, and Michel J. Dugas

Routledge
Taylor & Francis Group

NEW YORK AND LONDON

First published 2019
by Routledge
52 Vanderbilt Avenue, New York, NY 10017

and by Routledge
2 Park Square, Milton Park, Abingdon, Oxon, OX14 4RN

Routledge is an imprint of the Taylor & Francis Group, an informa business

Library of Congress Cataloging-in-Publication Data
Names: Robichaud, Melisa, author. | Koerner, Naomi, author. | Dugas,
    Michel J. (Michel Joseph), 1961– author.
Title: Cognitive behavioral treatment for generalized anxiety disorder :
    from science to practice / Melisa Robichaud, Naomi Koerner, and
    Michel J. Dugas.
Description: Second edition. | New York, NY : Routledge, 2019. | Revision
    of: Cognitive behavioral treatment for generalized anxiety disorder /
    Michel J. Dugas, Melisa Robichaud. | Includes bibliographical
    references and index.
Identifiers: LCCN 2018051631 (print) | LCCN 2018051912 (ebook) |
    ISBN 9781315709741 (E-book) | ISBN 9781138888067 (hardback : alk.
    paper) | ISBN 9781138888074 (pbk. : alk. paper)
Subjects: LCSH: Cognitive therapy. | Anxiety disorders—Treatment.
Classification: LCC RC489.C63 (ebook) | LCC RC489.C63 D84 2019
    (print) | DDC 616.89/1425—dc23
LC record available at https://lccn.loc.gov/2018051631

ISBN: 978-1-138-88806-7 (hbk)
ISBN: 978-1-138-88807-4 (pbk)
ISBN: 978-1-315-70974-1 (ebk)

Typeset in Minion
by Apex CoVantage, LLC

To Antony and Carolyn . . . as always—M.R.
To Richard and Dorothy—N.K.
À Céline, Jérémie et Sophie—M.J.D.

Contents

Tables and Appendices

Tables

Appendices

Preface

It has been over 10 years since we wrote the first edition of this book, so it should come as no surprise that our understanding and treatment of generalized anxiety disorder has evolved over time. New research conducted by our team, as well as other investigators, has impacted our theoretical conceptualization of GAD, which in turn allowed us to further refine our treatment protocol as a consequence.

Despite these changes, the goals that we originally devised when setting forth upon writing the first edition of this book have remained the same for this second edition. That is, we wanted this book to integrate the knowledge developed from both research and clinical work in order to be of interest and value to those who study GAD, as well as to those who treat it. Moreover, as scientist-practitioners, we have strived to improve upon our theoretical conceptualization of GAD and its corresponding psychological treatment, by allowing research findings to guide clinical interventions and by translating clinical observations into scientific studies. Hence, the title of our book remains unchanged from the first edition— *Cognitive Behavioral Treatment for Generalized Anxiety Disorder: From Science to Practice*. However, given the symbiotic relationship between research and clinical practice, there is certainly a case that can be made for changing the subtitle to "From Science to Practice and Back Again."

This book is primarily intended for psychotherapists working with individuals with GAD. As such, we have done our best to ensure (although one can never be sure of anything, but more on that later) that the content and style of the book continues to reflect the needs of clinicians. In Chapter 1, we present general information on GAD that sets the stage for the remainder of the book. In Chapter 2, we introduce a cognitive conceptualization of GAD that incorporates both the initial research that informed our understanding of GAD, and the more recent studies that have refined our current conceptualization of the disorder. We have made every effort to present the research findings in a way that "talks to clinicians" and is not overly technical (or overly statistical). We then describe an assessment strategy and present the main instruments for the evaluation of clients with GAD in Chapter 3. Again, although we typically use a comprehensive assessment strategy in our clinical trials, we have limited the presentation of instruments to those that therapists might find most useful in their day-to-day clinical practice. In Chapter 4, we present an overview of the treatment protocol and attempt to give the reader a sense of the "spirit" of therapy. Chapter 5 goes on to provide a step-by-step guide to treatment, with many examples of therapist–client dialogue that is designed to make the treatment "come to life." To increase the clinical usefulness of our guide to treatment, Chapter 5 also includes handouts for all between-session exercises. In Chapter 6, we review the data bearing on the treatment's efficacy. Specifically, the main results from several clinical trials are presented, and secondary findings with regard to treatment mechanisms are also reviewed. Finally, in Chapter 7, we present some of the main factors that can complicate treatment and discuss ways that therapists can address these factors. Throughout the book, we have attempted to strike a balance between the complexity of the research findings and the need for clinicians to have a clearly articulated model and treatment protocol to present to those struggling with GAD. In essence, despite the changes and updates that we have made to both our understanding of GAD and its treatment, our objective in this second edition remains the same. We endeavored to "translate" our research findings into clinical principles and procedures that both therapists and clients can relate to, and we sincerely hope we have reached this goal.

Acknowledgments

Many people have directly and indirectly contributed to this book. After all, our model and treatment are the result of over 25 years of collaborations! Although it is not possible to mention everyone, we would like to acknowledge those who have worked most closely with us. From 1992 to 1998, the GAD research program described herein was originally developed at l'Université Laval in Quebec City. At that time, Robert Ladouceur, Mark Freeston, Eliane Léger, and Patrick Gosselin played key roles in shaping the initial ideas put forth in this book. Since 1998, much of the research has been carried out at Concordia University, Sacré-Cœur Hospital in Montreal, Université du Québec en Outaouais, and Ryerson University. At Concordia University, all of the members of the Anxiety Disorders Laboratory have made valuable contributions to our clinical research program on GAD, including Kristin Buhr, Nina Laugesen, Kylie Francis, Kathryn Sexton, Elizabeth Hebert, Kristin Anderson, Sonya Deschênes, and Eleanor Donegan. Advancements to the clinical application of our GAD model also took place in Vancouver, at the University of British Columbia and the Vancouver CBT Centre. Special thanks go to Adam Radomsky, Sarah Newth, Maureen Whittal, Brandy McGee, Fjola Helgadottir, Jack Rachman, and Peter McLean. We would also like to acknowledge the members of the Cognition and Psychopathology Lab at Ryerson University—a special thanks to Katie Fracalanza, Elizabeth Pawluk, Emma MacDonald, Kathleen Tallon, Melina Ovanessian, Kathleen Stewart, and Bailee Malivoire, whose research and insights have influenced several of our newer ideas regarding the process and treatment of pathological worry. To those listed above, and to all those not listed who have contributed to our thinking on GAD, we sincerely thank you for your work, enthusiasm, and friendship. Without you, this book could not have been written.

CHAPTER 1

Description of Generalized Anxiety Disorder

Catherine was the first of three children. During her childhood, she had often been reminded that, as the eldest child, she should look out for her two younger siblings. By the time Catherine reached the third grade, she had begun worrying about her younger brothers. For example, if it was raining, she worried about whether one of them might catch a cold, or if they played rough games, she worried whether one of them might injure himself. She would often check on them several times a day to make sure that they were safe or to see if they needed anything. Although her worrying was not a problem, she was clearly less carefree than most of her friends. In high school, Catherine succeeded very well in academics and athletics. She always had good grades and was a member of the swimming and track teams. Despite worrying less about her younger brothers, she noticed that she had begun to worry more about the health of her parents, in particular her mother. For example, she had started calling her mother at work, sometimes several times a day, to ensure she was all right. Again, although Catherine did not feel that her worrying was a problem, she had definitely noticed that moderate levels of worry and anxiety were something she often had to deal with.

It was only when Catherine went away to college that her worry and anxiety began to get noticeably out of hand. Being away from home, she found herself worrying more than ever about her family. She had also begun to worry about other things such as her grades, financial situation, and friendships. She started having trouble sleeping, often lying in bed for hours before finally falling asleep. Although she continued to do well in school, she found that preparing for exams was extremely stressful, and this would typically result in Catherine speaking to her teachers or classmates several times to ensure her course notes were correct. In addition, writing papers seemed to take longer than usual because Catherine would read over what she had written several times to reassure herself that she had made no spelling or grammar mistakes.

After college, Catherine began a successful career in marketing, and eventually got married and had two children. Following the birth of her second child, her worry and anxiety began to "spiral out of control," and she decided that it might be time to receive some type of treatment. She described experiencing nearly constant feelings of fatigue, insomnia, and anxiety about "anything and everything."

She also noted that these feelings were beginning to interfere with her family and work life. Although she loved her children very much, she was so worried about their health and safety that she was usually tense and on edge while spending time with them. She found this to be extremely distressing, and she said that she could no longer enjoy happy moments in her life because she was so worried about any negative events that might take place in the future. She was also beginning to feel overwhelmed at work, yet she refused to delegate any responsibilities to other employees, stating that she could only be sure that the work was "done properly" if she did it herself.

Catherine was skeptical about the benefit of any form of psychological treatment, since she thought she had "the worrying gene" and was unlikely to change this part of her character. However, she was tired of "always feeling stressed out and anxious" and was willing to try anything to stop feeling this way. When she presented for treatment, she received an in-depth assessment. Based on her report of excessive worry about a number of daily life events, and her endorsement of somatic symptoms such as fatigue, sleep difficulties, and feelings of restlessness, she was given a diagnosis of generalized anxiety disorder (GAD).

As can be seen from the preceding illustration of Catherine, GAD can easily become quite debilitating, and can greatly reduce one's quality of life. Unfortunately, people afflicted with GAD rarely seek professional help, and when they do, clinicians often have difficulty recognizing the symptoms as being those of GAD. For these reasons, we will attempt to accomplish two major goals in this introductory chapter. The first is to provide a relatively thorough description of the characteristics of GAD. Specifically, we will discuss the history of the diagnostic category, the prevalence and associated features of the disorder, and the impairment that GAD typically engenders. The second goal is to present a "picture" of what GAD looks like from the clinician's point of view. What do we mean when we say "excessive worry and anxiety about a number of events or activities?" What is daily life like for someone with GAD? The above description of Catherine is only one example of the many ways in which GAD clients can present for treatment. It is our hope that, by thoroughly presenting information gathered over the course of our clinical practice, we can begin to provide a detailed picture of this fascinating and complex disorder.

Diagnosis of GAD

Generalized anxiety disorder is a diagnostic category that has undergone several changes within different editions of the *Diagnostic and Statistical Manual of Mental Disorders* (*DSM*; American Psychiatric Association, 1980, 1987, 1994, 2000, 2013). As such, it should come as no surprise that the diagnosis of GAD is at times confusing, even for anxiety disorder specialists. In the following section, we will review the evolution of GAD in the *DSM*, we will describe the changes that have been made to the criteria, and we will discuss the reasons behind these changes. The reader will likely note that while the current diagnostic definition in recent editions of the DSM is greatly improved from earlier editions, there is still much work to be done to arrive at a set of clear and reliable criteria that will increase the ease with which GAD is diagnosed.

History of the Diagnostic Category

The term *GAD* first emerged with the publication of the *DSM-III* (American Psychiatric Association, 1980). At that time, GAD was essentially viewed as a residual disorder because the diagnosis was not made if symptoms of panic disorder, obsessive-compulsive disorder, or phobias were present. The fundamental feature of the disorder was "persistent anxiety" for at least one month, with clients also required to endorse symptoms from three out of four categories, including motor tension, autonomic hyperactivity, apprehensive expectation, and vigilance/scanning.

To improve upon the broad and vague nature of the *DSM-III* diagnostic criteria for GAD, several important changes were made with the *DSM-III-R* (American Psychiatric Association, 1987). First, the core feature of the disorder shifted from persistent anxiety to excessive or unrealistic worry. Moreover, GAD could now be diagnosed in the presence of another mental disorder, so long as the worry and anxiety were unrelated to the other condition, thereby changing GAD from a residual problem to a primary diagnostic entity. The minimum duration required for a diagnosis was changed from one to six months, which is more consistent with the chronic nature of GAD. Despite these improvements, the vague somatic criteria remained, with clients requiring six out of 18 varied symptoms to meet diagnosis.

GAD in the DSM-IV and DSM-5

With the introduction of the *DSM-IV* in 1994, the diagnostic criteria for GAD became significantly streamlined and began to adequately reflect the independence of the disorder. Although excessive worry and anxiety was retained as the main feature of GAD, the term *unrealistic* was dropped and replaced with the notion that the worry is "difficult to control." In addition, the minimum duration requirement of 6 months was retained. Taken together, these two criteria clearly reflect the fundamental nature of GAD as a chronic condition that distinguishes itself from nonclinical worry by a *quantitative* difference in worry frequency and intensity, rather than by a qualitative difference (as was suggested by the term *unrealistic*). The criterion of "excessive and uncontrollable" worry reflects the clinical reality that individuals with GAD generally worry about the same types of things as everyone else does. The difference is that they worry more about them and it is harder to stop worrying once they have started. Indeed, the criterion of "uncontrollable" worry and anxiety was incorporated to distinguish GAD from nonpathological worry (Barlow & Wincze, 1998), highlighting the fact that the difference between GAD and "non-GAD" worry is primarily a matter of degree, not content.

Another notable revision to the criteria in the *DSM-IV* was the exclusion of many somatic symptoms from the diagnosis. Specifically, all the autonomic hyperactivity symptoms were removed, as well as a number of items from the motor tension and vigilance/scanning categories. The exclusion of the hyperactivity symptoms was particularly beneficial because they are more likely to be seen among individuals with panic disorder than those with GAD. As such, prior to this revision, distinguishing between panic disorder and GAD was a significant challenge for clinicians. In the *DSM-IV*, there were only six somatic symptoms linked to a GAD diagnosis, and although all but one (i.e., muscle tension) can also be endorsed by clients suffering from other depressive or anxiety disorders, the six symptoms are reliably found among GAD clients. These include feelings of restlessness or being keyed up, being easily fatigued, experiencing concentration difficulties or mind going blank, muscle tension, and sleep difficulties (typically problems falling or staying asleep).

A final noteworthy change to the *DSM-IV* was the inclusion of "significant distress and impairment" to the GAD criteria. Earlier editions of the *DSM* described GAD as a disorder that engenders only mild social and occupational impairment. The prevailing perception of individuals with GAD was as the "worried well," that is, as people who worry excessively yet are still able to accomplish most of their daily activities while maintaining acceptable levels of well-being and quality of life. Given that worry is a universal experience, it is not surprising that excessive worry might not be viewed as particularly disabling in one's day-to-day life. Yet, both research and clinical experience stand in contradiction to this belief. In fact, a more apt description of people with GAD is as "the walking wounded." Not only do they typically endure symptoms for many years without receiving treatment, but they may also experience significant social and economic disadvantages. For example, individuals with GAD are often divorced or not in a relationship, are more likely to have received disability payments at some time in their lives, and typically have very low annual incomes (e.g., Blazer, Hughes, George, Schwartz, & Boyer, 1991; Hunt, Issakidis, & Andrews, 2002). In addition, they frequently experience significant dissatisfaction with their professional and personal lives, as well as a diminished sense of well-being (Hoffman, Dukes, & Wittchen, 2008; Stein & Heimberg, 2004). As such, the *DSM-IV* revision to the impairment and distress criterion for GAD was more reflective of the actual presentation of the disorder.

It is striking that GAD was, and to some extent still is, viewed as a relatively mild disorder despite its association with poor quality of life, as well as social and occupational impairment. This inaccuracy is most likely due to the fact that the impairment associated with GAD is often compared to that seen in other anxiety disorders. For example, when discussing the interference in the daily lives of individuals with panic disorder, social anxiety disorder, or obsessive-compulsive disorder, the associated impairment is often quite obvious. Specifically, individuals with these disorders can engage in time-consuming and fear-driven behaviors as well as physical avoidance of specific places or events, rendering the disability apparent to both themselves and those around them. For example, an individual with obsessive-compulsive disorder characterized by contamination concerns might wash her hands so excessively that they bleed, or a person with panic disorder might become so fearful of having a panic attack that he rarely leaves the house. In contrast, the majority of individuals with GAD do not engage in behaviors that visibly demonstrate marked interference, nor do they necessarily appear particularly distressed or impaired by their symptoms. Rather, the lives of GAD clients are often fraught with subtle interference. For example, they might have difficulty concentrating on specific tasks at work because they are worrying about their retirement or fail to enjoy a weekend get-together with friends because they are concerned about the upcoming work week. Because these types of worries are commonplace among GAD clients, they have a considerable negative impact on productivity on a professional level (more on that later) and pleasure on a personal level (for example, clients are too preoccupied with potential problems to enjoy the pleasures of life). Further, due to the longstanding nature of the disorder, there is an additive effect to these interferences, and feelings of demoralization and exhaustion are often the end result of years of worrying. Consequently, although the impairments caused by GAD are sometimes less obvious, they are no less detrimental to one's quality of life and are therefore of significant clinical concern.

Although the *DSM-5* Working Group for anxiety and related disorders suggested a number of significant changes to the diagnostic criteria for GAD (see Andrews et al., 2010), ultimately the definition of GAD was (for all intents and purposes) unchanged in the fifth edition of the manual. Thus, the preceding discussion of the *DSM-IV* criteria for GAD also applies to the current conceptualization of the diagnosis of GAD.

In summary, it is clear that the way in which GAD is conceptualized (and ultimately diagnosed) has undergone sweeping changes since 1980 when it first appeared in the *DSM*. Successive editions of the *DSM* have attempted to define GAD in terms that are more specific, as well as more reflective of basic and applied research on worry, anxiety, and GAD. However, although our current ability to diagnose the disorder has definitely improved across revisions, GAD remains the anxiety disorder with the lowest diagnostic reliability (Brown, Di Nardo, Lehman, & Campbell, 2001). In other words, clinicians have considerable difficulty agreeing on the presence or absence of GAD, more so than for any other anxiety disorder. Thus, although the field has come a long way, much remains to be done before the reliability of the diagnosis of GAD reaches an ideal level.

Clinical Picture: What Does GAD Look Like?

As is evident from the prior section, the *DSM-5* sets out diagnostic criteria that are relatively helpful for the purposes of diagnosis; however, it does not fully capture the clinical presentation of GAD. In the following sections, we will describe some of the subtleties of the clinical picture of clients with GAD, with a special emphasis on their subjective experience.

Worry Themes

As noted previously, the cardinal feature of GAD is excessive and uncontrollable worry and anxiety about a number of events or activities. However, the criterion of excessive worry about "a number of events or activities" can be confusing to clinicians unfamiliar with GAD. Would an individual who worries excessively and uncontrollably about two situations (for example, health and social interactions) meet this diagnostic criterion? In our experience, the answer to this question is most often "no." We have observed that clients who report worry about a very limited number of subjects usually do not have GAD. As a result, it is best to be vigilant for other disorders that may better capture the presenting symptoms. For example, for someone who worries only about health and social interactions, separate diagnoses of illness anxiety disorder (health anxiety) and social anxiety disorder may be warranted.

Clients with GAD really do tend to worry about many different things. Often, when asked what they worry about, GAD clients will reply: "What *don't* I worry about?" In this sense, the "generalized" aspect of GAD is an apt moniker, as the content of their worries is generalized to almost everything in their lives. There are of course exceptions to this, where a client's worries focus on only two or three particular topics, but this is not the case for most GAD clients. Typically, a diagnosis of GAD implies that the client worries about "almost everything." In addition, the worries of GAD clients can spiral from one topic to another. For example, a client might begin worrying about his health ("What if I develop cancer?") and subsequently worry about his family and finances (for example, "Who will take care of my kids if I die? Will they be well provided for? What if my family can't afford the funeral?").

Clinicians will often ask what exactly GAD clients worry about. The short answer to this question is that they worry about the same things that everyone else does (hence, worry about daily life situations). That is, they frequently cite worry themes that include family, relationships, work/school, health, and finances. Both research findings and clinical experience indicate that the worries of GAD clients generally are not different in *content* from the worries of nonanxious individuals. There are, however, two subtle differences that have been observed in terms of GAD worry. First, it appears that people with GAD consistently worry more about *minor matters* than both nonclinical individuals and people with other anxiety disorders (Brown, Moras, Zinbarg, & Barlow, 1993; Hoyer, Becker, & Roth, 2001). In fact, minor matters seem to be the worry topic that is most sensitive to GAD. Indirect support for this was provided by Di Nardo (1991, cited in Brown, O'Leary, & Barlow, 1993), who found that a negative response to the question "Do you worry excessively about minor matters?" could effectively rule out a diagnosis of GAD.

GAD clients also tend to worry more about unlikely or remote future events than do other anxious individuals (Dugas, Freeston et al., 1998). For example, they might worry about their plane crashing even though the likelihood of this occurring is very slight or worry about how to pay for their unborn children's university education. Despite these differences (i.e., worry about minor matters and unlikely/remote future events), it can be said that individuals with GAD do not generally worry about topics that are particularly different or unique. Rather, for the most part, they simply worry *more* about the same things as everyone else.

Living in the Future

Individuals with GAD almost always report a poor quality of life, and much of this has to do with their tendency to live "in the future." Stated differently, they have great difficulty living in the moment. Even when they are involved in something pleasant, they often do not enjoy themselves because they are too busy worrying about various future events. For example, a client with GAD might spend an evening at a party worrying about the clean-up afterward or have difficulty falling asleep the night before a dental appointment because they are worried about being late for the appointment. The future orientation of individuals with GAD is often apparent right from the first therapy session. For example, the client might ask "Will this therapy work for me?" or "How long will it take before I feel better?" It may even be difficult for the clinician to obtain information about the client's current state because of this tendency to discuss the future.

Although some would argue that living in the future has advantages, such as being better prepared for situations that might occur, it is clear that an excessive future orientation prevents one from enjoying moments in the here and now. In fact, many clients with GAD report that they are unable to enjoy themselves because they are constantly thinking about what might happen next. Research has shown that individuals with GAD tend to have thoughts beginning with "What if . . .?" Clearly, it is difficult to enjoy the present moment when one is thinking thoughts such as, "What if I can't meet my deadline at work?"; "What if my child gets terribly sick?"; and "What if my husband decides to leave me?"

GAD Client Presentations

Although this topic will be discussed in greater detail in Chapter 3, it is of interest to know how GAD clients appear upon presentation. In terms of initial contact during assessment, many GAD clients do not appear particularly anxious or nervous. Unlike patients with panic disorder or obsessive-compulsive disorder, where the anxiety associated with presenting for treatment is often immediately visible (for example, the client is nervous/fidgety and expresses feelings of anxiety at the outset), GAD clients might initially appear calm and composed. However, one is struck by the second impression that begins to form once GAD clients are encouraged to discuss their worries. Some clients might disclose having gotten little or no sleep the night before as a result of worrying all evening about being late for the appointment. They may also describe elaborate worry chains and a nearly constant background of anxiety due to the frequency of their worries. Moreover, diagnostic interviews conducted with GAD clients can be quite lengthy because they often wish to provide exhaustive detail to all questions out of fear of providing insufficient or inaccurate information (e.g., "What if I forgot to mention something important? What if treatment does not go well because of something I didn't explain?").

As much as clients with the same diagnosis can exhibit a similarity in symptoms, so too can there be stark differences in their presentation. While many clients with

GAD can initially present as minimally anxious and only mildly impaired in their daily lives, a more severe presentation can at times also be observed. In such cases, clients may report marked anxiety, being easily overwhelmed by even minor tasks that were well managed in the past, or significant procrastination or avoidance of daily life obligations, as well as the emergence of depressive or dysthymic symptoms due to the longstanding nature of worry and anxiety. As noted earlier, GAD clients are often seen as the "worried well," and as a result more severe presentations can be misdiagnosed, with the assumption that the anxiety and associated distress and impairment is "too severe" to be attributable to GAD. Assessment techniques to correctly identify GAD irrespective of the presentation type will be discussed at length in Chapter 3.

Although the cardinal feature of GAD is excessive worry, it is noteworthy that it is not always described as such by clients. Specifically, clients will sometimes *not* use the term *worry* when describing their symptoms; therefore, clinicians will occasionally need to inquire about symptoms using different terminology. For example, in general it can be said that much of the excessive and uncontrollable worry that GAD clients engage in is done in an attempt to mentally plan and prepare for any eventuality in the future. As such, GAD worry can be seen as extensive "scenario building," which usually takes the following form: "What if X happens? Well, then I could do. . . . But what if Y happens? Well, then I might do . . ." Given this, if the clinician suspects the presence of GAD even though the client denies worrying, then the clinician can inquire about scenario building.

If clients do not always describe their symptoms as worries, to what do they refer to instead? Some GAD clients will describe their worries as fears, thereby making their problem appear to be a phobia rather than GAD. For example, an individual with GAD might describe a "fear" of driving, but upon further questioning the client voices this fear as a series of "what if" statements: "What if I get into an accident and end up in the hospital? What if we can't pay the hospital bills and have to sell the house? What if I lose my job from being out of work due to an accident?" Although the use of words such as *fear* or *anxiety* rather than *worry* is simply the particular way in which some clients express their symptoms, the avoidance of the term *worry* can also be due to the belief that worry is not a legitimate mental health complaint. That is, some clients might choose to describe their distress as *fear* or *anxiety* since these words may appear to be more indicative of a mental health disorder than the term *worry*.

The Case of Catherine

In keeping with our description of the clinical presentation of GAD, we will briefly review the course of Catherine's symptoms as depicted in the case illustration at the beginning of this chapter. Generally speaking, we can see an escalation of Catherine's worries and anxiety throughout her life. As a child, she worried about the health of her siblings, and although these worries diminished over the years, she developed new concerns consistent with the changes in her life. For example, her worries focused on academic performance when she was attending college;

however, her concerns shifted to work and the health of her children after she was employed and married with two kids. Her somatic symptoms also appear to have progressively increased over the years. While in college, Catherine began to experience significant sleep disturbance, "often lying in bed for hours before she finally fell asleep." After the birth of her second child, Catherine's somatic symptoms increased to an unmanageable level, as she reported near constant feelings of fatigue, tension, and restlessness. In our experience, it is the presence of increasingly severe and unmanageable somatic symptoms that often serves as the impetus for clients to ultimately seek treatment. This appears to be the case with Catherine, who stated that she was "sick and tired of always feeling stressed out and anxious." In fact, it is unlikely that she expected treatment to address her excessive worries in any way, as she stated that she believed herself to have "the worrying gene."

It is of interest to note that Catherine also engaged in many GAD-related safety behaviors over the years in an attempt to deal with or reduce her worries and anxiety. For example, when her worries about her mother's well-being escalated, she began calling her repeatedly during the day to ensure that she was all right. While in college, she began seeking excessive reassurance from her classmates and professors to ensure that her notes were correct, and she would often reread her papers to make sure that there were no mistakes. These safety behaviors later continued when she started working, where despite feeling overwhelmed by her responsibilities at work, Catherine would not delegate any tasks to other employees in order to ensure that the work was "done properly." These safety behaviors not only served to maintain her symptoms, but likely also exacerbated her feelings of fatigue and general anxiety.

One of the most noteworthy points in Catherine's case is the interference and distress caused by her symptoms. Specifically, we see a gradual decrease in her quality of life throughout the years, despite the high standard of performance she maintained in her professional and personal life (i.e., academic excellence, successful career, and rewarding family life). Early on, she described herself as feeling "less carefree" than other children who were her age, and as she advanced through high school and college, she appeared to be constantly struggling with chronic stress and anxiety. The decrease in her quality of life reached an apex following the birth of her second child, when she began feeling "tense and on edge" whenever she spent time with her children. Although some GAD clients can exhibit marked interference in their lives through social or occupational impairment (for example, interpersonal difficulties or job loss), Catherine's decreased joy and quality of life, despite her noticeable successes, is a good example of the at times paradoxical presentation of GAD. That is, some clients appear deceptively functional: They can outwardly present as high functioning through their ability to maintain a good career and family life but are nevertheless quite impaired by their symptoms. Many GAD clients describe feeling like a fraud because of the dichotomy of appearing outwardly functional despite being in great distress internally. Over time, individuals like Catherine might report extreme fatigue due to overwork and a need "to do everything" themselves. Ultimately, they can experience feelings of "burnout" as a result of their chronic worry and anxiety.

Epidemiology

Given that GAD is a chronic disorder that often leads to significant distress and impairment, research on the prevalence and associated features of the disorder can provide answers to vitally important questions. That is, how many people suffer from GAD? Are women or men more likely to be diagnosed with the disorder? When do symptoms typically begin to occur, how long do they last, and do they occur in isolation? The following sections will address these questions by presenting epidemiological data on GAD obtained in both community and clinical settings.

Prevalence in the General Population

Given the numerous changes to the diagnostic criteria of GAD over the years, one might expect that it would be difficult to report GAD prevalence rates with any accuracy. Specifically, many of the large-scale epidemiological studies on prevalence were conducted using the *DSM-III* and *DSM-III-R* criteria, which are quite different from the criteria seen in the *DSM-IV* and *DSM-5*. As such, it would not be surprising if the prevalence rates changed markedly from study to study. However, this does not appear to be the case. In terms of community studies, where individuals from the general population are queried about symptoms for various mental health disorders, the prevalence rates are *relatively* uniform. In terms of one-year prevalence rates, the likelihood of GAD is approximately between 2 and 4%, whereas lifetime prevalence rates hover between 4 and 7% (see Table 1.1 for actual rates across studies). In other words, 2 to 4% of the population will meet

Table 1.1 Prevalence Rates for GAD in Three Large-Scale Community Studies Using *DSM-III, DSM-III-R,* and *DSM-IV* Criteria

Study	One-Year GAD (%)	Lifetime GAD (%)
Epidemiologic Catchment Area (ECA) study[a] (*DSM-III* criteria)	2 – 3.6	4.1 – 6.6
National Comorbidity Survey (NCS)[b] (*DSM-III-R* criteria)	3.1	5.1
Australian National Survey of Mental Health and Well-Being[c] (*DSM-IV* criteria)	3.6	n/a
National Comorbidity Survey Replication (NCS-R)[d,e] (*DSM-IV* criteria)	3.1	5.7

[a] *Blazer et al. (1991).*
[b] *Wittchen, Zhao, Kessler, and Eaton (1994).*
[c] *Hunt et al. (2002).*
[d] *Kessler, Chiu, Demler, Merikangas, and Walters (2005).*
[e] *Kessler, Berglund, Demler, Jin, Merikangas, and Walters (2005).*

criteria for GAD in any given year, whereas 4 to 7% of the population will develop GAD at some point in their lives. While this does not make GAD the most common mental health problem, it is clear that a considerable proportion of the general population is at risk for either having GAD or developing it at some point in the future. In fact, the aforementioned rates might be an underestimation of the actual prevalence of GAD in the community. As noted by Kessler and colleagues (Kessler, Walters, & Wittchen, 2004) in their excellent review on the epidemiology of the disorder, some uncertainty still remains about the basic epidemiological characteristics of GAD. This appears to be the result of difficulties in cross-study comparisons due to changing *DSM* criteria, as well as continued debate over the appropriate criteria and thresholds for a diagnosis of GAD. The authors conjecture that the true point prevalence of the disorder in the community might actually be as high as 5 to 8%. Further studies are needed to determine the precise rate of GAD among the general population.

Prevalence in the Clinical Population

When we move from the community to primary care settings, there is a dramatic increase in the prevalence of GAD. Based on several investigations, including a multicenter study conducted by the World Health Organization, 8% of all people who seek primary care treatment meet diagnostic criteria for GAD (Maier et al., 2000; Üstün & Sartorius, 1995). Moreover, among individuals seeing their physicians for a mental health problem, 25% have a diagnosis of pure GAD (that is, no comorbid conditions). Indeed, GAD is the *most frequent* anxiety disorder, and the *second most frequent* of all mental disorders, in primary care facilities (Barrett, Oxman, & Gerber, 1988; Wittchen et al., 2002). GAD is therefore not only a debilitating disorder that is associated with poor quality of life; it is also a highly common problem, particularly in clinical settings.

Age of Onset, Course, and Remission

The age of onset for GAD has a bimodal distribution, with two periods when individuals are at greatest risk for developing the disorder. Approximately two-thirds of individuals with GAD experience an early onset of the disorder that occurs between the ages of 11 and the early 20s. However, a significant minority experiences a late onset of the disorder that develops in middle adulthood (Blazer, Hughes, & George, 1987; Brown, Barlow, & Liebowitz, 1994). In early onset GAD, there is usually no dramatic life stressor or shift from an earlier condition that precipitates the development of the disorder, although a gradual increase in responsibilities and transitional challenges characteristic of adolescence might play a significant role (Cole, Peeke, Martin, Truglio, & Seroczynski, 1998; Sprujit-Metz & Sprujit-Metz, 1997). In contrast to the insidious development of early-onset GAD, it appears that a significant life stressor (for example, the death of a loved one or a major life transition) is more likely to be the precipitating factor for late-onset GAD (Hoehn-Saric, Hazlett, & McLeod, 1993).

Irrespective of the age at which the disorder developed, the symptoms of GAD are generally chronic and unremitting in nature. Moreover, although there are fluctuations in the severity of GAD over time, with increases in GAD severity usually occurring in response to life stressors, episodes of the disorder commonly persist for over 10 years (Kessler, Keller, & Wittchen, 2001; Stein, 2004). Yet, despite the unremitting course of the disorder, many individuals with GAD will wait over 25 years before presenting for treatment (Rapee, 1991).

In terms of remission, GAD symptoms rarely abate naturally over time. In a large-scale study conducted by the Harvard/Brown Anxiety Research Program (HARP; Yonkers, Warshaw, Massion, & Keller, 1996) to investigate the natural history of GAD, only 15% of the participants showed full remission of their symptoms after one year, 25% showed remittance at two years, and 38% at five years. However, remission was determined if the participants were symptom-free for eight consecutive weeks. As GAD symptoms can wax and wane over time, these percentages are overestimations of actual remission rates. In fact, a substantial number of participants were later found to have "relapsed," highlighting the persistence of GAD symptoms and the chronicity of the disorder. In essence, unless individuals with GAD receive some form of treatment for their symptoms, they will likely continue to experience excessive worry and anxiety throughout most of their lives.

Age and Gender Differences

In terms of the gender makeup of GAD, it seems that the disorder is more commonly seen among women than it is among men, and this finding has been reliably and consistently shown in a great deal of research. For example, in the National Comorbidity Survey (NCS) and the Epidemiologic Catchment Area (ECA) study, both of which are large-scale U.S. investigations of mental health prevalence rates in the community, women reported virtually double the rates of GAD than did men. Specifically, in terms of one-year prevalence rates, approximately 4% of women were identified with GAD compared to 2% of men (Blazer et al., 1991; Wittchen et al., 1994).

The finding that women are more likely to have a diagnosis of GAD than men is consistent with the findings obtained for many other anxiety disorders. In the NCS, prevalence rates were found to be higher among women for panic disorder, agoraphobia, social anxiety disorder, and specific phobia. In fact, prevalence rates for having any anxiety disorder ranged from 22 to 30% for women, compared to 12 to 20% for men (Kessler et al., 1994), and this finding was maintained in the NCS Replication study, with a ratio of 1.9 to 1 for the development of any internalizing disorder (i.e., anxiety and depressive disorders) in women (Kessler, Chiu et al., 2005). A host of psychosocial and biological theories have been advanced to account for this gender difference, all of which may have an additive effect on the report of anxiety among women, but no definitive answer as to why women report more anxiety concerns than do men has yet been identified.

Although the relationship between gender and GAD seems to be relatively clear, age has a more complicated association with the disorder. For example, although several epidemiological studies found the highest prevalence rates for GAD in middle age (ages 35 to 55) and the lowest rates among older adults over the age of 55 (e.g., Blazer et al., 1991; Kessler, Berglund et al., 2005; Wittchen et al., 2002), studies on GAD and aging have revealed a different pattern. Specifically, GAD appears to be the most common disorder among older adults, and there might in fact be a steady increase of GAD rates with age, even for those over 65 (Beekman et al., 1998; Carter, Wittchen, Pfister, & Kessler, 2001). To further complicate the issue of age and GAD, a study on worry among older adults found that those in the 75 or older age category were significantly less worried than those in the 65 to 74 age category (Doucet, Ladouceur, Freeston, & Dugas, 1998), thereby contradicting the notion that GAD rates steadily increase into old age.

These discrepancies in the reported presence of GAD according to age group might be due to several factors. First, since GAD is a chronic disorder with a low rate of remission, it would be expected that middle-aged adults would have a higher lifetime risk for developing the disorder than others in younger age groups. Second, in terms of the discrepancy in the prevalence rates for older adults, it appears that anxiety disorders go undiagnosed in many older adults because they may also have health problems with symptoms that are similar enough to those seen in anxiety disorders to mask the presence of GAD (Stanley & Novy, 2000). As a result, the identification of GAD, and ultimately the reported rates, might differ from study to study, depending on the accuracy with which GAD is differentiated from physical health complaints. In practical terms, it is difficult to state with any confidence which age group is most likely to have a diagnosis of GAD. However, since we know that the disorder frequently begins in adolescence or early adulthood, and is both chronic and unlikely to remit on its own, we can assume that from middle adulthood onward the rates of GAD are likely to be relatively high.

Comorbidity

In epidemiological studies of GAD, a consistent finding has been that the vast majority of people with the disorder have other diagnosed problems as well. Specifically, over 90% of individuals who meet criteria for GAD in a given year will also have at least one other *DSM-IV* diagnosis (see Table 1.2 for a list of comorbid conditions). Depressive disorders are the most common comorbid conditions; however, more than half of GAD clients will have an additional anxiety disorder as well (for example, social anxiety disorder, panic disorder).

The fact that GAD has such a high rate of comorbidity with other disorders has led several anxiety disorder experts to debate whether GAD can actually be considered a distinct disorder in its own right. That is, because individuals with GAD rarely present without other problems, there is some controversy as to whether GAD is an independent disorder or simply a "prodromal" condition that serves to promote the development of other anxiety or depressive disorders (e.g., Akiskal, 1998; Maser, 1998; Roy-Byrne & Katon, 1997). Through several independent lines of inquiry, including studies on the specificity of symptoms to GAD (e.g., Brown, Chorpita, & Barlow, 1998; Maier et al., 2000), the contention that the disorder

Table 1.2 Prevalence of Comorbid *DSM-IV* Disorders for Individuals with GAD

DSM-IV *Disorder*	One-Month GAD (%)[a]	One-Year GAD (%)[b]
Alcohol abuse/dependence	8.2	6.4
Nicotine dependence	n/a	14.0
Drug abuse/dependence	5.8	1.4
Major depression	39.3	59.0
Dysthymia	17.7	36.2
Panic disorder	13.9	21.5
Agoraphobia without panic	5.2	11.3
Social anxiety disorder	21.2	28.9
Specific phobia	n/a	29.3
Phobia NOS	n/a	10.6
Obsessive-compulsive disorder	5.8	10.0
Post-traumatic stress disorder	12.4	n/a
Any somatoform disorder*	n/a	48.1
Any eating disorder	n/a	2.5
Any depressive disorder	44.9	70.6
Any anxiety disorder	37.4	55.9
Any of the above disorders	67.8	93.1

[a]*Data taken from the Australian National Survey of Mental Health and Well-Being:* Hunt et al. (2002).
[b]*Data taken from the Mental Health Supplement of the German National Health Interview:* Carter et al. (2001).
*The category "any somatoform disorder" includes pain disorder, hypochondriasis (illness anxiety disorder), and somatization.

is not a unique diagnostic entity has been largely disproved. First, when lifetime prevalence is considered, the rate of comorbidity among individuals with GAD is not any greater than what is seen in individuals with other anxiety disorders. In the NCS, although the great majority of individuals with lifetime GAD had at least one lifetime comorbid disorder, this was equally the case for those with other anxiety and depressive disorders. Second, research has shown that the temporal priority of GAD is similar to that seen for most other anxiety and depressive disorders. In other words, the onset of GAD does not *systematically* precede or follow the onset of comorbid conditions. The one exception to this rule appears to be that GAD often emerges as the first disorder for individuals who experience comorbid major depressive disorder (Kessler et al., 2004). Because of the chronic and unremitting nature of GAD, it should certainly come as no surprise that a longstanding struggle with GAD symptoms might have negative repercussions on one's mood. Put simply, feeling constantly worried and anxious for an extended amount of time is most likely quite depressing. To some extent, the fact that GAD often occurs prior to depression is consistent with this hypothesis.

The Cost of GAD

Despite early contentions that GAD leads to minimal functional impairment due to its subtle (yet insidious) presentation, GAD actually exerts a high cost on quality of life. Research into the burden of GAD on the individual has identified significant impairments on multiple quality of life indices, such as social and occupational functioning, on par with those seen in major depressive disorder and chronic medical conditions (Hoffman et al., 2008). However, beyond the cost to the individual suffering from GAD, there is also a significantly high cost to society as a whole. When examining the economic burden of mental health problems, two broad categories have typically been considered: direct and indirect costs (Dupont et al., 1996; Greenberg et al., 1999). Direct costs refer to health care utilization, including consultations with various medical and mental health practitioners, emergency room visits, and use of medication. Indirect costs typically relate to poor work productivity, absenteeism in the workplace, financial dependence (for example, social assistance, employment insurance), and caregiver burden. For GAD, the cost to society, both direct and indirect, is surprisingly substantial (see Koerner et al., 2004, for a review).

Direct Costs

Taking all anxiety disorders into consideration, it appears that a diagnosis of GAD is associated with one of the highest rates of health care use. In the NCS, 66% of individuals with GAD reported seeking professional help for their symptoms (Wittchen et al., 1994). A similar finding emerged in the Australian National Survey of Mental Health and Well-Being, where over half of individuals with a GAD diagnosis reported consulting with health care professionals. Interestingly, of those seeking help, only 14% consulted a mental health specialist (Hunt et al., 2002). Rather, when individuals with GAD seek help, they typically seek out the services of family physicians, nurses, and medical specialists, which often results in numerous unnecessary medical tests that are highly costly. In fact, GAD clients overuse these primary care resources at a surprisingly high rate, as they have been found to report double the average number of visits to primary care facilities when compared to depressed clients (Wittchen et al., 2002). In terms of visits to nonmental health specialists, the data show that individuals with GAD have very high consultation rates, in particular with cardiologists and gastroenterologists (Kennedy & Schwab, 1997; Logue et al., 1993). Most disturbing though is that despite their numerous medical visits, less than 10% of GAD clients receive adequate psychological or pharmacological treatment (Wittchen, 2002). This is likely due to the fact that the diagnosis of GAD is often "missed" in frontline care. In practical terms, these findings highlight the fact that a misdiagnosis of GAD is costly not only to the individual, who ends up suffering for years from a treatable condition, but also to society, as untreated GAD costs the health care system dearly in terms of time, money, and medical resources.

Indirect Costs

In addition to the burden of GAD on the health care system, undiagnosed and untreated GAD also has a deleterious impact on work productivity. In the Australian epidemiological study, more than half of the sample had taken at least one disability day in the past month that they attributed to their anxiety (Hunt et al., 2002). Another study showed that approximately one third of individuals with GAD showed a reduction in work productivity of 10% or more, and 11% decreased their work productivity by half as a result of their anxiety (Wittchen, Carter, Pfister, Montgomery, & Kessler, 2000). The impact of these indirect costs was underscored in a U.S. study on the annual cost of anxiety disorders in 1990. It was determined that $42 billion to $47 billion was spent that year alone as a result of anxiety disorders. Although most of that cost was attributed to psychiatric and nonpsychiatric medical treatment, reductions in work productivity accounted for 10% of that amount (that is, more than $4 billion; Greenberg et al., 1999). In a more recent study of the financial impact of anxiety on U.S. health care, it was estimated that over $33 billion was spent yearly on direct medical expenditures for anxiety disorders (Shirneshan et al., 2013). Despite the fact that these figures represent the cost of all anxiety disorders, the contribution of GAD is substantial. Given that a diagnosis of GAD is associated with the overuse of health care services and reduced productivity over years of employment (due to the chronicity of the disorder), it represents a significant burden on the economy and an important public health concern.

Summary and Concluding Remarks

GAD is unique among the anxiety disorders in that it is a relatively new diagnostic category. Its first official introduction into the mental health vernacular was in 1980 with the third edition of the *DSM*. Since then, GAD has gone through several revisions in its criteria, and it has been the subject of much debate, particularly in terms of its place in the *DSM* as a distinct diagnostic entity. Most interestingly, basic research and epidemiological studies have gradually changed the perception of GAD from a residual disorder with mild associated impairment to a highly prevalent, chronic, and disabling disorder that exerts a high economic burden on society.

GAD is also a disorder that exhibits the lowest diagnostic reliability of all the anxiety disorders and is frequently misdiagnosed and either treated inappropriately or not at all. Because so many GAD clients seem to be "slipping through the cracks" of the health care system (despite their overuse of that system), it is vital that clinicians become adept at identifying, understanding, and ultimately treating GAD. As such, the following chapters will be devoted to the following:

- We will endeavor to give clinicians an understanding of the cognitive behavioral processes that underlie the disorder through the exposition of an empirically supported model of GAD.

- We will provide helpful strategies and guidelines that will aid clinicians in recognizing the symptoms of GAD and enable them to conduct a thorough assessment.
- We will describe a treatment for GAD based on our cognitive behavioral model, with primary importance being placed on the role of intolerance of uncertainty in the maintenance of the disorder.
- We will review the data on the treatment's efficacy and provide potential solutions to the factors that can complicate treatment.

It is our hope that this book will be a helpful resource for clinicians working with GAD clients. Although their unique presentation is at times subtle, and a learning curve can be expected in terms of gaining proficiency in the assessment and treatment of the disorder, we believe that increased familiarity with the presentation and inner workings of GAD will properly demystify the disorder. We have attempted to incorporate as many practical tips and strategies as possible for the diagnosis and treatment of GAD, in order to maximize the benefit of this book for clinicians working with individuals suffering from GAD.

CHAPTER 2

A Cognitive Behavioral Conceptualization of Generalized Anxiety Disorder

In this chapter, we present the theoretical and empirical basis of our cognitive behavioral conceptualization of generalized anxiety disorder (GAD). Given that our main goal is to prepare the reader for subsequent chapters describing our cognitive behavioral treatment, we have chosen not to present other models of GAD here. The reader should keep in mind, however, that other biological, environmental, and psychological models of GAD have received considerable empirical support. By not formally presenting these models, we do not mean to imply that they have less scientific and clinical value than our conceptualization; only that they are not germane to the treatment described in this book. We refer to the work of others, of course, in instances where we have integrated their ideas into our own conceptualization of chronic worry.

Before we begin, we would like to tell the reader about the history and evolution of our cognitive behavioral conceptualization of GAD. The model, which we developed over 20 years ago, has one principal feature, intolerance of uncertainty, and three associated features which we regard as secondary: positive beliefs about worry, negative problem orientation, and cognitive avoidance (Dugas, Gagnon, Ladouceur, & Freeston, 1998).

From the start, we viewed intolerance of uncertainty as the "backbone" of the model. Accordingly, when our research group developed a conceptual diagram to depict our initial ideas regarding the interconnections among intolerance of uncertainty, positive beliefs about worry, negative problem orientation, and cognitive avoidance, we positioned intolerance of uncertainty in the backdrop of the figure (see Dugas, Gagnon et al., 1998). We always considered intolerance of uncertainty to be a *higher order, primary process* that contributes to the three other components. From an empirical point of view, many years of testing supported this conceptualization by showing that the relationship between GAD and the three other model components can be explained, at least partially, by level of intolerance of uncertainty. From a clinical perspective, the data suggested that intolerance of uncertainty should be addressed at all phases of therapy. Intolerance of uncertainty is undoubtedly the most important feature of our theoretical model. Accordingly, this is the component of the model we discuss most extensively in this chapter, and the one we continue to examine most intensively in our research.

In the following sections, we will present the research on each of the four components of the model. We chose to present each of the components in separate sections because it seemed like the most useful way of presenting the model to clinicians who are unfamiliar with our work. The reader should keep in mind, however, that the model components are *not* mutually exclusive and that they interact in complex ways that we are just beginning to understand.

Intolerance of Uncertainty

Intolerance of uncertainty, the central feature of our model, refers to *a dispositional characteristic that results from a set of negative beliefs about uncertainty and its implications.* Our research on intolerance of uncertainty suggests that there are two broad categories of negative beliefs about uncertainty that drive chronic, pathological worry: the belief that uncertainty has a negative impact on one's behavior and reflects poorly on the self, and the belief that uncertainty is unfair and spoils everything (Sexton & Dugas, 2009a). Although we have previously defined intolerance of uncertainty in other ways (e.g., Dugas, Gosselin, & Ladouceur, 2001; Freeston, Rhéaume, Letarte, Dugas, & Ladouceur, 1994), data from converging lines of research suggest that the term *dispositional characteristic* best describes its trait-like, fundamental nature.

Before reviewing the research on intolerance of uncertainty, we will briefly describe the clinical and empirical considerations that led us to this construct. As recently as the 1980s, behavioral and cognitive treatments for GAD fell primarily into two categories: (1) general anxiety reduction techniques such as progressive muscle relaxation and anxiety management training; and (2) cognitive interventions such as general cognitive restructuring or reevaluation. Although these interventions are efficacious for many clients with GAD, both the empirical literature and our clinical experience led us to the conclusion that they are not sufficient for the long-term management of GAD. In terms of general anxiety reduction interventions such as progressive muscle relaxation, data from treatment studies (e.g., Barlow, Rapee, & Brown, 1992; Öst & Breitholtz, 2000) suggested that they led to notable changes in GAD symptoms but that many clients were left with considerable residual symptoms. Our clinical experience, as well as our data, led us to a similar conclusion: although many clients were making significant gains early on in therapy, they often reached a plateau and found themselves continuing to experience important residual GAD symptoms following treatment.

As for general cognitive interventions, data from the same multitreatment studies (Barlow et al., 1992; Öst & Breitholtz, 2000) suggested that their efficacy was similar to that of relaxation techniques. In other words, general cognitive interventions appeared to lead to notable but insufficient change for many clients with GAD. One way to account for this may be that although there are many forms and variations of cognitive therapy for anxiety, most emphasize the reevaluation of probability and cost estimates related to feared outcomes. One of the aims of cognitive therapy is therefore to help anxious clients reevaluate both the probability that a feared outcome will take place and the consequences should it occur.

For example, imagine a client who fears job loss. The client might overestimate the probability of this loss taking place ("If I don't handle every assignment perfectly, I will lose my job"), as well as the probability of never finding another job should their current employment be terminated ("Other employers will know that I was fired from this job and will not want to hire me"). When using cognitive therapy, the therapist helps the client to reevaluate these thoughts and arrive at more realistic estimates of both the probability of job loss and the chances of never finding another job should the client get fired. According to the cognitive theory of anxiety, the reevaluation of the probability and costs of the feared outcome should lead to a corresponding decrease in worry and anxiety about the potential outcome. Specifically, the client might conclude that an occasional good but imperfect performance would probably not lead to being fired and that they would most likely be able to find another job if their current employment were lost.

When using "standard" cognitive therapy with clients who have GAD, we observed something that we had not expected. Specifically, we found that following the reevaluation of probability and cost estimates, our clients often reported that their worry and anxiety had *not* decreased. For example, one client had this to say about his fear of taking the airplane once he had reevaluated the chances of his plane crashing during his upcoming trip: "I know that there is only about one chance in five million that my plane will crash, but as long as there is a chance, no matter how small, I can't help but worry." Another client reported the following regarding her performance at work: "I know that I could probably deal with my boss being disappointed in my work performance, but I can't stop worrying about it because I just might be devastated." These examples illustrate what we experienced time and time again in our work with GAD clients: in order to not worry, they seemed to require absolute *certainty* that either a given event would not occur or that they would be able to deal with it should it take place. Thus, we came to the conclusion that standard cognitive therapy is insufficient for most individuals with GAD because the usual conclusion of cognitive reevaluation (that is, that a negative event is unlikely to happen and that the person would probably be able to cope with the occurrence of the event) is insufficient to help most clients with GAD significantly decrease their worry and anxiety about the event. Stated differently, the reevaluation of probability and cost estimates typically does not lead them to the conclusion they are looking for; namely, that a potential negative event would *definitely* not occur or that they would *unquestionably* be able to deal with the event should it occur. This line of reasoning led us to the idea that individuals with GAD might be *intolerant of uncertainty*.

Since coming to the conclusion that intolerance of uncertainty might play an important role in GAD, we, and other research teams, have tested this idea using a variety of approaches. In the following sections, we present the main research findings that bear on the relationship between intolerance of uncertainty, chronic worry, and GAD. As a general rule, the research on intolerance of uncertainty (and all other model components) has progressed from nonclinical studies to investigations in clinically anxious populations. The rationale behind this research strategy is the following: because nonclinical studies offer the advantage of testing new ideas in a relatively quick and cost-efficient fashion, they should be carried out first; clinical studies, which are much more time-consuming and expensive, can then focus on replicating and extending key nonclinical findings. Generally speaking, the literature on GAD supports this research strategy, as nonclinical findings have proven extremely useful in designing studies in clinical populations. Moreover, the vast majority of results pertaining to the processes involved in nonclinical worry have been replicated in samples of clients with GAD, suggesting that nonclinical research can be quite valuable in terms of understanding the etiology of GAD. Worry is a *dimensional* construct, meaning that all individuals engage in worry, just to varying degrees. For this reason, research on mild and moderate worry can shed light on processes involved in chronic, GAD-related worry. Along the same lines, discomfort with uncertainty is also a universal experience that exists on a continuum, which is why nonclinical investigations of intolerance of uncertainty can help us understand how individuals with GAD experience uncertainty.

We begin our review with studies examining the *specificity* of the relationship of intolerance of uncertainty to worry and GAD. We then turn our attention to the research that has explored the *nature* of these relationships; that is, the studies that address the question of whether intolerance of uncertainty is a risk factor for GAD. Finally, we summarize the research on *potential mechanisms* that link intolerance of uncertainty and chronic, pathological worry.

Specificity of Intolerance of Uncertainty

In our initial studies, we tested the relationship between intolerance of uncertainty and excessive worry in nonclinical individuals. Because worry and discomfort with uncertainty are relatively universal phenomena, we reasoned that if intolerance of uncertainty is involved in the etiology of pathological worry, we should be able to see a relationship between the two in people from the general population. Our early studies (e.g., Freeston et al., 1994) confirmed that intolerance of uncertainty and worry were in fact highly related among nonclinical individuals, a finding that has since been replicated many times by our research team, as well as other research groups, in studies with adults and adolescents (see Osmanağaoğlu, Creswell, & Dodd, 2018 for a review).

We also wanted to ensure that the relationship between intolerance of uncertainty and worry was not simply the result of their respective relationships with anxiety and depression. The findings from our early studies confirmed that this clearly was not the case (e.g., Dugas, Freeston, & Ladouceur, 1997). We then unpacked this finding by examining whether intolerance of uncertainty was more highly related to worry than to symptoms of non-GAD anxiety-related disorders. In a nonclinical study (Dugas, Gosselin et al., 2001), we found that although intolerance of uncertainty was related to symptoms of obsessive-compulsive disorder and panic disorder (which is not surprising given that different types of anxiety-related disorders share common vulnerabilities), it appeared to be more highly related to worry. Because worry and depression are related, we also compared the relationships between intolerance of uncertainty, worry, and depressive symptoms.

Again, we found that although intolerance of uncertainty was related to level of depressive symptoms in nonclinical individuals, it was more highly related to worry (Dugas, Schwartz, & Francis, 2004).

To further examine the question of specificity, we were interested in finding out if the relationship between intolerance of uncertainty and nonclinical worry could be accounted for by personal dispositions that are related to worry and anxiety. To address this question, we first examined the associations among worry, intolerance of uncertainty, perfectionism, and need for control (Buhr & Dugas, 2006). As expected, we found that worry was more highly related to intolerance of uncertainty than to perfectionism and need for control. In addition, the relationship between intolerance of uncertainty and worry was largely independent, whereas the relationships between worry and both perfectionism and need for control were for the most part accounted for by intolerance of uncertainty. Put simply, the contribution of perfectionism and need for control to the tendency to worry is largely explained by intolerance of uncertainty. From a theoretical perspective, these findings imply that perfectionism and need for control are not essential components within a cognitive behavioral model of GAD. From a clinical perspective, this suggests that helping clients with GAD become more tolerant of uncertainty should also help them to decrease their perfectionism and need for control. In a recent replication and extension of this study, we (Koerner, Mejia, & Kusec, 2017) also were able to determine that intolerance of uncertainty is not entirely the same as an aversion to risk, low curiosity, indecisiveness, or a need for predictability and closure. We also found that intolerance of uncertainty was more strongly associated with worry than were any of these other constructs. In the following paragraphs, we present the findings of our research examining intolerance of uncertainty in samples of clinically anxious clients.

In an initial clinical study, we compared levels of intolerance of uncertainty in clients with *DSM-IV* GAD, clients with various other *DSM-IV* anxiety disorders, and nonclinical control participants (Ladouceur et al., 1999). The mixed anxiety disorders group comprised mainly clients with obsessive-compulsive disorder, although social anxiety disorder, panic disorder, specific phobia, and posttraumatic stress disorder were also represented. As expected, we found that both clinically anxious groups had higher levels of intolerance of uncertainty than did the nonclinical control group. However, clients with GAD were more intolerant of uncertainty than were clients with other anxiety disorders.

Since that initial clinical study, we have compared levels of intolerance of uncertainty in GAD clients to those of panic disorder clients (Dugas, Marchand, & Ladouceur, 2005). We found that relative to the clients with panic disorder, those with GAD were more intolerant of uncertainty. Interestingly, when both groups were combined, intolerance of uncertainty was related to level of worry but was unrelated to panic-like symptoms. This implies that having difficulty tolerating and dealing with uncertainty predicts GAD-like symptoms in anxious clients who do not necessarily meet diagnostic criteria for GAD (at least, those with panic disorder).

In a further clinical test of specificity, we examined whether level of intolerance of uncertainty could predict the severity of symptoms in a group of individuals with

GAD (Dugas et al., 2007). Given that the variability of symptoms and processes within a group of GAD clients is limited (all have high levels of worry, anxiety, and intolerance of uncertainty), we did not necessarily expect to find any statistically significant relationships. Nonetheless, we found that clients with severe GAD had more difficulty tolerating uncertainty than did those with less severe forms of the disorder, lending further support to the sensitivity of the relation between intolerance of uncertainty and GAD.

Although the bulk of our research conducted in nonclinical and clinically anxious populations seems to suggest that intolerance of uncertainty has a sensitive and specific relationship to the symptoms of GAD (in particular chronic, excessive, and uncontrollable worry), readers should be aware that the more recent literature is mixed, with some studies suggesting that level of intolerance of uncertainty may *not* distinguish GAD from anxiety-related disorders, or depression. For example, in a recent study by our group (Anderson et al., 2012), average level of intolerance of uncertainty was higher in those with GAD than in those with other anxiety disorders, but the difference was not statistically significant. Other research groups have found levels of intolerance of uncertainty in social anxiety disorder and in major depressive disorder that are similar to what has been observed in GAD. These findings have led to the suggestion that intolerance of uncertainty may be a cross-cutting feature of many psychopathologies (Carleton, 2012). While it is entirely possible that intolerance of uncertainty is transdiagnostic, we propose that there may be aspects of intolerance of uncertainty that are specific to GAD, a point we return to toward the end of this section. We now turn our attention to the literature bearing on the *nature* of the relation between intolerance of uncertainty and pathological worry.

Evidence for Causality of Intolerance of Uncertainty

Before addressing the question of a potential causal link between intolerance of uncertainty and pathological worry, the criteria for establishing such a link will be reviewed. Helena Chmura Kraemer and her colleagues (1997) proposed a set of conditions to establish causality. The authors convincingly argued that the term *causal risk factor* should be used when describing a factor that has a causal influence on another because the term *cause* inaccurately suggests that only one factor is involved in the etiology of a second factor (which is almost never the case). Thus, the term *causal risk factor* will be used throughout this book when addressing the notion of causality. According to Kraemer and her associates, four conditions must be met for one factor (Factor A) to be considered a causal risk factor for a second factor (Factor B): (1) Factor A must be *correlated* with Factor B; (2) Factor A must *precede* Factor B; (3) Factor A must be *modifiable* (or else it is considered a fixed marker; e.g., year of birth); and (4) if modifiable, the experimental manipulation or induction of Factor A must lead to changes in, or the occurrence of, Factor B.

Although the previously reviewed studies show that intolerance of uncertainty and worry are closely related (Condition 1), they do not address the other three conditions required to establish that intolerance of uncertainty is a causal risk factor for pathological worry and GAD. We, and other researchers, have addressed the question of causality by tracking the progression of intolerance of uncertainty and excessive worry over time; by experimentally manipulating level of intolerance of uncertainty; and by examining change mechanisms during the treatment of GAD.

Intolerance of Uncertainty Predicts Increases in Excessive Worry Over Time

Although the *DSM-5* requires the symptoms of GAD to be present for at least 6 months before the diagnosis can be considered, people with GAD commonly report having struggled with excessive worry for many years and can remember worrying when they were very young. Therefore, studying children and adolescents can provide important insight into the development of clinically significant worry. Researchers have observed that intolerance of uncertainty distinguishes clinically anxious and nonanxious children (Comer et al., 2009). A strong correlation between intolerance of uncertainty and worry has been found in children (Comer et al., 2009; Cowie, Clementi, & Alfano, 2016) and in adolescents (Laugesen, Dugas, & Bukowski, 2003). Our group (Dugas, Laugesen, & Bukowski, 2012) conducted a 5-year, 10-wave longitudinal study in a large sample of adolescents to determine whether intolerance of uncertainty predicts the development of excessive worry over time. We found a bi-directional relationship, such that changes in intolerance of uncertainty preceded and predicted changes in worry over the course of adolescence, and vice versa. While this finding partially supports the idea of a causal relation of intolerance of uncertainty to worry, it also suggests that habitual worry reinforces (that is, strengthens) intolerance of uncertainty.

Heightening Intolerance of Uncertainty Momentarily Increases Worry

In a nonclinical laboratory study, we attempted to experimentally manipulate level of intolerance of uncertainty and assess the impact of changes in intolerance of uncertainty on level of worry (Ladouceur, Gosselin, & Dugas, 2000). Specifically, we used a gambling procedure to place participants in a situation that included uncertainty and asked them to place a series of bets where the chances of winning were one out of three. For half of the participants, we sought to *increase* their intolerance of uncertainty by having the experimenter repeatedly mention that the chances of winning were poorer in the present study compared to previous studies. The goal of this procedure was to have participants interpret their chances of winning as *unacceptable*. For the other half of the participants, we aimed to decrease their intolerance of uncertainty by having the experimenter frequently mention that the chances of winning in the current study were better than in previous studies. The goal of this procedure was to have participants interpret their chances of winning as *acceptable*. Unbeknownst to the participants, however, the gambling outcomes were programmed to be identical for everyone. All participants were told that if they managed to "break even," a donation would be made to a foundation for disadvantaged children. Following the gambling procedure, where none of the participants managed to break even, all were asked to complete a measure of intolerance of uncertainty as well as a measure of worry about the financial needs of the foundation. The results showed that the experimental manipulation was successful as participants in the increased intolerance of uncertainty condition reported higher levels of intolerance of uncertainty than did those in the decreased intolerance of uncertainty condition. Further, participants in the increased intolerance of uncertainty condition reported more worry about the needs of the foundation than did participants in the decreased intolerance of uncertainty condition.

In a sample of students in the United Kingdom, Meeten, Dash, Scarlet, and Davey (2012) used a vignette procedure to manipulate intolerance of uncertainty. Participants first read a story describing a character behaving in a manner that reflected either high intolerance of uncertainty or low intolerance of uncertainty. After reading their assigned story, participants were asked to think of an uncertain situation in their own life and to see the situation through the eyes of the character they had just read about. Participants spent 15 minutes writing down what they would think and feel if they were the character in the story. Then, participants answered a few questions to determine whether the experimental manipulation was effective in altering their attitude toward uncertainty. People assigned to read about a character high in intolerance of uncertainty prior to reflecting on their own personal experience of uncertainty reported being more concerned about their feelings of uncertainty than did participants in the comparison condition who read about a character low in intolerance of uncertainty. Moreover, those in the high intolerance of uncertainty condition reported a more negative mood state and produced a more elaborate chain of worries on a catastrophizing task than did individuals who were in the low intolerance of uncertainty condition.

Collectively, these studies provide support for the notion that level of intolerance of uncertainty can be modified and that a change in intolerance of uncertainty leads to change in worry, thereby satisfying Conditions 3 and 4 for a causal risk factor as set out by Kraemer and her colleagues (1997).

Improvement in Intolerance of Uncertainty Predicts Reduction in Worry During Treatment

In another test of the causality hypothesis, we investigated precedence of change over the course of treatment for clients with GAD. We reasoned that if intolerance of uncertainty is a causal risk factor for pathological worry, changes in intolerance of uncertainty should precede changes in worry during treatment. Stated differently, if intolerance of uncertainty is among the factors that lead to worry, it follows that individuals with GAD would have to succeed in better tolerating uncertainty before they could succeed in decreasing their worry. We addressed this issue by examining treatment data for 16 clients who received cognitive behavioral therapy (CBT) for GAD (Dugas, Langlois, Rhéaume, & Ladouceur, 1998). Participants were asked to rate their levels of intolerance of uncertainty and worry on a daily basis over the course of therapy (14 to 18 weeks). Following treatment completion, we used time-series analysis to examine the temporal relationship between intolerance of uncertainty and time spent worrying. We found that changes in intolerance of uncertainty preceded changes in level of worry for 11 clients, whereas changes in time spent worrying preceded changes in intolerance of uncertainty for only one client (no significant relationships were observed for four clients). Using different statistical techniques, other researchers have also found that changes in intolerance of uncertainty precede changes in worry over the course of cognitive behavioral therapy, even when the therapy contains strategies that target intolerance of uncertainty only indirectly (e.g., Bomyea et al., 2015).

Returning to the conditions set out by Kraemer and her colleagues (1997), the findings reviewed in this section show that the four conditions for identifying a causal risk factor have mostly been satisfied. Specifically, intolerance of uncertainty is closely related to worry (Condition 1); an increase in intolerance of uncertainty precedes the development of excessive worry (Condition 2); intolerance of uncertainty can be modified (Condition 3); and changes in intolerance of uncertainty typically precede changes in worry over the course of treatment (Condition 4).

Pathways from Intolerance of Uncertainty to Pathological Worry

Given that the data accumulated thus far are consistent with the idea that intolerance of uncertainty is a causal risk factor for pathological worry, we now turn our attention to the issue of *how* intolerance of uncertainty might lead to frequent, prolonged, or intense episodes of worry. First, we will provide an overview of our conceptualization of intolerance of uncertainty and its relationship with worry, and then we will review research that has informed this conceptualization.

The beginning point for excessive worry is confrontation of, or exposure to a *novel, unpredictable, or ambiguous* situation. Such a situation will elicit *uncertainty*, a cognitive-affective state that is triggered by the unknown elements of the situation. Uncertainty is a normal response to situations that are novel, unpredictable, or ambiguous. However, people high in intolerance of uncertainty are more reactive to their own feelings of uncertainty and experience them as more intense and difficult to withstand. Accordingly, they make *catastrophic interpretations of uncertainty* (for example, "I hate this feeling of uncertainty"; "It's not fair that I am being kept in the dark"; "I can't stand the uncertainty"). Regardless of whether or not the triggering situation actually has a realistic potential for a bad outcome, intolerance of uncertainty causes individuals to *expect that uncertainty-inducing situations will result in negative outcomes, and that these outcomes will be catastrophic and beyond their abilities to cope.* Even situations that are accepted by most people as safe, or that are relatively free of threat, can be anxiety provoking for people who are high in intolerance of uncertainty, provided that these situations induce a state of uncertainty. The uncertainty that these situations elicit is more distressing than the potential for a bad outcome, especially when individuals perceive that they are being made to feel uncertain, that their feelings of uncertainty are uncontrollable, or that uncertainty is prolonged. Catastrophic interpretations in response to uncertainty-inducing situations elicit a range of emotions, notably fear and anxiety. The activation of intense emotions sets into motion unhelpful behavior to control or eliminate the state of uncertainty and the emotional and physical discomfort that accompanies it. Chief among these behaviors is perseverative worrying. The act of worrying is similar to engaging in rapid-fire mental simulation of all the things that could go wrong in an uncertainty-inducing situation. People will also engage in *safety behaviors*, strategies designed to reduce or terminate uncertainty and anxiety. These behaviors alleviate discomfort in the short-term, but have the unintended effect of strengthening the "program" of maladaptive responses to novel, unpredictable, or ambiguous situations that intolerance of uncertainty and resultant catastrophic interpretations initiate. This is because safety behaviors prevent individuals from learning (1) that most uncertainty-inducing situations are manageable and are within their ability to cope effectively; (2) that they are capable of waiting out and withstanding a period of uncertainty; and (3) that uncertainty is normal, manageable, and can sometimes even be pleasant. As a consequence of safety behaviors, individuals continue to expect that novel, unpredictable, and ambiguous situations will result in negative outcomes that are costly and insurmountable; the perception of uncertainty as threatening persists; and negative beliefs about uncertainty remain resistant to disconfirmation. Common safety-behaviors include, but are not limited to, excessive information seeking, repeated reassurance seeking, delayed action (for example, procrastination), and impulsive action. When possible, individuals high in intolerance of uncertainty may also engage in preemptive avoidance of uncertainty-inducing situations so as not to trigger discomfort in the first place.

In the following paragraphs, we review research that has informed our conceptualization of intolerance of uncertainty. Together, these lines of research begin to paint a portrait of the many interacting and dynamic pathways leading from intolerance of uncertainty to chronic worry and GAD.

Interpretation Bias in Response to Uncertainty-Inducing Situations

Studies of *interpretation bias* support information processing as a pathway leading from intolerance of uncertainty to pathological worry. Interpretation bias is the tendency to appraise or explain events in a way that is consistent with one's existing beliefs or schemas about the self, others, and the world. In the early days of research on GAD, Gillian Butler and Andrew Mathews (1983) proposed that people with GAD view the world as an unsafe place and perceive more danger than actually exists. To test this idea, they presented participants with descriptions of scenarios that were ambiguous (e.g., "You wake up with a start in the middle of the night, thinking you heard a noise, but all is quiet—what do you think woke you up?") along with possible explanations ranging from benign to threatening. Butler and Mathews observed that relative to participants low in worry and anxiety, those with GAD tended to report that the most threatening explanation ("It could be a burglar") was the one that came to mind first. Using various methodologies, many studies went on to show that individuals with GAD indeed have an exaggerated tendency to make *threatening interpretations of ambiguous situations that contain the possibility of a negative outcome* (e.g., Eysenck, Mogg, May, Richards, & Mathews, 1991; Hazlett-Stevens & Borkovec, 2004; Mogg, Bradley, Miller, & Potts, 1994). Thus, when faced with a situation that contains the possibility of two or more outcomes (with at least one of them being negative), individuals with GAD tend to jump to the conclusion that the worst outcome will ensue. For example, they may conclude very quickly that their plane will crash if they experience turbulence during a flight; that they will be late for a meeting if their taxi is temporarily stuck in traffic; or that their romantic partner has been in an accident if they do not answer their mobile phone.

On the surface, the finding that individuals with GAD tend to make threatening interpretations of ambiguous information certainly seems consistent with the notion that they have difficulty tolerating uncertainty. In fact, it may be that strongly held negative beliefs about uncertainty "drive" the tendency to make threatening interpretations of unclear information. In other words, intolerance of uncertainty may be the factor that best explains this bias in individuals with GAD.

To test this hypothesis, we examined the relationship between intolerance of uncertainty and the tendency to make threatening interpretations of everyday ambiguous situations containing the possibility of a negative outcome or a benign outcome. In initial studies, we looked at the relationship between intolerance of uncertainty and interpretations of these kinds of ambiguous situations in nonclinical volunteers (Dugas, Hedayati et al., 2005; Koerner & Dugas, 2008). Participants were instructed to read a series of fictional diary entries, imagine them as though they were their own, and rate each entry in terms of its threat value. Half of the diary entries were ambiguous ("While on my way out tonight I was stopped in the street") and the other half of the entries were divided between overtly positive ones ("I was really pleased when I passed my driving test today; this calls for a big celebration") and overtly negative ones ("We had invited some friends to join us for a barbecue, but no one turned up"). As expected, the participants with high levels of intolerance of uncertainty rated the ambiguous diary entries as more threatening. More importantly, threat ratings of ambiguous entries were more highly related to intolerance of uncertainty than to levels of anxiety, depression, and worry. Furthermore, the relation between intolerance of uncertainty and threat ratings was independent of mood ratings.

We administered the same fictional diary entries to clients at an anxiety disorders clinic. We found again that higher intolerance of uncertainty was associated with negative appraisals of ambiguous information, and that this relationship could not be entirely explained by candidate third variables like depressed mood or the general propensity to be anxious (that is, being high in trait anxiety; Anderson et al., 2012). Thus, it appears that in nonclinical individuals and in people with anxiety disorders, intolerance of uncertainty may be at the root of biased interpretations of ambiguous information. This conclusion is in line with the cognitive theory of psychopathology that states that pre-existing beliefs (and not symptoms such as anxiety or depression) have a direct impact on the way we process information from our environment (Beck & Clark, 1997).

What is clear from the aforementioned research is that individuals high in intolerance of uncertainty become distressed when they encounter ambiguous situations that contain the possibility of a negative outcome. However, we have observed that individuals high in intolerance of uncertainty *also* express significantly more distress than do those low in intolerance of uncertainty in response to situations that most people view as *benign or safe* (Koerner & Dugas, 2008). Why might this be? Researchers (Brosschot, Verkuil, & Thayer, 2016; Woody & Rachman, 1994) have suggested that individuals who are high in intolerance of uncertainty, especially those with GAD, need complete evidence of safety. As long as there is any ambiguity, even if slight, situations that are safe will also arouse uncertainty and anxiety. Recent research supports this idea. Pepperdine and colleagues (2018) presented nonclinical participants with uncertainty-inducing negative and positive/benign scenarios (that respondents in a pilot study had rated as very likely to end in a negative outcome or a positive/safe outcome, respectively) and asked them to answer several questions in response to each one, including how much they would be bothered by the uncertainty. An example of a positive situation was: "Your best friend tells you to book your birthday off work as they have arranged a day out. You know they always have your best interests at heart and you have often had fun together. You don't know where you will be going or what you will be doing. You do as they ask and your birthday is next week." The researchers found that those higher in intolerance of uncertainty reported being more highly bothered by the positive/benign scenarios than did those lower in intolerance of uncertainty. Interestingly, those higher in intolerance of uncertainty reported being more bothered by the uncertainty elicited by the positive/benign situations than by the uncertainty elicited by the negative situations, suggesting that people high in intolerance of uncertainty experience discomfort in ambiguous situations that most people accept as safe/benign (such as a friend planning a birthday surprise). Seen through the lens of intolerance of uncertainty, such situations still contain a modicum of threat, even if not apparent, making them a cause for worry and anxiety.

Thus far, we have discussed the appraisals and interpretations that uncertainty-inducing situations can trigger. While it is clear that individuals with high intolerance of uncertainty will tend to experience anxiety and fear in these situations, what may seem less evident to readers is that such situations can also elicit anger. We propose that this is more likely to be the case when an expectation of certainty has been violated. We tested this idea in a study with undergraduate students (Anderson, Deschênes, & Dugas, 2016) and indeed found that violations of expectations of certainty elicited anger *and* anxiety, particularly when individuals were being deprived of information that another person possessed. Also, participants holding a stronger belief that uncertainty is unfair experienced significantly more anger in response to avoidable uncertainty than did the other participants. Therefore, one pathway by which intolerance of uncertainty leads to chronic worry is that individuals who are intolerant of uncertainty have a strong tendency to make threatening interpretations in novel, unpredictable, or ambiguous situations, even when there is little to no apparent threat of a negative outcome. These interpretations may lead to elevated levels of anxiety, fear, and possibly anger, and initiate worry and unhelpful behaviors to control, reduce, or eliminate uncertainty.

Decision Making

Related to the study of information processing, a number of researchers have examined the impact of level of worry and anxiety on laboratory decision making. Although intolerance of uncertainty was not assessed in many of these studies, they are nonetheless quite informative in terms of understanding the potential role of intolerance of uncertainty in excessive worry.

Richard Metzger and his colleagues (Metzger, Miller, Cohen, Sofka, & Borkovec, 1990) set out to examine differences between high and low worriers in terms of decision making, by comparing both groups of participants on a categorization task that varied in level of ambiguity. Participants were asked to decide whether or not variations in figures were members of a novel category. The level of ambiguity was manipulated by modifying one or more features of the figures. The results showed that high worriers did not differ from low worriers when the level of ambiguity was low (manipulation of only one feature). However, for elevated levels of ambiguity (manipulation of more than one feature), the high worriers took longer than did the low worriers to reach a decision. Thus, it appears that high worriers have greater difficulty dealing with the uncertainty of highly ambiguous situations.

In a related study, Frank Tallis and his colleagues (Tallis, Eysenck, & Mathews, 1991) used a computerized search task to compare high and low worriers. Participants viewed randomly distributed letters on the computer screen and were asked to determine if a target (the letter "E") was among the displayed letters. When the target was present, there were no differences between the groups. However, when the target was absent, the high worriers took longer to respond than did the low worriers. Tallis and colleagues concluded that high worriers required more evidence than did low worriers when making a decision involving greater levels of ambiguity or uncertainty. Although both studies reviewed above did not specifically address the role of intolerance of uncertainty, their findings can be interpreted as showing that high worriers have difficulty dealing with the uncertainty inherent in ambiguous situations. Because high worriers typically have elevated levels of intolerance of uncertainty, one can speculate that intolerance of uncertainty is closely related to the disparity in performance on the unambiguous and ambiguous tasks.

Having considered the findings of the decision-making studies described earlier, we directly examined the impact of intolerance of uncertainty on decision making. In an initial study, we used a series of three laboratory tasks to investigate the relationship between intolerance of uncertainty and decision making in nonclinical participants (Ladouceur, Talbot, & Dugas, 1997). The first task was a completely unambiguous task that varied only on level of difficulty. In the second and third tasks, we manipulated the level of ambiguity to be moderate or high. As expected, we found that intolerance of uncertainty was unrelated to performance on the first task, regardless of how difficult it was. However, intolerance of uncertainty was related to performance at moderate levels of ambiguity on the second and third tasks, with the high intolerance of uncertainty participants doing more poorly. Thus, it appears that intolerance of uncertainty has its greatest effects in moderately ambiguous situations. This seems logical when one considers that categorically unambiguous situations generally present little threat to all individuals (including those high in intolerance of uncertainty) and that highly ambiguous situations are typically threatening for most people (including those low in intolerance of uncertainty). Many situations in everyday life are characterized by moderate levels of ambiguity and these situations are especially anxiety provoking for those who have high levels of intolerance of uncertainty, given that their threshold for uncertainty is lower than it is for those more tolerant of uncertainty.

Other researchers have also examined the role of intolerance of uncertainty in decision making. In a clever experiment (Luhmann, Ishida, & Hajcak, 2011), student participants completed a computerized decision task that involved multiple trials in which they had to make a choice between two monetary rewards. The first reward was always smaller *and* less probable. Participants could decide to immediately accept this reward with the knowledge that there was a 50% chance of obtaining it, or they could wait several seconds to see the second reward. The task was set up so that the second reward was always larger and more probable, at 70%. So, participants stood a better chance of making bigger wins by declining the first reward. The researchers found that participants higher in intolerance of uncertainty more frequently accepted the smaller rewards than the larger rewards even though the smaller rewards were not only lower in value, but also less probable. In addition, the researchers were able to establish that those higher in intolerance of uncertainty made their choices more quickly than did people lower in intolerance of uncertainty, suggesting that they were more impulsive in their decision making, perhaps because they could not tolerate waiting for larger rewards. Finally, the researchers were able to establish that the findings were not better accounted for by differences in trait anxiety. In fact, variations in trait anxiety did not relate to how people made choices in this task. What this study shows is that people who are higher in intolerance of uncertainty are uncomfortable waiting it out when they are confronted with uncertainty or multiple options, which can lead to worry and anxiety, and consequently disadvantageous decision making.

We have since shown that intolerance of uncertainty and higher GAD symptoms are associated with two unhelpful decision-making styles: one that is slow, overly deliberate, and leads to inaction, and one that is impulsive and leads to rash action (Pawluk & Koerner, 2013; Pawluk & Koerner, 2016). The idea that uncertainty can elicit rash action in people with GAD is not immediately obvious given that worrying typically reflects a premeditative orientation. Under what circumstances might people with GAD show impulsive behavior? Our research suggests that rash action is motivated by an immediate need to reduce or eliminate intense emotional discomfort. We propose that being in a state of uncertainty is unbearable and anxiety provoking for people high in intolerance of uncertainty, and accordingly this may prompt urgent maladaptive action to terminate it. Therefore, another pathway leading from intolerance of uncertainty to chronic worry is that individuals who are intolerant of uncertainty may (1) require more information when making decisions in moderately ambiguous situations and (2) make hasty decisions when confronted with uncertainty. In either case, their goal is to reduce their uncertainty and the discomfort that accompanies it. However, safety behaviors in the form of inaction, slow action, or impulsive action may only reinforce chronic worry and anxiety.

In line with other cognitive behavioral models of psychopathology, our model is based on the idea that beliefs (in this case, about uncertainty) are fully activated when the individual is in a negative mood state. Others (e.g., Beck & Emery, 1985) have referred to this as the activation of latent schemas. Although we prefer the term *belief* to *schema*, we agree with the notion that negative cognition and emotion can interact to contribute to the development and maintenance of psychopathology. Given the potential interaction between beliefs and emotional state, we examined the interaction between intolerance of uncertainty and state anxiety in nonclinical participants (Talbot, Dugas, & Ladouceur, 1999). In this study, half of the participants were subjected to the Public Speaking Task, a state anxiety manipulation where they were told that they would be speaking in front of a small group of graduate students (although they did not actually have to make the speech). Participants then completed a laboratory task that included various levels of ambiguity. Although level of intolerance of uncertainty and state anxiety were unrelated to task performance at all levels of ambiguity, they were related to certainty about having made correct decisions on the task. In particular, participants with high levels of intolerance of uncertainty who had received the anxiety manipulation were less confident about their performance than were the other participants, including those who had received the anxiety manipulation but were low in intolerance of uncertainty. These results imply that the combination of high intolerance of uncertainty and high anxiety leads to lower levels of certainty (confidence) in at least some decision-making situations. Consequently, another pathway leading from intolerance of uncertainty to chronic worry is that individuals who are intolerant of uncertainty, when anxious, have less confidence in their decisions in ambiguous situations, which may lead to worry and anxiety about the implications of their decisions.

In summary, the data accumulated thus far suggest that individuals who are intolerant of uncertainty may be at risk for developing chronic pathological worry because they tend to: (1) make threatening interpretations of uncertainty in novel, unpredictable, or ambiguous situations, even when there is no apparent threat in these situations; (2) make disadvantageous decisions in moderately ambiguous, uncertainty-inducing situations, especially when uncertainty is prolonged; and (3) have particularly low confidence in their decisions when anxious. Although future research will undoubtedly uncover many other pathways leading from intolerance of uncertainty to chronic, pathological worry, there is good reason to believe that investigations into the way individuals with varying levels of intolerance of uncertainty process information will continue to be highly useful in furthering our understanding of chronic worry and GAD.

Questions about Intolerance of Uncertainty

Although it is fairly clear that a high intolerance of uncertainty plays a major role in chronic worry and GAD, there remains much to be learned. One question, which we alluded to earlier, is whether intolerance of uncertainty is specific to GAD, or is a characteristic that is fairly common across many psychological disorders. We propose that both are true, but that the way intolerance of uncertainty has been measured in research has made it challenging to uncover those aspects that may distinguish GAD from other psychological disorders. Although the Intolerance of Uncertainty Scale (described further in Chapter 3) is a very useful tool for the measurement of one's general inability to withstand uncertainty, it may not quite capture aspects of intolerance of uncertainty that may be specific to GAD. In a recent study, we interviewed people with GAD and people low in anxiety and worry about their attitudes toward uncertainty and their behaviors in uncertainty-inducing situations, to arrive at hypotheses about aspects of intolerance of uncertainty that may be most relevant to persons with GAD (Fracalanza, Koerner, McShane, & Antony, 2013). One finding was that *all* participants with GAD reported that being uncertain meant something about them as a person; whereas, only a quarter of people low in worry and anxiety reported this. Personal meanings fell into three themes: (1) being uncertain means that I am incompetent; (2) being uncertain means I am abnormal; and (3) being uncertain means I am not prepared. Rather than viewing uncertainty as the result of a situation or as a transient psychological state, it seemed that participants with GAD were thinking about uncertainty as an undesirable or abnormal personality characteristic. Based on this, we hypothesize that for persons with GAD in particular, uncertainty is intimately connected with a negative self-concept, whereas for others, it is not. A follow-up study with a clinical comparison group is needed to determine whether other groups also connect uncertainty with self-concept; however, for the moment, it is interesting to consider that people with GAD may be more inclined than other groups to pathologize the experience of uncertainty and to engage in self-denigration when they experience uncertainty. Another question worth exploring is whether individuals with GAD have a more generalized sensitivity to, or a lower threshold for, uncertainty-inducing situations than do people with other forms of psychopathology.

Positive Beliefs about Worry

The beliefs that individuals with GAD hold about worry have also received considerable study. In this section, we focus on the research on *positive beliefs about worry* because this line of study has direct implications for the treatment that is presented in the following chapters. However, the reader should keep in mind that negative beliefs about worry have received formidable empirical support (e.g., Wells & Carter, 1999), and that other cognitive behavioral treatments focus on changing these particular beliefs to help individuals with GAD.

Early in the study of GAD, Thomas Borkovec and colleagues (see Borkovec & Roemer, 1995) observed that nonclinical and clinical high worriers hold beliefs about the usefulness of worrying; for example, that it allows one to have control over events. Our research on positive beliefs about worry was initially the result of our interest in conditioning theory. In line with operant conditioning principles, we reasoned that positive beliefs about worry could develop and be maintained by the processes of positive and negative reinforcement. Specifically, if a person notices that the act of worrying is followed by the attainment of desired outcomes (positive reinforcement) or the avoidance of undesirable outcomes (negative reinforcement), that person would be likely to develop positive beliefs about worry (and thereby continue to worry). With this in mind, we and other researchers have set out to examine positive beliefs about worry in nonclinical and clinical populations.

In our initial studies, we assessed positive beliefs about worry that fell into two broad categories: (1) worrying can prevent or minimize negative outcomes (negative reinforcement), and (2) worrying is a positive action for finding a solution (positive reinforcement). We first found that nonclinical individuals meeting some GAD criteria reported greater positive beliefs about worry than did nonclinical individuals meeting none of the criteria (Freeston et al., 1994). We also found that the relationship between positive beliefs and level of worry was independent of anxiety and depression, which suggests that these beliefs make a unique contribution to the explanation of how much people worry. In a second study, we assessed the same positive beliefs about worry and found that GAD clients reported stronger beliefs than did nonclinical moderate worriers (Ladouceur, Blais, Freeston, & Dugas, 1998). Subsequently, we examined these positive beliefs in GAD clients, other anxiety disorder clients, and nonclinical individuals (Ladouceur et al., 1999). Although the GAD clients reported more positive beliefs about worry than did the nonclinical individuals, both clinical groups reported similar levels of positive beliefs. These results suggest that although GAD clients have higher levels of worry than do clients with other anxiety disorders, they do not hold stronger beliefs about the usefulness of worrying. These findings were replicated in a study comparing GAD clients to panic disorder clients (Dugas, Marchand et al., 2005), lending further support to the idea that positive beliefs about worry are a characteristic of clinically anxious individuals as opposed to being a GAD-specific feature.

In an effort to attain a more comprehensive and clinically useful understanding of positive beliefs about worry, our group revised our conceptualization to include five types of positive beliefs: (1) worrying helps to find solutions to problems; (2) worrying increases motivation to get things done; (3) worrying protects against negative emotions; (4) worrying, in and of itself, can prevent bad things from happening (this has been referred to as magical thinking or thought–action fusion); and (5) worrying is a positive personality trait (e.g., it shows that one is a responsible and caring person). Since conceptualizing positive beliefs along these lines, we have developed and validated a questionnaire measuring these five positive beliefs about worry (the Why Worry-II, which is presented in Chapter 3). In studies using this questionnaire, we have found that the degree to which nonclinical individuals endorse the combination of these beliefs is associated with the presence of excessive and uncontrollable worry (Hebert et al., 2014; Laugesen et al., 2003; Robichaud, Dugas, & Conway, 2003). In terms of specific beliefs, it appears that the beliefs that worry facilitates problem-solving, protects against negative emotions, and is a positive personality trait are the best predictors of excessive worry, at least in a nonclinical population (Bakerman, Buhr, Koerner, & Dugas, 2004; Hebert et al., 2014).

Other research groups have also used the Why Worry-II. In a nonclinical study (Crouch, Lewis, Erickson, & Newman, 2017), participants completed the scale of the Why Worry-II that measures the belief that worrying protects against negative emotions and then kept a weekly diary in which they recorded the details of the worst event of the week. In reference to this situation, participants were asked to rate the extent to which the event involved the experience of a negative emotional contrast (e.g., "I got my hopes up and then was disappointed"). The researchers found that those who held a stronger belief that worrying protects against negative emotions were more likely to report in their diary that the worst event of their week involved an unexpected shift into a negative mood state, which supports the idea, albeit indirectly, that people with GAD try to avoid being caught off guard and that worrying may be one strategy that they use to remain on guard against negative emotions.

It is important to point out, however, that there are mixed findings in the literature with regard to the role of positive beliefs about worry. In a nonclinical study, researchers (Thielsch, Andor, & Ehring, 2015) found that endorsement of positive beliefs about worry on the Why Worry-II did *not* relate to worry intensity as measured by a 1-week daily diary, whereas negative beliefs about worry did. Individuals who held strong beliefs about the negative consequences of worrying reported more intense daily worrying. Although this finding seems to suggest that positive beliefs about worry may *not* be that important to the experience of chronic worry, researchers have suggested that the role of positive beliefs may be easier to observe in detailed analyses of individual worry episodes (Thielsch et al., 2015). In line with this, researchers at the University of Sussex (Davey, Startup, MacDonald, Jenkins, & Patterson, 2005) have provided indirect evidence for the role of positive beliefs about worry in perseveration during worry episodes. In one study, participants were engaged in simulated worry via a "catastrophizing interview," which involved elaborating on worry out loud in response to sequenced prompts from an interviewer (e.g., "If X happened, what would happen next? And what would happen next?"). In one condition of the experiment, participants were told to ask themselves during the interview, "Have I reached the goal of exploring my worry?" and to continue to elaborate on their worry until satisfied that they had. Participants assigned to the other condition of the experiment were told to ask themselves, "Do I feel like I want to continue with this interview?" and to continue to elaborate on their worry until they no longer felt like it. Those who were instructed to ask themselves whether they had fully explored their worry generated more elaborate worry chains than did those in the "feel like it" condition. Although we cannot know which of the five positive beliefs about worry motivated the worry elaborations in this study, what the findings do tell is that when people enter an episode of worry believing that that they must stay with it until they have achieved some personal end, they tend to remain "stuck" in their worry.

We performed an analysis of data from one of our clinical trials (Dugas et al., 2010) to see the extent to which positive beliefs about worry decline with the treatment of GAD. We found that four of the five positive beliefs significantly decreased over the course of therapy for clients receiving CBT. Only the second belief (worrying increases motivation to get things done) did not change during CBT. Interestingly, for clients receiving the other treatment, applied relaxation, none of the five beliefs decreased over the course of therapy. Thus, it appears that targeting positive beliefs about worry in treatment makes a difference; these beliefs do not change unless the therapist and client directly address them.

In summary, the data show that positive beliefs about worry are related to level of worry and GAD. The nature of their relations to chronic worry and GAD awaits clarification via experimental manipulations and longitudinal studies. Although we propose that these beliefs play a role in the development and maintenance of GAD, we see these beliefs as playing a secondary role in the maintenance of chronic worry.

Negative Problem Orientation

According to current models of problem solving (D'Zurilla & Nezu, 2006), the problem-solving process can be broken down into two major constituents: problem orientation and problem-solving skills. Problem orientation refers to an individual's general cognitive set when faced with a problem. As such, it includes perceptions of problems, appraisals of oneself as a problem-solving agent, and expectations regarding problem-solving outcomes. Problem-solving skills, on the other hand, refer to the actual skills required to successfully solve everyday problems. These skills include: (1) defining the problem and formulating problem-solving goals; (2) generating alternative solutions; (3) choosing a solution; and (4) implementing the chosen solution and assessing its effectiveness. Overall, research has shown that worry and GAD are closely related to having a negative problem orientation, but that they are largely unrelated to knowledge of problem-solving skills. Thus, it appears that although individuals with GAD generally know how to solve their problems, they have difficulty successfully doing so because they have a negative cognitive set when faced with a problem. That is, they tend to view problems as threatening, to doubt their problem-solving ability, and to be pessimistic about problem-solving outcomes. Thus, the third component of our cognitive model of GAD is *negative problem orientation*. In the following paragraphs, we review the findings from studies using problem-solving questionnaires as well as those from a study using a novel structured interview.

Questionnaire Studies of Problem Solving

In our initial studies, we assessed the relationship between problem solving and worry in nonclinical volunteers using self-report questionnaires (Dugas et al.,

1997; Dugas, Letarte, Rhéaume, Freeston, & Ladouceur, 1995). In both studies, we found that although level of worry was strongly related to having a negative problem orientation, it was unrelated to knowledge of problem-solving skills. In the first study (Dugas et al., 1995), the findings showed that negative problem orientation continued to predict worry scores when anxiety and depression were statistically controlled. That is, the relationship between problem orientation and worry was not explained by their respective relationships with anxiety and depression. In the second study (Dugas et al., 1997), we added a measure of intolerance of uncertainty and found further evidence for the specificity of the relationship between negative problem orientation and excessive worry. Negative problem orientation maintained its relationship with worry when anxiety, depression, and intolerance of uncertainty were statistically controlled.

Given that negative problem orientation overlaps to some extent with the personality characteristics of pessimism, low self-mastery, and neuroticism, we examined their respective relationships with excessive worry (Robichaud & Dugas, 2005b). In terms of our model, the main finding was that the relation between negative problem orientation and worry was largely independent of all personality characteristics assessed in our study. In other words, negative problem orientation made a specific contribution to the prediction of worry, which could not simply be explained by the more general personality features of pessimism, low self-mastery, and neuroticism. Another important finding of this study was that negative problem orientation was a stronger predictor of worry than of depression when the above-mentioned personality characteristics were taken into account. Thus, although negative problem orientation has also been shown to predict depressive symptoms, it appears to be a stronger predictor of the tendency to worry. Taken together, the findings from the nonclinical questionnaire studies of problem solving suggest that negative problem orientation is a sensitive and specific marker of chronic and excessive worry.

For the most part, the findings of our clinical studies have supported those of our nonclinical studies. For example, we found that although clients with GAD and nonclinical control participants had relatively equivalent knowledge of problem-solving skills, the GAD clients had a more negative problem orientation (Dugas, Gagnon et al., 1998). In terms of comparisons between different clinical groups, we found that clients with GAD had a more negative problem orientation than clients with various other anxiety disorders, most of whom had primary obsessive-compulsive disorder (Ladouceur et al., 1999). However, we also found that clients with GAD and those with panic disorder had a similar problem orientation (Dugas, Marchand et al., 2005). Thus, it may be that GAD clients have a more negative problem orientation than some but not all other clients with anxiety-related disorders. Although the preliminary data point to this conclusion, further research is required to properly address the question of diagnostic specificity.

In a previous section of this chapter, we reported a study showing that level of intolerance of uncertainty was related to the severity of GAD *within* a sample of GAD clients (Dugas et al., 2007). In the same study, we found that level of negative problem orientation was also related to the severity of GAD symptoms.

In fact, intolerance of uncertainty and negative problem orientation were the only model components that predicted the severity of GAD. These findings suggest that, although negative problem orientation may not be specific to a diagnosis of GAD relative to all other anxiety disorder diagnoses, it does seem to be quite sensitive to the presence and severity of GAD. Clinically, therefore, negative problem orientation appears to be an important secondary target in the treatment of clients with GAD.

Interview Study of Problem Solving

According to D'Zurilla and Nezu's (2006) model of problem solving, individuals with adequate problem-solving skills will not be efficient problem solvers if they have a negative problem orientation, because having a negative problem orientation can interfere with the proper application of one's problem-solving skills. For individuals with GAD, this certainly appears to be the case. Although research shows that they possess problem-solving skills that are roughly equivalent to those of nonclinical individuals, clinical experience suggests that they often have difficulty dealing with relatively minor day-to-day problems. But how does having a negative problem orientation *actually* interfere with solving one's problems effectively? Does negative problem orientation always interfere with successful problem solving or does it only interfere under certain conditions? Does negative problem orientation prohibit the proper application of all problem-solving skills or only a subset of the skills? To begin addressing these questions, we developed a comprehensive interview procedure that allows us to examine the impact of problem orientation on each step of the problem-solving process for different types of problems.

Generally speaking, the Problem-Solving Interview asks participants to describe exactly what they would do at each stage of the problem-solving process (problem definition and goal formulation, generation of alternative solutions, decision making, and solution implementation and verification). Furthermore, participants are asked to go through the problem-solving process for two different problems: a hypothetical problem and a real-life problem they are currently experiencing. We asked nonclinical participants to complete the Problem-Solving Interview and a series of questionnaires, including the Negative Problem Orientation Questionnaire and the Intolerance of Uncertainty Scale (Robichaud, 2005). Overall, the findings showed that having a negative problem orientation was related to poor problem-solving performance under certain circumstances. In terms of specific results, three findings are particularly important for our model and treatment. First, regardless of the participants' level of intolerance of uncertainty, negative problem orientation was unrelated to performance at all problem-solving steps for the hypothetical problem. Second, for participants with low levels of intolerance of uncertainty, negative problem orientation was related to poor performance on *one* problem-solving step (that is, decision making) for the real-life problem. Finally, for participants with high levels of intolerance of uncertainty, negative problem orientation was related to poor performance on *all* problem-solving steps for the real-life problem. Consequently, it appears that having a negative problem orientation interferes most with the proper use of problem-solving skills when individuals who are intolerant of uncertainty have to deal with current problems that have personal relevance. Given that individuals with GAD typically have high levels of intolerance of uncertainty, it may be that their negative problem orientation has a particularly negative impact on their ability to deal with their personally relevant, day-to-day problems.

The findings of the interview study described above fit nicely with the clinical procedures described in Chapters 4 and 5, which include training in both problem orientation and problem-solving skills. Namely, it appears that offering training in the specific steps required to successfully deal with personally relevant problems can be important when treating GAD clients (who typically have a negative problem orientation *and* are intolerant of uncertainty). Therefore, the decision to include problem-solving training as an ancillary intervention in the treatment of GAD is supported by research that takes into account the complex interrelations between negative problem orientation, problem-solving skills, intolerance of uncertainty, and problem relevance.

Cognitive Avoidance

The final component of our model is *cognitive avoidance*. Like positive beliefs about worry and a negative problem orientation, it is a secondary process in our theoretical model. Cognitive avoidance refers to a variety of strategies that individuals with GAD use to avoid threatening cognitive and emotional content. These include suppressing thoughts that may lead to a worry cycle; substituting neutral or positive thoughts for worry; using distraction as a way to interrupt worry; avoiding situations that can trigger thoughts or mental images about worry-provoking situations; and thinking about disturbing events in words rather than in mental images. Research has substantiated that each of these cognitive avoidance strategies is independently related to excessive and catastrophic worry (e.g., Gosselin et al., 2002; Sexton & Dugas, 2008); however, we will focus our discussion mainly on the last strategy, avoidance of mental imagery of disturbing events. Thomas Borkovec was the first to observe that when individuals engage in chronic worry, they do so mainly in very vague words, statements, and questions (e.g., "What if *something* bad happens—what will I do? What if *things* don't work out?") and with a relative absence of mental imagery (Borkovec & Inz, 1990; Stöber & Borkovec, 2002). To fully grasp the clinical relevance of this finding, one must consider the effects of worrying in vague words and statements.

Research shows that thinking about emotionally evocative situations in vague, abstract words and statements elicits less subjective emotion and physiological responding than does picturing those same situations in vivid, concrete detail (Vrana, Cuthbert, & Lang, 1986). Research in cognitive psychology and social cognition suggests that there may be some "advantages" to thinking about situations in a fuzzy or blurry way, especially when these situations are frightening. Notably, thinking in this way increases the psychological distance between the individual and a feared hypothetical event (Trope & Liberman, 2010), making the event feel less real and less probable. Several lines of research in cognitive psychology also demonstrate however that vague, abstract thinking in response to problems (real or perceived) can have many negative consequences: (1) it reduces attentional control and restricts working memory capacity, making it difficult for people to focus on the task at hand; (2) it reduces the quality of problem solving; and (3) it actually makes people feel overwhelmed and emotionally reactive. But how do these findings help us understand pathological worry and GAD?

Individuals with GAD report that they adopt a vague, abstract mode of processing when they worry, so as to avoid seeing clearly, in their mind's eye, the situations that they fear. This likely makes frightening situations feel more distant and therefore less probable, at least in the moment. Studies with individuals high in pathological worry generally support the negative consequences of vague, abstract, verbal thinking as demonstrated in nonclinical research: GAD-type worry dysregulates attention and restricts working memory capacity, making it difficult to concentrate on a competing task. As discussed in the previous section, individuals with GAD also display challenges with problem solving. There is considerable research showing that individuals with GAD are reactive to emotional discomfort and experience challenges with the regulation of emotion. Finally, Stöber and Borkovec (2002) found that clients who showed the greatest improvements following treatment for GAD were those who had shifted to describing their worries in a more concrete, visually descriptive way, which suggests thinking style is important to the psychopathology of GAD.

Given the negative effects of vague, abstract worry, and the finding that shifting to a more concrete mode of thinking is associated with better outcomes, strategies to enhance a more concrete, specific mode of processing may be helpful for reducing worry. Research suggests that *concrete writing* evokes "vivid action scenes" in the mind's eye (Paivio, 1991); accordingly, in several controlled proof-of-concept experiments (Goldman, Dugas, Sexton, & Gervais, 2007; Fracalanza, Koerner, & Antony, 2014; Koerner & Prusaczyk, 2016; Ovanessian, Koerner, Antony, & Dugas, 2018) we have examined whether *writing* vividly and concretely about one's most feared hypothetical situation leads to a reduction in worry.

In each of these studies, participants high in pathological worry were guided to write a coherent narrative or story about their most feared hypothetical situation. To start, participants identified their worst worry and were then taken through a brief catastrophizing interview (e.g., "What is it about X that worries you? If X happened, what would happen next? What about X would you find frightening or bad if it did happen?"; Vasey & Borkovec, 1992) that allowed us to uncover their worst fear. In a thematic analysis of these interviews (Koerner, Fitzpatrick, Fracalanza, & McShane, 2016), we observed that in all cases, what people described as their worst worry was only superficially connected to their worst fear. For example, a participant initially reported that her worries were mainly in the area of romantic relationships and through the interview, it was discovered that she actually feared ending up homeless and alone in a shelter as a result of not being with her partner, and that she feared this more than the dissolution of the relationship. After identification of their personal fear narrative, participants were asked to write about their feared scenario in a style that is antithetical to the abstract, vague thinking that characterizes worry. Specifically, participants were instructed to write in the present tense and to write about their deepest thoughts and feelings, as well as their mind's eye sensory experiences. Writing about one's worst fear in accordance with these instructions for 20–30 minutes on each of 3 to 5 days was associated with moderate-to-large reductions in worry in the days following the writing intervention. Participants also reported being less afraid of holding in mind a mental image of their worst fear, suggesting that they were less motivated to avoid this content. From these results, it appears that writing repeatedly and concretely about a feared situation leads to fairly immediate reductions in worry and cognitive avoidance in people who are prone to pathological worry. But, how does this writing intervention produce these changes?

We propose that shifting into a more concrete mode of processing while elaborating on worries about feared situations *reduces negative beliefs about emotion*, particularly anxiety. Our work, as well as the work of others, suggests that individuals with GAD have a strong tendency to fear the experience of intense emotions, especially their own anxious responding (e.g., Buhr & Dugas, 2009; Mennin, Heimberg, Turk, & Fresco, 2002; Olatunji, Moretz, & Zlomke, 2010; Roemer, Salters, Raffa, & Orsillo, 2005; Sexton & Dugas, 2009b). By actively engaging in cognitive avoidance strategies, individuals with GAD succeed in temporarily dampening or eliminating intense emotion. However, this only strengthens negative beliefs about emotion because individuals do not learn to deal with their emotional responding. They do not learn that they can "handle" feeling anxious, for example, and they do not develop adaptive strategies to regulate strong emotions. We propose that training a more concrete mode of processing counteracts avoidance by evoking mental imagery, uncomfortable emotions, and uncertainty about how one will deal with these emotions; consequently, it targets negative beliefs about emotion by providing individuals with concrete, experiential evidence that they can in fact handle difficult, intense emotions without any loss of control. Indeed, in a study in which we asked participants to make predictions about what would happen in writing about their worst fear coming true (Koerner & Prusaczyk, 2016), many participants predicted that they would experience uncomfortable and unabating emotions. When these same participants were subsequently asked what they learned from writing about their feared hypothetical situation, they said that engaging in the writing exercise caused them to realize that they were more afraid of their sensations and emotional reactions, than of the situation itself. In a separate study, participants reported being less afraid of their anxiety (and other emotions, such as anger) in the days after writing repeatedly and concretely about their worst fear coming true (Ovanessian et al., 2018).

We also propose that writing concretely and repeatedly about one's worst fear *shifts individuals' perceptions of their feared hypothetical situations and their ability to cope with them*. In the aforementioned study in which we asked participants to make predictions about what would occur in writing about their worst fear, many participants also reported being afraid that thinking intentionally and concretely about their feared situation would somehow make it more likely to come true. After writing about their feared scenario, many participants did not perceive their feared scenario as any more or less probable, but reported realizing that their scenario was unrealistically "bad," and that even if it did occur, they could do something to change it or lessen its impact. These findings suggest that taking the time to write concretely and intentionally about the worst-case scenario impacts information processing by allowing individuals to appraise the situation differently and to consider less catastrophic alternatives.

Together, the findings of our experiments support concrete writing as an ancillary intervention in the treatment of GAD. Specifically, the findings suggest that in addition to reducing worry and cognitive avoidance in relation to feared hypothetical situations, writing concretely about the worst-case scenario provides individuals with important insights about what they may *actually* fear (e.g., for some people with GAD, it is losing control over emotions), experiential evidence that difficult emotions are tolerable, and an opportunity to gain perspective on their feared situation and their ability to cope with it.

Concluding Remarks

As mentioned at the beginning of this chapter, our main objective in developing and validating a cognitive behavioral model of GAD was to come up with a framework that would assist clinicians in working with GAD clients. We have tried to achieve a balance between "following the data" and formulating a model that has heuristic value in terms of clinical work. Although our model and treatment continue to evolve as more knowledge accrues, we believe that the model, as it now stands, is neither too complex nor overly simplistic for most clients seeking help for their worry and anxiety.

CHAPTER 3

Diagnosis and Assessment

As discussed in Chapter 1, the identification of generalized anxiety disorder (GAD) can present quite a challenge, even for the seasoned clinician. In fact, anxiety disorder specialists often find it difficult to recognize GAD, so it comes as no surprise that GAD has the lowest diagnostic reliability of all the anxiety disorders. In this chapter, we will provide a detailed outline of strategies that are helpful for the assessment of GAD in a clinical interview format, particularly in terms of the differential diagnosis of GAD from other anxiety-related disorders. In addition, because the use of standardized instruments is very important in establishing a diagnosis of GAD, useful diagnostic interviews and self-report questionnaires will be reviewed. Finally, in presenting each instrument we will add a discussion of the strengths and weaknesses of each one, as well as integrate thoughts about our experience with these different measures.

The Clinical Interview

When perusing the *DSM-5*, one is quickly struck by the overlap between virtually all of the GAD-associated symptoms (that is, restlessness or feeling keyed up or on edge, being easily fatigued, difficulty concentrating or mind going blank, irritability, and sleep disturbance) and the symptoms of other anxiety and depressive disorders. In fact, of all the associated symptoms included as criteria for GAD, only muscle tension is not included in the criteria for at least one other anxiety or depressive disorder. This highlights the fact that a focus on associated symptoms is generally not recommended when attempting to establish a GAD diagnosis, or any anxiety disorder diagnosis for that matter. The physiological experience of anxiety is largely similar across anxiety disorders, such that the client endorsement of GAD-associated symptoms is usually not very helpful with respect to the correct assessment of a particular anxiety disorder. Stated simply, anxiety "feels" like anxiety irrespective of the diagnosis: it is what triggers the anxiety that is most salient in terms of correctly identifying the problem. Clinicians should therefore focus their assessment on the client's cognitions, in this case excessive worry, in an attempt to establish a GAD diagnosis, rather than focusing on the associated symptoms. This is also a useful tip for clinicians assessing a client who has not been specifically referred for GAD, since simply asking whether a client has been worrying a great deal about a number of daily events can increase the chances of recognizing GAD if the disorder is in fact present.

One of the tricky aspects involved in the diagnosis of GAD is attempting to determine whether a client's worry is *excessive and uncontrollable*. Because it is fundamentally a subjective call whether a client is worrying to an excessive or uncontrollable degree, clinicians will have to weigh client report with their own judgment to determine the pathological nature of a client's worry. Although this may seem like a daunting task, we have elaborated some useful diagnostic questions that can help clinicians assess worry on these two dimensions.

GAD Worry

Given that excessive worry is subjective and highly dependent upon an individual's life circumstances, it is important to begin with an assessment of the stressors, changes, or difficulties in a client's life. This is necessary because a client's worries do not occur in a vacuum: they may be a normal response to a stressful situation. For example, a client may be worrying excessively about his mother's health, but if his mother was recently diagnosed with a life-threatening illness or is slated to undergo surgery in the near future, the level of worry the client is experiencing may be appropriate to his current situation. With this in mind, clients should be queried about possible stressors across various areas of life (i.e., family, finances, work/school). In addition, it is important to ask about changes in clients' lives, including positive ones (for example, a move, graduation from school, or a wedding), as these transitions can also be stressful, and it is normal to worry more in relation to these events.

Taking into consideration the backdrop of clients' current life circumstances and potential stressors, there are three properties of worry that should be the focus of assessment: frequency, excess, and control. Because the hallmark of GAD is worry about a number of events or activities, clinicians should first take the time to go through each major life area to get an idea of the frequency with which clients worry about each topic. This includes family, interpersonal relationships, work/school, health, finances, and day-to-day minor matters. In practical terms, clinicians should try to get an idea of how frequently clients worried about each topic *over the last six months.*

As noted above, clients may worry a great deal about a given topic, but their worry might not be considered excessive if current life circumstances account for the frequency. As such, placed within the context of situational stressors, worry can be deemed excessive if it is greater than what one might expect for a given topic. To determine the excessiveness of frequent worry topics, clinicians can ask several different questions. First, clients can be asked whether they feel that their worry is excessive: "Does your worry about X strike you as excessive? That is, do you think that you worry too much about X?" If clients experience difficulty with this, it can be helpful to remind them that this is a subjective question and that the goal is to try to get an idea of their own perceptions. There is no right or wrong answer to the question. Second, to address the role of potential stressors that may be exacerbating worry about a particular topic, clinicians might ask: "If everything is going all right with X, do you still worry a great deal about this topic?" Alternatively, a specific stressor can be incorporated into the question. For example, "I know that you mentioned your mother is ill right now, which is obviously causing you to worry a great deal about her, but do you find that you worry a lot about your family's health even when everyone is doing well?" A third way in which to tap excessiveness is to ask clients to compare their worry to that of others. That is, "If someone else were in your shoes, would they worry as much about X as you do?" or "Do others tell you that you worry too much about X?" In this manner, clinicians should begin to develop a good picture of what worry topics are particularly problematic for clients.

The third property of worry that warrants assessment is the client's sense of control over worry. Individuals with GAD will often describe their worries as spinning out of control, with one worry ("What if I get into a car accident one day?") engendering others ("What if it's a serious accident and I don't recover? What will happen to my children?"). This *chaining effect* of worry, and the resultant feeling of uncontrollability that is characteristic of GAD, can be addressed through the analogy of a freight train. That is, "Is it difficult to control your worry about X? Does it feel like a freight train, in that it is difficult to put on the brakes once it has really started up?" Once again, the clinician should ask these questions about each worry topic. This is important not only to satisfy the criterion of excessive and uncontrollable worry about a number of events, but also to allow for differential diagnosis. Since individuals with various other anxiety disorders will typically report worrying about their primary fear, it is necessary to make certain that a client with suspected GAD is truly worrying about a number of topics.

GAD-Associated Symptoms

In order to be formally diagnosed with GAD, clients need to endorse at least three of the following six associated symptoms: restlessness or feeling keyed up or on edge, being easily fatigued, difficulty concentrating or mind going blank, irritability, muscle tension, and sleep disturbance. Identified symptoms must also be experienced chronically, for at least 6 months, in order to satisfy GAD diagnostic criteria. As noted earlier, other than the experience of muscle tension, all of the GAD-associated symptoms can be found among the criteria for other mental health disorders. This is particularly the case for depressive disorders, where a client with major depressive disorder or persistent depressive disorder (i.e., dysthymia) might endorse concentration difficulties, fatigue, and sleep disturbance. Because of this, it is a good idea for clinicians to question clients further about these symptoms to determine whether they are in fact GAD-related. For example, when querying about muscle tension, clients can be asked: "Do you find that most of the muscle tension is in your neck and shoulders?" Since chronic anxiety often leads to tension in that part of the body, individuals with GAD will usually endorse this symptom. In addition, specifying a particular location of tension gives clients the feeling that they are "in the right place." That is, that they are speaking with someone who really understands their specific difficulties.

When asking about concentration difficulties, clients can be asked to expand on their answer if they endorse this symptom: "Why do you think you have concentration problems? Does it feel like your mind is running at 100 miles an hour with various worries and that as a result, it is hard to focus or concentrate?" Finally, in terms of sleeping difficulties, it is a good idea to get a sense of the type of sleeping problem (that is, problems falling asleep, staying asleep, or restless sleep), because for GAD sufferers this is most likely due to excessive worry. For example, if a client endorses difficulties falling asleep, they can be queried: "Do you find that your mind starts spinning with worries the moment you put your head to the pillow?" Alternatively, clients who endorse difficulties staying asleep or restless sleep can be asked: "Do you find that you are so preoccupied with worries that you wake up throughout the night?" By asking clients to provide additional information about how they experience their associated symptoms, the clinician will be in a much better position to determine if the symptoms are part of the GAD diagnosis or if they reflect the presence of another disorder.

Safety Behaviors in GAD

Although not formally a part of the GAD diagnosis, identifying the presence of GAD-related safety behaviors can help clinicians gain further confidence in their diagnostic decision, as well as set the stage for the treatment to follow. Safety behaviors are deliberate actions (or mental acts) that individuals engage in as an attempt to reduce anxiety and avoid or prevent a feared outcome (Salkovskis, 1991). The type of safety behaviors individuals engage in is dependent upon the particular feared outcome, or theme of threat, they wish to avoid. Since the themes of threat can vary across the anxiety disorders, a different set of behaviors can be expected according to the particular anxiety disorder. For example, one theme of threat seen in social anxiety disorder (SAD) is a fear of being viewed poorly by others. Individuals with SAD can engage in a range of safety behaviors including avoiding social situations, averting their gaze, speaking as little as possible, or rehearsing small talk prior to attending a social outing (Clark & Wells, 1995), all of which involve avoiding or reducing potential negative judgment from others.

Although we will expand on this in later chapters, the primary theme of threat in GAD is the fear of uncertainty. Individuals with GAD tend to engage in behaviors designed to avoid or reduce uncertainty in daily life situations, either by attempting to reduce the uncertain elements in a given situation or avoiding those situations altogether. Examples of GAD safety behaviors can include seeking out excessive reassurance or information, procrastination, excessive planning and preparing, keeping a very predictable routine, and doing everything by oneself (i.e., refusing to delegate tasks to others).

With respect to the assessment of GAD, it is a good idea to inquire about the safety behaviors that clients engage in to cope with their worries, as it can provide further evidence for the validity of a GAD diagnosis. There are several ways that clients can be queried about safety behaviors. Depending upon the level of insight, clients can be asked directly or indirectly about their methods of coping. Specifically, some people can readily identify their particular coping behaviors when asked, "What do you tend to do when you are worrying excessively?" In this case, individuals might volunteer some of the ways that they attempt to reduce their worry and anxiety, including keeping a predictable routine, avoiding situations that are novel or for which the outcome is unclear, or double-checking tasks repeatedly to ensure that they were correctly completed. However, many clients do not always realize that these behaviors are tied to their excessive worries. As such, it can also be helpful to ask specific questions about safety behaviors. For example, clients can be queried, "Do you find that you make lots of lists to make sure that you don't forget anything, seek out excessive information or reassurance before making even minor decisions, or procrastinate or avoid situations that lead to worry and anxiety?" It is recommended that clinicians keep the behaviors that clients endorse in mind, as they will be of use when subsequently embarking upon treatment.

Impairment and Distress

The final criterion required to ascribe a diagnosis of GAD is the presence of significant distress or interference in an individual's life as a result of their symptoms. This can certainly be determined by simply asking clients whether they experience mild, moderate, or severe distress and interference due to their worry and anxiety; however, this is also an opportunity to gather additional information about the impact of the disorder on the client's life. As will be discussed at length in later chapters, there is a certain amount of ambivalence that clients often experience with regard to reducing their worries. Since many view themselves as "born worriers," it can be difficult for them to imagine a life without excessive worry. As such, it will be important for clinicians to have an understanding of the negative impact that worry has had on the client's life, as this is further information that can be used later in treatment.

In order to get a good picture of the GAD-related impairment, it might be helpful to probe specific aspects of the client's life. For example, how is this impacting upon the person's relationships with family and friends? Is the person constantly giving advice to others to the degree that it is causing tension? Problems may also arise at work or in school. Are assignments getting done on time, or is the individual spending so much time worrying about small details that work productivity is suffering? Another highly revelatory aspect is that of quality of life. Is the client enjoying life? More specifically, when engaging in a pleasant activity, is the client so preoccupied by worries about future events that they can't enjoy the moment? Allowing clients to discuss the repercussions of worry on their lives can strengthen their motivation for treatment and give them the feeling of being understood.

In summary, there are numerous aspects to consider when making a GAD diagnosis, the most time-consuming of which is the assessment of worry. Since worry is a universal human phenomenon, it is important to verify that the client's worries are frequent, excessive, and difficult to control, as well as related to several different events or activities of daily life. Moreover, the worry must be chronic and longstanding, and not simply the result of external stressors. The detail described herein can often result in a rather lengthy clinical interview, particularly when time is taken to gather specific information about each major worry topic. However, there are several benefits to spending a full session or two on information gathering. First, it will increase the clinician's confidence in a GAD diagnosis if one is given, and considering its low diagnostic reliability, it is important to take the time to really understand a client's presenting complaints. Second, it allows for a complete "picture" of the client, which will be quite helpful during the treatment phase. Finally, clients are more likely to feel that they are understood by the clinician, which can help to establish a good rapport right from the initial assessment stage.

Obstacles to the Diagnosis of GAD

GAD clients are like most people who present for treatment with mental health issues in that they are rarely "textbook cases." Few, if any, will walk into the clinician's office and state that they are experiencing excessive and uncontrollable worry. Unless specifically referred for GAD, the majority of clients will not even think to mention worry as their primary complaint. The following are some obstacles to diagnosis, as well as some practical suggestions to address them.

"I'm Not a Worrier"

For various reasons, clients with GAD might deny that their problem is excessive worry. This can be due to the belief that worry is not a legitimate complaint, is socially undesirable, or does not reflect the intensity of the individual's suffering. As a result, the clinician's task will involve ascertaining what words the client is using to describe worry and providing a more expansive definition of worry that the client can accept and endorse. As mentioned in Chapter 1, frequent alternate terminologies that clients use in place of worry are: "anxiety," "fear," and "phobia." For example, "I am fearful of everything! I have a phobia about travel, storms, and even driving a car. I also get really anxious in social situations." From this description, the client could indeed have several specific phobias, as well as some social anxiety. However, by probing into the reasons underlying these fears, it can quickly become apparent that these are worries rather than phobias. For example, when asked why he is fearful about travel, the client might respond: "I'm afraid that there might be a problem with the plane. What if it crashed? What would happen to my children? How would my wife cope with being a single parent?" Given that this response looks like a worry chain, it is recommended that the clinician probe about other "fears" to determine whether they are also mislabeled worries.

When clients are reluctant to describe their problems in terms of worry, we have found it helpful to explain what we mean when we talk about worry. A useful explanation is as follows:

> When I talk about worry, I'm not referring to the kind of worrying that almost all of us do in our daily lives to some extent. I'm talking about excessive worry, which is essentially a form of elaborate *scenario building*. That is,

taking anything uncertain in your life and trying to think of every possible eventuality so that nothing comes as a surprise. For example, "What if X happens? Well, then I might do this. . . . But what if Y happens? Well in that case, I might try to do this. . . ." Some people describe this type of scenario building as "fear" or "anxiety," but it is still worry. Does this sound like what you do?

By providing an alternate way of describing worry, clinicians can not only better establish a diagnosis of GAD when that is in fact the problem, but they can also lay some of the groundwork for the forthcoming treatment. Clients need to be able to recognize that they are in fact worrying, or they might not see a treatment that targets excessive worry as appropriate for their particular distress.

"Yes, I Have That Too . . ."

Given that individuals with GAD often describe worrying about "everything," it should come as no surprise that some would be very worried about whether they are describing their symptoms properly (that is, "What if I don't explain myself well and I'm misdiagnosed?"). As a result, some GAD clients can feel the need to provide exhaustive detail in response to each question, as well as endorse symptoms from many other anxiety disorders that they are not currently experiencing. That is, if they have ever experienced symptoms from any particular diagnostic category (as we all do sometimes), they will respond in the affirmative to questions about those symptoms. For example, a GAD client queried about social anxiety might endorse fears of being negatively evaluated by others in social situations even if this is not causing any particular distress or interference. Obviously, if a client is endorsing symptoms from every diagnostic category, the interview can become extremely lengthy, and the challenge of distinguishing clinically significant problems from those that are not increases exponentially.

How can a clinician deal with a client who is endorsing virtually every symptom he or she is asked about, while still maintaining rapport and identifying multiple concurrent disorders if comorbidity is present? First, the clinician can discuss this issue at the outset. Clients can be told that they will be asked about a variety of symptoms, many of which probably will not apply to them, and only those symptoms that they are actually experiencing (or have experienced in the past) will be discussed in more detail. It is also a good idea to discuss the difference between experiencing a symptom (which is common to most people) and having the symptom as a serious problem for the individual. One way to address this is by saying the following:

We are going to be discussing a lot of different types of symptoms today so that we can determine which ones are problematic for you and which ones aren't. I will always start off by asking some general questions that require a yes or no answer. If the symptom applies to you, I will ask you about it in more detail, but if it doesn't apply to you, we will simply move on to the next. I want to remind you that most of the symptoms that I will be talking to you about today are things that many people experience to some degree from time to time in their lives. For example, many people are afraid of snakes, but we wouldn't classify this fear as a "disorder" unless it significantly interfered with their lives and caused them great distress. That means that when I ask you about particular symptoms, it is best to say yes to a question only if I am describing something that you experience quite often and that is really bothering you or interfering with your life. Do you have any questions about that?

By taking the time to "set the stage" for the interview, clients are less likely to endorse almost every symptom. As a result, identifying the disorders that are actually a problem for the individual can become clearer and the length of the interview can be reduced as well. However, if clients are still endorsing virtually every symptom throughout the clinical interview, clinicians might want to ask: "Is this something that you experience excessively or severely and is it causing you great distress?" Eventually, clients can be expected to focus more specifically on their clinically significant problems. As stated beforehand, GAD clients will occasionally engage in this overreporting behavior out of a concern that if they fail to disclose anything, they might be improperly diagnosed. It is important for clinicians not to lose patience with clients, but to bring them back on course gently in order to maintain a good working relationship at this initial therapeutic stage.

Misdiagnosing Symptoms as GAD

Another common problem in diagnosis is the labeling of GAD when the disorder is not in fact present. Although this will be discussed in greater detail in the differential diagnosis section, a frequent reason for this problem is due to the introduction of mental health terms into the common vernacular. That is, more and more, clients will describe increases in anxiety as "panicking," bouts of low mood as "depression," and ruminations as "obsessing." In the case of GAD, just as it is likely for clients to describe their worries as fears, it is also common for clients with other anxiety or depressive disorders to state, "I worry about many different things." Because of this, clinicians always need to sub-question clients about their worries in order to ensure that the theme of threat underlying an individual's worries is clear. For example, a client might state that they worry about school, work, and social situations. On the surface, this is suggestive of worry about several different daily life events (which is characteristic of GAD), but the underlying theme of threat for these disparate situations might be a fear of negative evaluation that is better accounted for by a diagnosis of social anxiety disorder. Such a potential misdiagnosis underscores the importance of not only being thorough in the assessment of GAD, but also in the evaluation of other anxiety, depressive, and related disorders as well.

Differential Diagnosis

As noted previously, of all the anxiety disorders, GAD can be one of the trickiest diagnoses to make. Even in anxiety clinics where clinicians are expecting to encounter GAD, it is not an obvious or straightforward diagnosis. Certainly, for clinicians in nonspecialized settings, it can be even more of a challenge to identify. The problem is aggravated by the fact that when medical practitioners refer anxious clients for psychological treatment, they will occasionally note only "generalized anxiety" in the referral. This highlights a frequent misunderstanding of GAD as a diagnosis for individuals who are simply "generally anxious," rather than a problem in its own right. However, in these cases, "generalized anxiety" can refer to any of the anxiety disorders, not necessarily GAD, as the locus of the anxiety was probably not thoroughly assessed. In essence, clients who are described as having "generalized anxiety" may be suffering from an anxiety disorder other than GAD, and clients with GAD may be misdiagnosed as having another anxiety, depressive, or related disorder. For this reason, it is helpful to have some guidelines to aid in the differential diagnosis of GAD in relation to other disorders.

Illness Anxiety Disorder (Health Anxiety)

In the *DSM-5*, illness anxiety disorder (IAD) is classified under "Somatic Symptom and Related Disorders" (APA, 2013). IAD has also been called health anxiety (previously known as hypochondriasis), and it is defined as an excessive preoccupation with having or acquiring a serious disease or illness. The disorder is the result of a catastrophic misinterpretation of physical symptoms and bodily sensations. For example, a persistent cough or a small bump on a part of the body may be erroneously interpreted as signs of cancer. Most individuals with IAD will engage in care-seeking behaviors, wherein they frequently consult with medical specialists for their feared illnesses, although the reassurance they receive from these visits is typically short-lived, as they tend to persist in their belief that the disease or illness is in fact present although undiagnosed. Some clients with IAD will instead engage in care-avoidant behavior, wherein despite fears of having a serious illness, they nonetheless avoid medical visits out of a fear of medical testing and severe diagnoses.

Because of the excessive preoccupation and worry about health, illness anxiety can resemble GAD. As such, if a client reports excessive and uncontrollable worry about her health, the clinician is faced with a dilemma: does the client have GAD, IAD, or both disorders? If the client only reports excessive worry about her health, that is, she does not list worries about any topics other than her fears about having contracted a specific disease, then a diagnosis of IAD would likely be warranted. However, if a client reports excessive worries about other topics in addition to concerns about health, then the primary issue becomes the discrimination between a diagnosis of GAD or a diagnosis of GAD and IAD (with the primary disorder being established based on which problem is causing the individual greater distress and interference).

To aid in this discrimination, there are several useful questions that clinicians can ask. First, a primary distinction between both disorders relates to the belief that the feared disease or illness is already present. With GAD, individuals tend to report excessive worries about one day developing a serious disease such as cancer; thus, the focus is on the *possibility* of developing the disease. With illness anxiety, individuals tend to focus on their conviction that they may have *already developed* the disease, and as a result, numerous medical consultations are typically sought out to identify and begin treating the feared illness. Although the *DSM-5* states that IAD is defined by the preoccupation with having *or acquiring* a serious illness, our experience suggests that in the vast majority of cases, these individuals believe they have already developed the illness. Clients can therefore be asked the following question: "Do you think that you may already have a serious disease or illness that has simply not been diagnosed yet, or are you mostly worried about potentially getting this disease in the future?" If clients report that the main focus of their health concerns is the possibility of developing a health condition in the future (and the consequences thereof), then a diagnosis of IAD can be ruled out, as the concerns are most consistent with a diagnosis of GAD. If clients instead report the conviction that they have already contracted a disease not yet identified, then a diagnosis of IAD might be more appropriate.

Other useful questions relate to the erroneous interpretations of physical symptoms or bodily changes. Individuals with illness anxiety have a tendency to catastrophically misinterpret any physical change as evidence of a serious illness. As such, a slight discoloration of the skin, a rash, or a cough is taken as proof of having contracted a disease. Clients can therefore be asked the following: "Do you often perceive changes in your body or physical symptoms as evidence that you have in fact contracted a serious illness?" As stated previously, GAD clients might worry excessively about their health and the possibility of becoming ill, but they are less likely to focus on the interpretation of minor physical symptoms.

In terms of medical consultations, individuals with IAD can present for the same tests on several occasions, out of a conviction that a specific disease is present but unidentified. Often, the medical visits are for very frivolous or minor concerns, and although individuals with GAD will also frequently consult with medical specialists, they are less likely to return for the same tests multiple times. With respect to IAD, all of these behaviors provide only brief reassurance. For example, clients might feel relieved following a medical visit where no illness was found; however, that relief is short-lived; before long, the individual with IAD will once again become convinced that the feared disease is present. GAD clients, however, might see several medical specialists for their concerns, but the worries are assuaged once the results of medical tests are provided. If clients are care-avoidant, refusing to see a physician to receive medical testing, the rationale for this decision typically differs for GAD and IAD clients. Individuals with IAD will on occasion avoid medical consults out of a significant fear of having a dire diagnosis confirmed, whereas GAD clients are more likely to believe that additional medical tests are unnecessary, despite their worries. In the latter case, the avoidance of medical care is typically not due to a fear of having confirmation of a serious illness.

As a final note, if the clinician determines that a client merits a diagnosis of illness anxiety in addition to GAD, a simple way to determine which disorder is primary is to ask the client which problem is most distressing. This can be accomplished with a pie chart, where clients are asked: "If this pie represents all the problems that you are struggling with now, how much of the pie would the illness anxiety take? How much would GAD take?" In this manner, clinicians can determine whether GAD should be the focus of treatment or whether it is secondary to another condition.

Social Anxiety Disorder

Social anxiety disorder is characterized by an intense fear of social or performance situations, where one might be judged or thought of negatively. Individuals with social anxiety tend to engage in significant avoidance of feared social situations, and they typically experience extreme anxiety when anticipating an upcoming social event or activity. It is an anxiety disorder that can manifest itself in multiple situations, including parties, business meetings, one-on-one conversations, or crowded areas where one might be prone to be judged or observed by others. Because of both the heterogeneity of situations where an individual with social anxiety might feel anxious, and the tendency to worry about these situations prior to entering them, the disorder can appear quite similar to GAD.

As with illness anxiety, if worries are relegated exclusively to concerns about being judged or negatively evaluated in social situations, then a diagnosis of GAD is easily ruled out. However, it can be a challenge to determine whether disparate worries about various situations are in fact subsumed under a diagnosis of social anxiety disorder. A primary distinction between GAD and social anxiety is the theme of threat. If, for example, a client reports worrying about several situations (e.g., work, school, interpersonal/relationships), clinicians should ask specific details about what the individual is worried about in order to better understand the fear that is motivating the worry. Clients with social anxiety will consistently endorse a fear that they might be observed or evaluated by others, or that they will do something embarrassing or humiliating in front of others. For example, an individual with social anxiety might report worry about an upcoming presentation at work. However, additional queries might reveal that the main thrust of the worry is that the presentation will be viewed poorly, and that others will think the individual is stupid, awkward, or incompetent as a result. In this case, the theme of threat of negative evaluation can clearly be seen. Although GAD clients can also endorse this type of worry, they will likewise endorse other concerns as well, thereby satisfying the criterion of "worries about a number of daily events."

The picture becomes more complex if clients appear to report GAD worries in addition to social concerns. The question then becomes: does the client have a diagnosis of GAD where one of the worry topics is social/interpersonal situations, or is an additional diagnosis of social anxiety disorder merited? A good way to determine this is to ask about avoidance behavior. One of the hallmarks of social anxiety disorder is significant avoidance of social situations, the extent of which is distressing to the individual and interferes with his or her life. For example, a client with social anxiety might avoid initiating conversations with others, attending social gatherings with friends, or eating and writing in public. Although GAD clients might engage in a certain amount of avoidance of triggers for their worries, it is their excessive worry and anxiety that is causing most of their distress and impairment, not the avoidance behavior. As such, clients can be asked the following: "When you think about your fear of social situations, what would you say is most distressing and interfering for you: the fact that you worry excessively about these situations or the fact that you avoid them?" GAD clients will frequently endorse greater distress and impairment from their worries, whereas individuals with an additional diagnosis of social anxiety disorder will often endorse avoidance.

Obsessive-Compulsive Disorder

Obsessive-compulsive disorder (OCD), formerly categorized as an anxiety disorder, is currently under the category "Obsessive-Compulsive and Related Disorders" in the *DSM-5* (APA, 2013). It is characterized by the presence of obsessions or compulsions that cause significant interference and distress. Because obsessions are intrusive and recurrent thoughts, they can at times appear quite similar to GAD worries, once again rendering the discrimination between GAD and another disorder a challenge. In terms of overt behavioral compulsions such as excessive hand washing, touching or tapping of objects in a ritualistic manner, or excessive checking of locks and appliances, the presence of these behaviors is clearly specific to OCD. As such, if clients endorse these types of overt compulsions, a diagnosis of OCD is warranted. However, individuals with OCD can also experience solely the presence of obsessions without associated observable compulsions. Since both obsessions and worries are essentially cognitive intrusions, the distinction between these two is not immediately evident. Although there are certain obsessions that are more obviously distinct from GAD worries, such as an obsessional impulse to stab a loved one compared to an excessive worry about completing work tasks on time, there are cognitive intrusions that are less easily distinguishable. For example, thoughts about harm occurring to one's child can be viewed as either an obsession or a worry. Discriminating between the two can be effectively done by querying clients along several dimensions about their thoughts.

First, the content of worries tends to be about real-life daily events (e.g., work or school performance, punctuality, interpersonal relationships). In contrast, obsessions are typically considered odd or inappropriate, such as sexual or blasphemous thoughts. Moreover, although obsessions can take the form of thoughts (for example, "What if I hit someone with my car while driving?"), they can also be experienced as vivid visual images (for example, an image of punching someone) or impulses (for example, an urge to scream obscenities in church). Worries, on the other hand, are experienced mostly as thoughts and rarely take the form of images or impulses. Second, obsessive thoughts are seen by the client as unwanted and intrusive. That is, they are experienced as highly unpleasant and distressing, and the client will typically make a concerted effort to resist or avoid the thoughts. This is not the case with GAD worries. The content of the worries is not typically viewed as inappropriate and is largely ego-syntonic. In fact, as will be discussed in later chapters, many worries experienced by GAD clients are viewed as serving a positive function (for example, "The fact that I worry about the health of my children shows that I am a caring mother"). Finally, the content of obsessions tends to be static in nature. That is, individuals with OCD typically experience repeated intrusions of the same distressing thought, image, or impulse. Worries, however, are largely dynamic in nature, as the content will shift from day to day, and they are experienced as a continually evolving scenario. For example, worries about the health of one's child ("What if my child gets injured at school?") will typically lead to other worries ("What if the injury is serious, and my child never recovers? What if my child's performance at school and ability to make friends is affected? How will this impact my family?"). As such, through a careful assessment of the content and the nature of a client's thoughts, clinicians can differentiate between GAD and OCD with confidence.

Major Depressive Disorder and Persistent Depressive Disorder

Major depressive disorder (or depression) is characterized by persistent feelings of sadness and loss of interest in previously enjoyed activities for a period of at least two weeks. Persistent depressive disorder (previously dysthymia) is a more chronic form of depression, as symptoms must be present for at least two years. There are two main reasons why discriminating between these disorders and GAD can prove to be a challenge. First, there is an overlap in terms of associated symptoms. Specifically, poor concentration, sleeping difficulties, and fatigue are associated with GAD, depression, and dysthymia. Second, depressed or dysthymic individuals are prone to rumination, that is, a passive and repetitive focus on one's distress and the meaning of that distress (Nolen-Hoeksema, 1998). This kind of dwelling thought process could easily resemble GAD worry. Moreover, GAD and depression/dysthymia have been found to co-occur quite frequently. As such, it is important to determine whether clients are suffering from either one or both disorders in order to begin developing a proper treatment strategy.

In terms of GAD-associated symptoms, the experience of muscle tension, particularly in the neck and shoulders, has been found to be specific to GAD. As a consequence, participants who endorse this symptom, in addition to other GAD-associated symptoms, are likely to merit a diagnosis of GAD. However, not all GAD clients endorse significant muscle tension, and because of the considerable overlap between the disorders, clinicians should ultimately place the diagnostic focus on the client's thought content rather than their associated symptoms. That is, the emphasis should be placed on distinguishing between GAD worries and depressive ruminations. A primary distinction between worries and ruminations is the temporal focus. Individuals who worry tend to focus on potential negative events in the future (that is, negative things that *might* happen), whereas those who ruminate tend to focus on negative events that have taken place in the past (that is, negative things that have *already* happened). One potential complication with this distinction is the fact that worries can occasionally relate to past events. For example, a client might be preoccupied about an exam that they failed the week before. On its surface, this thought appears to be a depressive rumination as it involves a negative event in the past. However, whether it is a worry or a rumination will depend on why the client is focusing on that particular concern. That is, this may in fact be a GAD worry if the individual is thinking about a past event in terms of its *future* repercussions, whereas it is more likely to reflect depression if the individual is dwelling on the event as yet another example of failure. For example, dwelling on a failed exam and what this says about the individual (e.g., "I'm an idiot; there's no point in trying") is more characteristic of depression. However, worrying about whether the failed exam will impact whether the individual passes the course and ultimately graduates (e.g., "What if I fail the class? What if I have to complete an additional semester before completing my degree?") is more characteristic of worry. As with other disorders, the best way to confidently diagnose GAD is to obtain detailed information about the content of the client's thoughts and the process underlying their troublesome thoughts (see Table 3.1 for an overview of the differential diagnosis of GAD and the previously discussed disorders).

In summary, differential diagnosis with respect to GAD can be quite a challenge. This is due not only to the inclusion of relatively subjective criteria for the disorder (that is, excessive and uncontrollable worry) and the absence of specific GAD safety behaviors in the *DSM-5*, but also to the high comorbidity rates between GAD and other disorders. As such, it is extremely important to take the time to properly assess the thought content of clients. Although this process of assessment might seem

Table 3.1 Differential Diagnosis: Tips for Discriminating between GAD and Other Anxiety, Depressive, and Related Disorders

GAD	Illness Anxiety Disorder
1. Excessive worry about several topics, which might include disease or illness	1. Excessive preoccupation with disease or illness
2. Worry about potentially contracting a disease in the future, but no conviction that it is already present but undiagnosed	2. Belief that one has already contracted the feared disease (in most cases)
3. May present for medical consultations, but visits are not excessive regarding feared disease	3. Excessive medical consultations and reassurance-seeking; reassurance provided is short-lived
4. No presence of persistent misinterpretation of bodily symptoms or changes	4. Physical symptoms are erroneously interpreted as signs of a serious illness (despite evidence to the contrary)
GAD	Social Anxiety Disorder
1. Worry about several different events in daily life that can include social/interactional situations	1. Worries exclusively relate to situations where the individual might be judged negatively by others for behaving in a socially inept or awkward manner
2. Worries are not confined to negative social evaluation concerns	2. Underlying fear of all worries is of being judged or evaluated negatively by others
3. Worries about social situations are more distressing and impairing than avoidance	3. Avoidance of social situations causes significant distress and impairment

GAD	Obsessive-Compulsive Disorder
1. Worries about real-life daily events	1. The content of obsessions is considered odd or inappropriate
2. Worries are not seen as inappropriate; the content is often ego-syntonic (e.g., worries about family can be viewed as evidence of the individual's caring and empathy toward others)	2. Obsessions are seen as intrusive and unwanted; the content of which causes significant distress
3. Content of worries is dynamic (i.e., takes the form of a continually evolving scenario)	3. Content of obsessions is typically static (i.e., repetition of the same thought, image, or urge)

GAD	Depression and Dysthymia
1. Muscle tension as a unique GAD-associated symptom	1. Muscle tension is not a symptom associated with depression or dysthymia
2. Cognitive content is worry	2. Cognitive content is depressive rumination
3. Focus is on negative events that may occur in the future	3. Focus is on negative events that have occurred in the past

lengthy, the information derived is invaluable both to the clinician and to the client. Clinicians can feel confident that when a diagnosis is made, it accurately reflects the symptom presentation of their clients, and clients can leave the assessment with a better understanding of themselves and their distress. Although the previous information was primarily described in a clinical interview format, it is our belief that the use of structured diagnostic tools is vital to a complete and thorough assessment. As such, the following section will address the various structured assessment tools that are most relevant to GAD and to our particular treatment protocol.

Structured Diagnostic Interviews

Although many clinicians prefer to use unstructured clinical interviews when assessing their clients, our experience has been that the use of structured diagnostic interviewing is highly beneficial when attempting to identify GAD. We have found that clients respond very well to the structured nature of the interview, and often interpret the highly structured and in-depth nature of the interview as a sign that they are "in the right place." In fact, many clients have never had a thorough investigation of their anxiety and welcome the opportunity to discuss the many facets of their anxiety and anxiety-related problems.

The main advantage of structured diagnostic interviewing is that the clinician is less likely to make the mistake of not going beyond clients' presenting complaints. By inquiring about a broad range of emotional problems, the clinician may discover that what appeared to be a simple case of GAD is in fact a case of many comorbid conditions. This is particularly the case with clients who are experiencing a great deal of distress as a result of their primary presenting complaint. Their focus on the most disruptive symptoms can lead them to ignore or fail to disclose other concurrent problems unless specifically queried. As noted previously, not only is GAD a disorder with a high comorbidity rate, but disentangling GAD from other secondary diagnoses can be a challenge. It is therefore highly advantageous to use a structured assessment tool in order to ensure that all other relevant disorders are properly queried.

Another advantage of structured diagnostic interviewing is that it provides information that can be used to establish a "baseline," which can then be used as a comparison point for changes over time in treatment and thereafter. This is useful not only for the clinician to monitor progress in treatment, but also for clients themselves, as over the course of treatment they might be unaware or dismissive of the extent of positive changes they have made. A final advantage worthy of mention is that structured diagnostic interviews prevent the clinician from "drifting" away from standard diagnostic criteria to a more idiosyncratic or personal interpretation of the criteria for the specific disorders contained in the different classification systems. Thus, there are a number of important advantages to structured diagnostic interviewing that more than compensate for the disadvantages of using this methodology. There are, however, at least two disadvantages to using these interviews.

The first and most obvious disadvantage of structured diagnostic interviewing is that the interviews can take a considerable amount of time to administer, anywhere from 30 minutes to 2 hours depending on the interview used and the client's problems. Although this does not necessarily present a difficulty in the context of research, it is definitely an important consideration for clinicians working in non-research settings, whether they work in the public or the private sector. The second disadvantage worthy of mention is that there is an important learning curve to the proper use of diagnostic interviews. Until the clinician becomes accustomed to using an interview, there is a chance that the interview will feel "artificial" and may even interfere with the establishment of a sound working relationship with the client (although, in our experience, this is quite rare). Thus, clinicians should expect that they might feel awkward the first few times that they use an interview. Overall, however, the advantages of structured diagnostic interviewing outweigh the disadvantages. It is important, though, that clinicians follow certain guidelines when using structured diagnostic interviews. In the following paragraphs, we will describe the main guidelines for using most assessment interviews. Although the list is not meant to be exhaustive (interviews typically come with clinician manuals that describe the guidelines in detail), it is meant to give the reader a sense of the "spirit" that goes into structured diagnostic interviewing.

Guidelines for Using Structured Diagnostic Interviews

When using structured diagnostic interviews, clinicians should take five or 10 minutes before beginning the interview to explain why a structured approach is helpful for the diagnosis and conceptualization of the client's problem. The client should be prepared for the structure and organization of the interview by the provision of a general description of how it will proceed. For example, the clinician may want to present the following notions:

> Today, I will be using a structured interview to help us to gain a better understanding of your difficulties. As you will see, I will ask a wide variety of questions, some of which will be relevant to your situation and some of which will not. It is important that I ask you all of these questions because it is easy to focus on just one problem without verifying if you have other problems that might be related to your presenting complaint. In other words, we need to ascertain if there are problems that may not be so obvious to you that are contributing to your difficulties. That is why I will be asking you about so many different things today. Does that seem reasonable to you? Do you have any questions before we proceed with the interview?

Another important point that clinicians should keep in mind is that they should not be apologetic for using a structured diagnostic interview (which is what most clinicians tend to do the first few times they conduct a structured interview). In our experience, it is important that the clinician model confidence when using a validated assessment strategy. Although lengthy, the interview should be presented as a valuable tool that will not only allow the clinician to thoroughly understand the client's problems, but also allow the client to leave the session with a better understanding of themselves. In terms of the actual interview process, the clinician should pose each question as it is formulated in the interview. Only if the client does not fully understand the question should a different formulation of the question be used. If the clinician is not clear on the meaning of the client's answer, additional explanations should be sought. For example, the clinician may ask what clients mean when they say that they are "panicked at work." As mentioned previously, clinicians should also not be overly reliant on clients' answers to their questions. For example, when the client's answers appear to contradict earlier information, the clinician should point this out and ask for clarification. In addition, if difficulties arise in discriminating between disorders, some of the suggestions provided in the differential diagnosis section can be used.

Description of Structured Diagnostic Interviews

What follows is a description of two diagnostic interviews that can be used for the identification of GAD. The interviews that are described represent the most commonly used instruments to diagnose GAD as well as various other disorders.

Anxiety and Related Disorders Interview Schedule for DSM-5

The Anxiety and Related Disorders Interview Schedule for *DSM-5*, Adult Version (ADIS-5; Brown & Barlow, 2014), is the newest version of a semi-structured interview commonly used by researchers and practitioners to assess all anxiety and related disorders, as well as screen for other serious mental health and medical problems. Although the ADIS-5 also exists in a Lifetime Version, the Current Version of the ADIS-5 provides sufficient information for a comprehensive assessment of most clients. The interview yields information on the presence of conditions previously known as Axis I disorders with severity ratings on a 9-point Likert scale (0–8). Research on the earlier version of the measure, the ADIS-IV, has shown that the diagnostic reliability of the anxiety disorders is satisfactory, with improvements over the ADIS-III-R (Brown et al., 2001). The main advantage of the ADIS-5 (as well as earlier versions of the ADIS) is that it includes a Clinician's Severity Rating Scale that allows for an evaluation of the severity of each condition that is identified. This information allows the clinician to establish the severity of each disorder, to determine which is the primary disorder when multiple disorders are diagnosed (with primary disorder meaning the most severe disorder), and to ascertain a baseline level of severity that can be used as a comparison point for treatment progress. In addition, the questions to be posed for the different anxiety disorders are in-depth enough to get a relatively rich picture of each of the client's problems if comorbidity is present. The main disadvantages of the ADIS-5 are that it does not cover certain disorders that are often comorbid with anxiety (such as feeding and eating disorders) and that it can take anywhere from 30 minutes to 2 hours to administer.

Structured Clinical Interview for DSM-5

The Structured Clinical Interview for *DSM-5* Disorders, Clinician Version (SCID-5-CV; First, Williams, Karg, & Spitzer, 2016) is the most current version of the SCID, and reflects the diagnostic categories of the *DSM-5*. It contains modules for anxiety disorders, obsessive-compulsive, trauma, and related disorders, depressive disorders, psychotic disorders, substance use disorders, somatic symptom and related disorders, and feeding and eating disorders. In terms of its psychometric properties, given that the SCID-5-CV has only recently been updated to conform to the *DSM-5*, the research examining its psychometric properties has yet to be published at this time. However, research with earlier versions of the SCID for Axis I disorders shows that it has acceptable psychometric properties (Williams et al., 1992; Zanarini et al., 2000). The main advantage of the SCID-5-CV is that it covers a broad range of disorders, particularly when compared to the ADIS-5, which focuses more extensively on the anxiety and depressive disorders. The main disadvantage of the SCID-5-CV is that unlike the ADIS-5, it does not provide ratings of severity. Rather, it exclusively provides information about the presence/absence of disorders. Moreover, questions related to the assessment of the anxiety disorders, particularly GAD, are not as detailed and specific as those found in the ADIS-5. Because of this, discriminating among the anxiety disorders may be more difficult when using the SCID.

Self-Report Questionnaires

Self-report questionnaires are an extremely useful assessment modality because they are both highly informative and very practical. As these measures are easily administered, many of them are standardized with clear guidelines for their inter-pretation. What follows is a selection of the main self-report questionnaires for the assessment of GAD symptoms and relevant cognitive processes (measures of associated anxiety, depression, and quality of life are also briefly discussed). It is worth noting that we will focus solely on the measures used by our research group. Although there are many other excellent self-report questionnaires for the assess-ment of the symptoms and processes involved in GAD, we will restrict the follow-ing presentation to the instruments that directly map onto our treatment rather than attempting to present a comprehensive list of measures for GAD.

Guidelines for Using Self-Report Measures

In our experience, the flexible use of self-report measures greatly facilitates the assessment of treatment progress. A general strategy for using self-report ques-tionnaires might be to administer a comprehensive battery of questionnaires before beginning treatment, to select a limited number of questionnaires that the client will complete every week or so during treatment, and to re-administer all questionnaires following treatment. A typical example of this strategy would be to give the client all questionnaires described below as a between-session exercise before the first and last treatment sessions, and to have the client complete the measures of worry and intolerance of uncertainty in the waiting room before each treatment session. Filling out the measures of worry and intolerance of uncer-tainty on a weekly basis can provide extremely useful information about the cli-ent's progress and the required treatment length. In terms of the interpretation of the client's responses to the self-report questionnaires, some general guidelines are provided below. However, clinicians should keep in mind that responses to individual items may be just as informative as the total score in terms of helping to establish treatment priorities. Moreover, the clinician should review the responses to the self-report questionnaires with the client in order to show the client that their answers are being taken into account for treatment planning. For example, simply discussing the items scored highest on each questionnaire can go a long way in helping the client see the usefulness of the comprehensive assessment.

Self-Report Measures of GAD Symptoms

Worry and Anxiety Questionnaire

The Worry and Anxiety Questionnaire (WAQ) (Dugas, Freeston et al., 2001) is made up of 11 items covering *DSM-IV* diagnostic criteria for GAD; however, given that the core symptoms of GAD are unchanged in *DSM-5*, the WAQ continues to be a valid measure. Items such as "Do your worries seem excessive or exaggerated?" and "To what extent does worry or anxiety interfere with your life, for example, your work, social activities, family life, etc.?" are rated on a 9-point Likert scale (0–8). The WAQ has satisfactory test-retest reliability and good known-groups validity (Dugas, Freeston et al., 2001). Our research indicates that the WAQ, when used as a diagnostic instrument, leads to many false positives but few false negatives. Stated differently, many individuals meeting GAD diagnostic criteria on the WAQ will not meet the same criteria on a structured diagnostic interview (false positive). However, rarely will an individual who does not meet GAD diagnostic criteria on the WAQ meet the same criteria on a diagnostic interview (false negative). Given that our group developed the WAQ as a screening instrument for GAD, the fact that the WAQ is more inclusive than actual diagnostic measures is consistent with our intent; there is little cost to a false positive (having to further assess the individual before rejecting the diagnosis of GAD) whereas there are great costs associated with a false negative (for example, not providing the appropriate treatment to someone suffering from GAD; see Appendix 3.1).

Penn State Worry Questionnaire

The Penn State Worry Questionnaire (PSWQ; Meyer, Miller, Metzger, & Borkovec, 1990) is comprised of 16 items designed to evaluate the tendency to engage in excessive and uncontrollable worry. Items are rated on a 5-point Likert scale ranging from 1 ("not at all typical of me") to 5 ("very typical of me"). Examples of items are "My worries overwhelm me" and "I know I shouldn't worry about things but I just can't help it." The PSWQ has high internal consistency (α = .86 to .95), and very good four-week test-retest reliability, r = .74 to .93. The questionnaire also shows evidence of convergent and divergent validity, as it is more highly correlated with other measures of worry than with measures of anxiety and depression (Molina & Borkovec, 1994).

Since its development, the PSWQ has established itself as the gold standard for the assessment of worry. Over the past several decades, the majority of studies on worry and GAD have used the PSWQ. One advantage of the PSWQ is that it offers a quick, valid, and reliable assessment of the tendency to engage in excessive and uncontrollable worry. There is also a great deal of normative data available on the measure, which makes the interpretation of the client's score easier and more meaningful. One minor disadvantage of the PSWQ is that it contains five inverted items (items that measure the absence of worry such as "I find it easy to dismiss worrisome thoughts" and "I never worry about anything"). Thus, clients need to be particularly attentive to the formulation of items when responding to the PSWQ, and clinicians need to ensure that they are correctly scoring the measure. A copy of the PSWQ is provided in Appendix 3.2.

Self-Report Measures of GAD Cognitive Processes

Intolerance of Uncertainty Scale

The Intolerance of Uncertainty Scale (IUS; Original French version: Freeston et al., 1994; English translation: Buhr & Dugas, 2002) consists of 27 items assessing negative beliefs about uncertainty. The IUS has two subscales: (1) uncertainty has negative behavioral and self-referent implications; and (2) uncertainty is unfair and spoils everything (Sexton & Dugas, 2009a). Items are rated on a 5-point Likert scale ranging from 1 ("not at all characteristic of me") to 5 ("entirely characteristic of me"). Items from the IUS include "When it's time to act, uncertainty paralyses me" (Subscale 1) and "It's unfair not having any guarantees in life" (Subscale 2). Like the original French version, the English translation of the IUS shows excellent internal consistency, $\alpha = .94$, good test-retest reliability over a five-week period, $r = .74$, and good convergent and divergent validity when assessed against measures of worry, depression, and anxiety (Buhr & Dugas, 2002).

Carleton and colleagues (2007) developed a short version of the IUS, which consists of 12 of the 27 items from the original questionnaire. Like the full-scale IUS, the IUS-12 has two subscales: (1) prospective IU—which is similar to IUS Subscale 2; and (2) inhibitory IU—which is comparable to IUS Subscale 1. Because the IUS-12 has psychometric properties that are similar to those of the full-scale IUS (while requiring less time to complete), it has been increasingly used in clinical and experimental contexts over the past decade.

Since the inception of our research program on GAD, the IUS has consistently outperformed measures of other anxiety-related constructs such as perfectionism and need for control in terms of predicting levels of worry and identifying individuals with GAD. Furthermore, the IUS is sensitive to changes over treatment (Ladouceur, Dugas et al., 2000). Thus, the main advantage of the IUS resides in its sensitivity and specificity to excessive worry as well as to the presence and severity of GAD. It is a good measure to administer weekly to clients, because reductions in IUS scores can indicate good treatment progress. See Appendix 3.3 for a copy of the IUS.

Why Worry-II

The Why Worry-II (WW-II; Original French version: Gosselin, Ladouceur, Langlois et al., 2003; English translation: Hebert et al., 2014) is a 25-item revised English version of the Why Worry (WW) questionnaire (Freeston et al., 1994), designed to assess positive beliefs about the function of worry. Items are rated on a 5-point Likert scale from 1 ("not at all true of me") to 5 ("absolutely true of me"). Its design incorporates five subscales that reflect different dimensions of beliefs about worry. These five subscales include beliefs that: (1) worry aids in problem solving (e.g., "The fact that I worry helps me plan my actions to solve a problem"); (2) worry helps motivate (e.g., "The fact that I worry motivates me to do the things I must do"); (3) worrying protects the individual from difficult emotions in the event of a negative outcome (e.g., "If I worry, I will be less unhappy when a negative event occurs"); (4) the act of worrying itself prevents negative outcomes (e.g., "My worries can, by themselves, reduce the risks of danger"); and (5) worry is a positive personality trait (e.g., "The fact that I worry shows that I am a good person"). The English version of the WW-II shows a high internal consistency ($\alpha = .93$), good test-retest reliability at six weeks ($r = .72$), and convergent and divergent validity with other measures of positive and negative beliefs about worry (Hebert et al., 2014).

Although there exist other measures of positive beliefs about worry such as the Positive Beliefs subscale of the Consequences of Worrying Scale (Davey, Tallis, & Capuzzo, 1996), the WW-II is the only questionnaire entirely devoted to the assessment of beliefs about the usefulness of worrying (or positive beliefs about worry). Furthermore, the WW-II taps the five types of beliefs that have been identified in our previous research and that are specifically targeted by our treatment. Thus, there are some important advantages to using the WW-II for the assessment of positive beliefs about worry. The main disadvantage of using the WW-II is that self-report may not be the optimal format for identifying these beliefs. Not surprisingly, we have found that many clients are not fully aware of their beliefs about worry and that some clients who are aware may not wish to disclose these beliefs because they represent a form of secondary gain from having GAD. Thus, for a client reporting few positive beliefs about worry, the clinician may want to investigate these beliefs further during the session to ensure that the responses on the questionnaire are in fact indicative of the client's true beliefs. The WW-II is reproduced in Appendix 3.4.

Negative Problem Orientation Questionnaire

The Negative Problem Orientation Questionnaire (NPOQ; Original French version: Gosselin, Ladouceur, & Pelletier, 2001; English translation: Robichaud & Dugas, 2005a) is a 12-item measure that assesses a dysfunctional cognitive set toward problems and perceived problem-solving ability. Participants rate each item on a 5-point Likert scale ranging from 1 ("not at all true of me") to 5 ("extremely true of me"), according to how they react or think when confronted with a problem. Sample items include "I see problems as a threat to my well-being" and "I often see problems as bigger than they really are." An initial psychometric evaluation of the measure suggests that the NPOQ is unifactorial, with excellent internal consistency ($\alpha = .92$), high test-retest reliability over five weeks ($r = .80$), and good convergent and discriminant validity (Robichaud & Dugas, 2005a).

The NPOQ was developed as a specific measure of problem orientation. Other questionnaires assessing problem orientation embedded the construct within a larger measure that assessed many facets of problem solving, including knowledge of problem-solving skills. Given that the self-report of problem-solving skills has been found to be unrelated to worry and GAD (Davey, 1994; Dugas et al., 1997; Dugas, Gagnon et al., 1998), it appeared that a measure exclusively assessing problem orientation was called for. The main advantage of the NPOQ is that it is brief and easy to administer. Furthermore, unlike previous self-report measures of negative problem orientation (e.g., Social Problem-Solving Inventory-Revised; D'Zurilla, Nezu, & Maydeu-Olivares, 1998), the NPOQ is comprised solely of items that reflect the cognitive process or predisposition of negative problem orientation. Specifically, it is devoid of items that reflect the potential emotional, behavioral, and cognitive *consequences* of having a negative problem orientation (e.g., feelings of frustration regarding problem solving, avoidance of solving one's problems). The main disadvantage of the NPOQ is that validation data using clinical samples has yet to be systematically collected. A copy of the NPOQ is provided in Appendix 3.5.

Cognitive Avoidance Questionnaire

The Cognitive Avoidance Questionnaire (CAQ; Original French version: Gosselin et al., 2002; English translation: Sexton & Dugas, 2008) contains 25 items assessing the tendency to use five types of cognitive avoidance strategies: (1) suppressing worrisome thoughts (e.g., "There are things I try not to think about"); (2) substituting neutral or positive thoughts for worries (e.g., "I think about trivial details so as not to think about important subjects that worry me"); (3) using distraction as a way to interrupt worrying (e.g., "I often do things to distract myself from my thoughts"); (4) avoiding actions/situations that can lead to worrisome thinking (e.g., "I avoid actions that remind me of things I do not want to think about"); and (5) transforming mental images into verbal-linguistic thoughts (e.g., "When I have mental images that are upsetting, I say things to myself in my head to replace the images"). Items are rated on a 5-point Likert scale ranging from 1 ("not at all typical of me") to 5 ("entirely typical of me"). The CAQ has good internal consistency, $\alpha = .95$ for the total scale, and very good test-retest reliability over four to six weeks ($r = .85$). The CAQ also shows evidence of convergent and divergent validity when used with measures of worry, thought suppression, and dispositional coping styles (Sexton & Dugas, 2008).

The main advantage of the CAQ is that it covers a broad range of cognitive avoidance strategies. But like the NPOQ, its psychometric properties have yet to be adequately explored in clinical samples of individuals with GAD or other anxiety and depressive disorders. Although the original French version of the CAQ has shown promise in clinical samples, the English translation awaits further testing. The CAQ is reproduced in Appendix 3.6.

Self-Report Measures of Associated Symptoms

There are many ancillary self-report measures that can be used to complement the assessment of GAD, including measures of associated anxiety, depression, and quality of life. In our experience, it is important to assess for somatic anxiety with a self-report measure such as the Beck Anxiety Inventory (Beck, Epstein, Brown, & Steer, 1988). Even though GAD is not associated with exceptionally high levels of somatic anxiety, a significant minority of individuals with GAD have a more somatic profile than would normally be expected. Furthermore, our data suggest that many individuals with GAD also present with subclinical levels of panic disorder symptoms. Thus, the assessment of somatic anxiety provides valuable information in terms of treatment issues.

With respect to symptoms of depression, a self-report questionnaire such as the Beck Depression Inventory-II (Beck, Steer, & Brown, 1996) can be very useful. Data from a number of studies show that individuals with GAD often have high levels of depressive symptoms. In fact, it may be that many individuals with GAD only decide to seek professional help when they become demoralized or depressed due to their constant worry and anxiety.

In the field of psychotherapy (and pharmacotherapy), there is increasing emphasis on the assessment of nondisorder-specific variables such as quality of life. There is good reason for this trend because simply being free of *DSM*-defined symptoms does not necessarily mean that the client has attained a quality of life that is comparable to that of individuals from the general population. The assessment of quality of life with measures such as the Quality of Life Inventory (Frisch, 1994) also fits well with current models of wellness that emphasize that the absence of disorders does not necessarily imply that a person is healthy and well.

Summary and Concluding Remarks

A comprehensive assessment of GAD is important for many reasons. First, given that the diagnostic reliability of GAD is lower than that of most other anxiety disorders, a careful and complete assessment is warranted. In theory, the identification of GAD may seem relatively straightforward; however, in practice this is not usually the case. Second, because individuals with GAD often meet diagnostic criteria for other disorders as well, it is important to determine not only what, if any, other problems a given client is suffering from, but also which problem is most severe and requires immediate attention. Third, a comprehensive assessment provides a broad range of baseline scores that can be used to measure the client's progress in areas such as symptoms, processes, general psychopathology, and quality of life.

One of the criticisms of the scientist-practitioner model is that treatment research is not always informative for clinicians because the methods used in research are not thought to be amenable to everyday clinical practice. Perhaps nowhere is this more apparent than for assessment. However, it may be that this situation is in part attributable to clinician perceptions of what clients are willing to engage in for the proper assessment of their difficulties. Our own experience has been that most clients appreciate receiving a thorough assessment and understand its importance. Moreover, by having clients complete most of the self-report measures as between-session exercises, the burden of assessment can be significantly reduced.

Worry and Anxiety Questionnaire (WAQ)

1. What subjects do you worry about most often?

   a) _____   d) _____

   b) _____   e) _____

   c) _____   f) _____

For the following numbers, please circle the corresponding number (0–8).

2. Do your worries seem excessive or exaggerated?

0	1	2	3	4	5	6	7	8
Not at all excessive				Moderately Excessive			Totally excessive	

3. Over the past six months, how many days have you been bothered by excessive worry?

0	1	2	3	4	5	6	7	8
Never				1 day out of 2			Every day	

4. Do you have difficulty controlling your worries? For example, when you start worrying about something, do you have difficulty stopping?

0	1	2	3	4	5	6	7	8
No difficulty				Moderate difficulty			Extreme difficulty	

5. Over the past six months, to what extent have you been disturbed by the following sensations when you were worried or anxious? (Rate each sensation with the following scale.)

0	1	2	3	4	5	6	7	8
Not at all				Moderately			Very severely	

   _____ Restlessness or feeling keyed up or on edge

   _____ Being easily fatigued

   _____ Difficulty concentrating or mind going blank

   _____ Irritability

   _____ Muscle tension

   _____ Sleep disturbance (difficulty falling or staying asleep, or restless unsatisfying sleep)

6. To what extent does worry or anxiety interfere with your life? For example, your work, social activities, family life, etc.?*

0	1	2	3	4	5	6	7	8
Not at all				Moderately			Very severely	

*English translation of original French version, from: Dugas, M. J., Freeston, M. H., Provencher, M. D., Lachance, S., Ladouceur, R., & Gosselin, P. (2001). Validation dans des échantillons non cliniques et cliniques. [The Worry and Anxiety Questionnaire: Validation in clinical and nonclinical samples]. *Journal de Thérapie Comportementale et Cognitive, 11*, 31–36.

Penn State Worry Questionnaire (PSWQ)*

Please enter a number (1 to 5) that best describes how typical or characteristic each item is of you.

1	2	3	4	5
Not at all typical		Somewhat typical		Very typical

1. _____ If I don't have enough time to do everything, I don't worry about it
2. _____ My worries overwhelm me
3. _____ I don't tend to worry about things
4. _____ Many situations make me worry
5. _____ I know I shouldn't worry about things but I just can't help it
6. _____ When I'm under pressure, I worry a lot
7. _____ I am always worrying about something
8. _____ I find it easy to dismiss worrisome thoughts
9. _____ As soon as I finish one task, I start to worry about everything else I have to do
10. _____ I never worry about anything
11. _____ When there is nothing more that I can do about a concern, I don't worry about it anymore
12. _____ I've been a worrier all my life
13. _____ I notice that I have been worrying about things
14. _____ Once I start worrying, I can't stop
15. _____ I worry all the time
16. _____ I worry about projects until they are all done

Reversed items: 1, 3, 8, 10, 11

*Reprinted from Meyer, T. J., Miller, M. L., Metzger, R. L., & Borkovec, T. D. (1990). Development and validation of the Penn State Worry Questionnaire, *Behaviour Research and Therapy, 28*, 487–495. (With permission from Elsevier.)

Intolerance of Uncertainty Scale (IUS)

You will find below a series of statements which describe how people may react to the uncertainties of life. Please use the scale below to describe to what extent each item is characteristic of you. Please enter a number (1 to 5) that describes you best.

1	2	3	4	5
Not at all characteristic of me		Somewhat characteristic of me		Entirely characteristic of me

1. _____ Uncertainty stops me from having a firm opinion
2. _____ Being uncertain means that a person is disorganized
3. _____ Uncertainty makes life intolerable
4. _____ It's unfair not having any guarantees in life
5. _____ My mind can't be relaxed if I don't know what will happen tomorrow
6. _____ Uncertainty makes me uneasy, anxious, or stressed
7. _____ Unforeseen events upset me greatly
8. _____ It frustrates me not having all the information I need
9. _____ Uncertainty keeps me from living a full life
10. _____ One should always look ahead so as to avoid surprises
11. _____ A small unforeseen event can spoil everything, even with the best of planning
12. _____ When it's time to act, uncertainty paralyses me
13. _____ Being uncertain means that I am not first rate
14. _____ When I am uncertain, I can't go forward
15. _____ When I am uncertain, I can't function very well
16. _____ Unlike me, others always seem to know where they are going with their lives
17. _____ Uncertainty makes me vulnerable, unhappy, or sad
18. _____ I always want to know what the future has in store for me
19. _____ I can't stand being taken by surprise
20. _____ The smallest doubt can stop me from acting
21. _____ I should be able to organize everything in advance
22. _____ Being uncertain means that I lack confidence
23. _____ I think it's unfair that other people seem sure about their future
24. _____ Uncertainty keeps me from sleeping soundly
25. _____ I must get away from all uncertain situations

26. _____ The ambiguities in life stress me

27. _____ I can't stand being undecided about my future*

*Reprinted from Buhr, K., & Dugas, M. J. (2002). The Intolerance of Uncertainty Scale: Psychometric properties of the English version, *Behaviour Research and Therapy, 40*, 931–945. (With permission from Elsevier.)

Why Worry-II (WW-II)

Below are a series of statements that can be related to worry. Please think back to times when you are worried, and indicate by entering a number (1 to 5) to what extent these statements are true for you.

1	2	3	4	5
Not at all true	Slightly true	Somewhat true	Very true	Absolutely true

1. _____ If I did not worry, I would be careless and irresponsible

2. _____ If I worry, I will be less disturbed when unforeseen events occur

3. _____ I worry in order to know what to do

4. _____ If I worry in advance, I will be less disappointed if something serious occurs

5. _____ The fact that I worry helps me plan my actions to solve a problem

6. _____ The act of worrying itself can prevent mishaps from occurring

7. _____ If I did not worry, it would make me a negligent person

8. _____ It is by worrying that I finally undertake the work that I must do

9. _____ I worry because I think it can help me find a solution to my problem

10. _____ The fact that I worry shows that I am a person who takes care of their affairs

11. _____ Thinking too much about positive things can prevent them from occurring

12. _____ The fact that I worry confirms that I am a prudent person

13. _____ If misfortune comes, I will feel less responsible if I have been worrying about it beforehand

14. _____ By worrying, I can find a better way to do things

15. _____ Worrying stimulates me and makes me more effective

16. _____ The fact that I worry incites me to act

17. _____ The act of worrying itself reduces the risk that something serious will occur

18. _____ By worrying, I do certain things which I would not decide to do otherwise

19. _____ The fact that I worry motivates me to do the things I must do

20. _____ My worries can, by themselves, reduce the risks of danger

21. _____ If I worry less, I decrease my chances of finding the best solution

22. _____ The fact that I worry will allow me to feel less guilty if something serious occurs

23. _____ If I worry, I will be less unhappy when a negative event occurs

24. _____ By not worrying, one can attract misfortune

25. _____ The fact that I worry shows that I am a good person

WW-II Subscales:

Worry aids in problem solving: items 3, 5, 10, 14, 21

Worry helps motivate: items: 8, 15, 16, 18, 19

Worrying protects the individual from difficult emotions in the event of a negative outcome: items: 2, 4, 13, 22, 23

The act of worrying itself prevents negative outcomes: items: 6, 11, 17, 20, 24

Worry is a positive personality trait: items: 1, 7, 9, 12, 25

Negative Problem Orientation
Questionnaire (NPOQ)*

People react in different ways when faced with problems in their daily lives (e.g., health problems, arguments, lack of time, etc.). Please use the scale below to indicate to what extent each of the following items correspond to the way you react or think when confronted with a problem. Please enter the number that best corresponds to you for each item.

1	2	3	4	5
Not at all true of me	Slightly true of me	Moderately true of me	Very true of me	Extremely true of me

1. _____ I see problems as a threat to my well-being

2. _____ I often doubt my capacity to solve problems

3. _____ Often before even trying to find a solution, I tell myself that it is difficult to solve problems

4. _____ My problems often seem insurmountable

5. _____ When I attempt to solve a problem, I often question my abilities

6. _____ I often have the impression that my problems cannot be solved

7. _____ Even if I manage to find some solutions to my problems, I doubt that they will be easily resolved

8. _____ I have a tendency to see problems as a danger

9. _____ My first reaction when faced with a problem is to question my abilities

10. _____ I often see my problems as bigger than they really are

11. _____ Even if I have looked at a problem from all possible angles, I still wonder if the solution I decided on will be effective

12. _____ I consider problems to be obstacles that interfere with my functioning

*Reprinted from Robichaud, M., & Dugas, M. J. (2005). Negative problem orientation (part I): Psychometric properties of a new measure. *Behaviour Research and Therapy, 43*, 391–401. (With permission from Elsevier.)

Cognitive Avoidance Questionnaire (CAQ)

People react differently to certain types of thoughts. Using the following scale, please indicate to what extent each of the following statements is typical of the way that you respond to certain thoughts. Please enter the appropriate number (1 to 5).

1	2	3	4	5
Not at all typical	A little typical	Somewhat typical	Very typical	Completely typical

1. _____ There are things that I would rather not think about

2. _____ I avoid certain situations that lead me to pay attention to things I don't want to think about

3. _____ I replace threatening mental images with things I say to myself in my mind

4. _____ I think about things that concern me as if they were occurring to someone else

5. _____ I have thoughts that I try to avoid

6. _____ I try not to think about the most upsetting aspects of some situation so as not to be too afraid

7. _____ I sometimes avoid objects that can trigger upsetting thoughts

8. _____ I distract myself to avoid thinking about certain disturbing subjects

9. _____ I avoid people who make me think about things that I do not want to think about

10. _____ I often do things to distract myself from my thoughts

11. _____ I think about trivial details so as not to think about important subjects that worry me

12. _____ Sometimes I throw myself into an activity so as not to think about certain things

13. _____ To avoid thinking about subjects that upset me, I force myself to think about something else

14. _____ There are things I try not to think about

15. _____ I keep saying things to myself in my head to avoid visualizing scenarios (a series of mental images) that frighten me

16. _____ Sometimes I avoid places that make me think about things I would prefer not to think about

17. _____ I think about past events so as not to think about future events that make me feel insecure

18. _____ I avoid actions that remind me of things I do not want to think about

19. _____ When I have mental images that are upsetting, I say things to myself in my head to replace the images

20. _____ I think about many little things so as not to think about more important matters

21. _____ Sometimes I keep myself occupied just to prevent thoughts from popping up in my mind

22. _____ I avoid situations that involve people who make me think about unpleasant things

23. _____ Rather than having images of upsetting events form in my mind, I try to describe the events using an internal monologue (things that I say to myself in my head)

24. _____ I push away the mental images related to a threatening situation by trying to describe the situation using an internal monologue

25. _____ I think about things that are worrying other people rather than thinking about my own worries

CAQ Subscales:

Suppressing worrisome thoughts: items 4, 11, 17, 20, 25
Substituting neutral or positive thoughts for worries: items 3, 15, 19, 23, 24
Using distraction as a way to interrupt worrying: items 8, 10, 12, 13, 21
Avoiding action/situation that can lead to worrisome thoughts: items 7, 9, 16, 18, 22
Transforming mental images into verbal-linguistic thought: items 1, 2, 5, 6, 14

CHAPTER 4

Treatment Overview

Over the years, a number of psychological treatments have been developed for generalized anxiety disorder (GAD). Many of these treatments are based on theoretically derived accounts of GAD (e.g., Borkovec, 2006; Mennin, Heimberg, Turk, & Fresco, 2005; Roemer & Orsillo, 2002; Wells, 2006), and have received empirical support in randomized controlled trials (e.g., Borkovec, Newman, Pincus, & Lytle, 2002; Mennin, Fresco, O'Toole, & Heimberg, 2018; Roemer, Orsillo, & Salters-Pedneault, 2008; van der Heiden, Muris, & van der Molen, 2012). Among those shown to be efficacious in controlled treatment studies, either the treatments in their entirety, or significant components thereof, can be subsumed under the heading of cognitive behavioral therapy (CBT). Our treatment, which we shall describe at length in the following two chapters, is one such treatment. It is based on an evolving theoretical model of GAD that has been empirically supported (see Chapter 2) and the efficacy of our protocol has been supported by several randomized controlled trials (see Chapter 6). The present chapter will provide an overview of our treatment by discussing its core modules, thereby paving the way for the next chapter, which describes the actual implementation of the treatment strategies.

Treatment Outline

The term *CBT* is used to describe a broad range of therapeutic modalities. Although most psychological treatments that have been shown to be effective for GAD carry the CBT label, they differ greatly from one another in terms of underlying models, treatment targets, and procedures. For example, in the CBT protocol "Mastery of Your Anxiety and Worry" (2nd Edition) developed by Zinbarg, Craske, and Barlow (2006), treatment components include relaxation, probability estimation, and decatastrophizing, all of which are considered cognitive behavioral interventions. However, none of these techniques is employed in our treatment package. This is due to several factors: first and foremost, we consider the process *underlying* excessive worry to be the primary focus of treatment, rather than worry itself. Given that worry content tends to shift daily for GAD clients, we view strategies that directly target the content of worry as akin to "chasing a moving target," since they would need to be used for each subsequent worry. As such, although decatastrophizing and probability estimation can be helpful CBT strategies, they tend to be less effective as a whole when it comes to the excessive worry in GAD. Second, we view the associated symptoms of GAD (e.g., muscle tension, sleep disturbance) as being largely the result of pathological worry. The noteworthy consequence of such a conceptualization is that the treatment *does not* directly target the associated symptoms of GAD, and therefore strategies like applied relaxation and anxiety management training are not part of the treatment described in this book. Rather, all treatment modules bear directly on excessive worry and its underlying mechanisms, with concomitant reductions in associated symptoms expected to occur as a function of reductions in worry. Data from our clinical trials support this contention, as it was found that decreases in worry lead to decreases in the associated symptoms of GAD (see Chapter 6 for more detail).

Overall Goal of Treatment

Although the treatment described in this book aims to achieve several therapeutic goals, the ultimate goal of our treatment is to help clients reevaluate their catastrophic interpretations about uncertainty and its consequences. This is accomplished by shifting their beliefs about the threat of uncertainty present in daily life situations from a series of negative beliefs to a more balanced perspective. Our research suggests that individuals with GAD tend to inflate the likelihood and severity of a negative outcome in novel, unpredictable, and ambiguous situations, underestimate their ability to cope with potential negative outcomes, and view the experience of uncertainty in daily life as unpleasant, unacceptable, and unfair. Without a doubt, having the ability to view the uncertainty in various situations as normal, as often benign in its outcome, and as manageable, is incompatible with the excessive and uncontrollable worry seen in GAD. One way to view worry is as an elaborate form of scenario building, where individuals mentally review every potential outcome of an uncertainty-inducing situation in order to control or be fully prepared for each outcome. Worry can therefore be construed as an attempt to reduce or eliminate the state of uncertainty induced in a given situation. If individuals with GAD can shift their beliefs to view uncertainty as less threatening (and even embrace uncertainty on occasion), the extensive "mental preparation" of worry no longer becomes necessary. As such, helping clients to reevaluate and shift their negative beliefs about uncertainty is the overarching focus of the treatment.

With the primary focus of treatment in mind, Module 3 targets negative beliefs about uncertainty directly by helping clients to test out their beliefs through the use of behavioral experiments. Clients are encouraged to recognize their own beliefs about the threat of uncertainty in daily life situations and to become familiar with the GAD-related safety behaviors they engage in as a consequence. These safety behaviors (e.g., reassurance seeking, over-preparation, avoidance) are then deliberately and strategically eliminated in order to observe in an experiential manner what actually occurs when uncertainty is invited into one's life.

Modules 2, 4, and 5 also target negative beliefs about uncertainty, albeit indirectly. Although they address specific components that are both impacted by uncertainty beliefs and serve to maintain or exacerbate excessive worry, these three modules also address secondary treatment goals. Module 2 primarily serves a motivational function by assisting clients in recognizing and challenging any positive beliefs they might have about the usefulness of worry. Modules 4 and 5 involve a shift in focus to specific strategies that target worry content and are meant to address any lingering excessive or problematic worries that might remain subsequent to targeting negative beliefs about uncertainty. Module 4 targets worries about current problems by teaching clients how to shift their orientation toward problem solving, as well as how to effectively apply their problem-solving skills. This module targets negative beliefs about uncertainty indirectly due to the inherent relationship between uncertainty and problem solving. Addressing one's problems rather than simply worrying about them allows clients to both actively target specific worries and directly challenge their beliefs about a potential negative outcome in an uncertainty-inducing situation. Finally, Module 5 involves written exposure, a therapeutic strategy designed to address ongoing or lingering excessive worries about feared hypothetical situations (e.g., "What if I develop a serious illness and everyone abandons me?"). This module also indirectly addresses negative beliefs about uncertainty by having clients face the uncertainty involved in their worst fears through repeatedly writing them out and ultimately challenging the veracity and likelihood of their beliefs. Throughout treatment, learning to reevaluate the actual threat of uncertainty in novel, unpredictable, and ambiguous situations is a constant undercurrent, and issues related to negative beliefs about uncertainty are discussed and dealt with accordingly.

Treatment Modules

The treatment includes the following modules: (1) psychoeducation and worry awareness training; (2) reevaluation of the usefulness of worry; (3) reevaluation of negative beliefs about uncertainty; (4) problem-solving training; (5) written exposure; and (6) relapse prevention. This chapter presents the rationale and "spirit" of each module, whereas Chapter 5 will present the "nuts and bolts" of the treatment. It is important for the reader to keep in mind that the treatment strategies described in Chapter 5 are in fact examples of ways to target the processes believed to underlie GAD. They are by no means exhaustive or even ideal for all clients. By clearly understanding the principles laid out in this chapter, the therapist will be in a position to adapt the treatment to clients' specific needs while continuing to target the underlying processes involved in maintaining GAD.

Module 1: Psychoeducation and Worry Awareness Training

As with most CBT protocols, the first few sessions of treatment are devoted to psychoeducation. The therapist provides clients with information about the structure of sessions, the guiding principles of cognitive behavioral interventions, and the primary role of worry in GAD. In addition, clients learn to monitor their worrying on a day-to-day basis.

Psychoeducation about CBT

Although the interventions used in CBT differ according to the disorder and the particular treatment protocol being used, there are certain general principles of CBT that are important to impart to clients. Some of the principles will come as a surprise to many clients, as they may have preconceived notions about psychological treatment or may be unfamiliar with CBT. It is therefore necessary to take the time to explain what CBT involves so that clients are fully aware of what will take place in treatment and what is expected of them. We recommend that the following principles be addressed at the outset of therapy:

- *CBT is based on a model that emphasizes the relationship between thoughts, behaviors, and emotions.* Given that there is a bi-directional interplay between our thoughts, behaviors, and emotions (that is, subjective affect and physiological responses), effecting change in one area can lead to changes in the others. As such, clients can willfully alter their cognitive, behavioral, and emotional reactions to situations when provided with the proper tools to do so. However, clients will primarily focus on changes to their thoughts and behaviors throughout the course of therapy, as they are often the most amenable to direct intervention (i.e., it is more difficult to manipulate or change one's emotional state in a volitional manner).
- *CBT provides a new way of understanding the problem.* Many clients begin treatment with the perception that their problem is impossible to control because it is the direct result of their genetic makeup or of deep-seated unconscious conflicts. CBT is designed to give clients a greater sense of control and mastery by helping them to understand their problem in a new way. This is done through a gradual process of guided discovery, where new concepts are presented to clients as hypotheses they can test using behavioral experiments. CBT is therefore a very empowering treatment approach, as clients are not simply "given" an explanation of their problem, but rather encouraged to test the validity of different hypotheses (with a gentle nudge in the right direction from the therapist).
- *CBT relies on active collaboration between clients and therapists.* Some clients might come into treatment with the expectation that therapists will "cure" them of their problem with little effort on their part. This is certainly not the case with CBT. Both client and therapist work together in order to effect change. If clients do not participate in their own treatment, it is very unlikely that they will see any substantive improvement in their symptoms.
- *CBT aims to provide clients with tools that allow them to deal with the problem independently.* In keeping with the collaborative nature of treatment, one of the tasks of the therapist is to assist clients in acquiring skills that will help them manage their problem. Of course, it is the client's responsibility to learn and to

practice the skills taught in session. Symptom reduction is largely due to the effort clients put into acquiring the necessary skills and implementing them accordingly. There is no magic cure for GAD, and clients need to be aware that it is only through their own diligence that they will improve.

- *CBT is brief and time-limited.* The number of sessions for CBT typically ranges from 12 to 20, depending upon the particular diagnosis and severity of the problem. This is done for a very good reason: the ultimate goal of CBT is to teach clients to become *their own therapist*. As such, treatment should last long enough to ensure that clients have properly acquired the necessary skills, but not so long as to foster dependency, or lead the client to believe that they cannot manage their worries without their therapist's assistance. By encouraging autonomy in clients, CBT enables them to leave treatment with a clear and concrete plan for maintaining their gains (with the possibility of making further progress).

- *CBT is structured and directive.* Given that CBT is a skill-based approach that is also time-limited, sessions are relatively structured. As such, therapists set an agenda for sessions that typically includes reviewing the exercises carried out in the past week, revisiting material discussed in previous sessions, presenting and discussing new material, and assigning exercises for the following week. Given that this format for treatment may seem unfamiliar to certain clients, it is important to make them aware of the typical session plan.

- *CBT is based on the here and now.* A central tenet of CBT is that treatment focuses on factors that contribute to maintaining the problem (for example, what the client is doing, thinking, and feeling *now*), rather than emphasizing the factors that contributed to the initial development of the problem (e.g., family history, childhood conflicts). The reason for this is that identifying the origins of a problem does not, in and of itself, *solve* the problem. This is particularly true with respect to anxiety disorders, as what is maintaining the anxiety in the present might be very different from what originally led to its development. This is not to say that the therapist should never devote time to a discussion of the origins of the problem, only that it is not necessary to do so in order to help clients with their current problem.

- *Between-session exercises are an integral part of CBT.* The hallmark of CBT is the prescription of exercises to all clients from session to session (we will use the term *between-session exercises* throughout this book in lieu of the more common *homework exercises* because the latter has a negative undertone for many clients). It is important that clients be made aware of this at the outset, and queried about their willingness to devote time and attention to home exercises throughout the duration of treatment. Clients who are unwilling to complete between-session exercises are unlikely to show substantial progress in therapy. Since CBT is skill-based, mastery of the skills discussed in treatment will only occur through repeated practice between sessions. Without the completion of home exercises, any symptom reduction that occurs might be tenuous at best because the skills are likely to be poorly acquired, rendering the client vulnerable to relapse following cessation of treatment.

Despite the fact that there are many principles to be considered, which may seem a little overwhelming, it is nevertheless necessary to review them at the outset for two major reasons. First, prior to starting any treatment, clients should be fully aware of what treatment will involve and what is expected of them. They ultimately must decide whether the proposed treatment is a good match for them or not. Second, given that clients will be expected to contribute significantly to their own treatment, both in and out of session, it is important that they agree to put forth the effort. Clients who appear to have low treatment motivation should be queried extensively about this, in order to discriminate between an unwillingness to work in treatment and a fear of what will be required of them. In the case of the former, CBT might not be appropriate (at least at that time) since it is unlikely that clients will progress if they are unwilling, or not yet ready, to engage in treatment. In the latter case however, the therapist might choose to discuss clients' particular fears and explain that nothing will be asked of them unless they understand the rationale behind the request, feel able to do it (albeit on occasion with difficulty), and agree to it.

Psychoeducation about GAD

The second major psychoeducational component involves the provision of information about GAD. This should include two parts; specifically, a description of the diagnosis of GAD and an introduction to a model of the disorder. In terms of explaining the diagnosis, the therapist should strive to describe GAD and its associated symptoms in simple and easily comprehensible terms. Clients might have been told in the past that they have a diagnosis of GAD, but they will often be unclear about what that means. As such, it is important to take the time to explain that GAD is an anxiety disorder that is characterized by excessive and uncontrollable worry about a number of daily events, and to review the associated symptoms of the disorder. In addition, it can be beneficial to describe anxiety problems (and certainly excessive worry) as existing on a continuum. The majority of clients are likely to view their problem within a medical framework, where GAD is a disease that can be "cured." From a CBT perspective, this is not only inaccurate, but it lays the groundwork for unrealistic expectations about treatment (that is, "I will be cured of my worry"). By presenting GAD and excessive worry along a continuum, clients can see their problem as an excessive manifestation of a normal phenomenon, with all individuals scattered along the worry continuum (as opposed to being clustered at each end). Moreover, it allows the therapist to discuss the realistic expectation of moving one's worry level away from the pathological dimension (that is, excessive worry) to a more manageable, or normal, level.

The second part of GAD psychoeducation involves the presentation of a model of the disorder (which is a standard element of most CBT protocols). It is essential that clients understand the role that their own thoughts, behaviors, and emotions have in keeping their problem alive, and this phenomenon is highlighted using a pictorial model. Although we describe our theoretical model in Chapter 2, within our treatment protocol we present clients with an evolving clinical model of the disorder that emphasizes the primary role of negative beliefs about uncertainty in the development and maintenance of excessive worry. By presenting a model that highlights the focus of the treatment and visually depicts the impact of negative beliefs about uncertainty on thoughts, feelings, and behaviors, clients are more likely to understand the model and place themselves within it, without becoming overwhelmed at the outset.

Our initial clinical model of GAD presented to clients includes the symptoms associated with a diagnosis of GAD. The therapist elaborates upon the types of situations that trigger a worry cycle (i.e., novel, unpredictable, and ambiguous situations), and then subsequently describes "what if" questions, worry, anxiety, and GAD-related safety behaviors. The emphasis in this first model of GAD is on helping clients to understand the cyclical and self-perpetuating relationship between worries, anxiety, and safety behaviors. The therapist also provides clients with a simple, clinically useful definition of worry that differentiates it from anxiety. Given that worry is an internal event, it is important that both the client and therapist agree on a definition of worry so that there is a common language and a common goal in treatment.

Worry Awareness Training

Worry awareness training is the first between-session exercise provided to clients, and it involves encouraging them to become more aware of the content of their thoughts, as well as the link between their worries and their feelings and actions. During this phase of treatment, the between-session exercise involves the following: three times a day, clients are asked to stop what they are doing and take note of any worries they may be experiencing "in the moment," their level of anxiety, and any behaviors they engaged in to cope with their worry. Learning to identify worry episodes as they occur, as well as recognizing worry's link to anxiety and behavior, is a key component of this exercise.

Module 2: Reevaluation of the Usefulness of Worry

In Module 2, the primary goal is to assist clients in identifying their beliefs about the usefulness of worry and to begin reevaluating them. This treatment target might seem counterintuitive at first glance, particularly since clients have deliberately sought help for their excessive worry and anxiety. The reader might therefore question whether clients actually hold positive beliefs about the usefulness of worry. In fact, many clients are unaware of, or hesitant to discuss, the positive beliefs they have about their worries. However, the therapist should be careful not to hastily conclude that clients do not see any usefulness in their worries. As discussed in Chapter 2, our research suggests that individuals with GAD hold positive beliefs about worry from any of the five following categories: (1) worry helps them find solutions to their problems; (2) worrying can serve a motivating function, thereby aiding them in getting things done; (3) worry can serve as a buffer for negative emotions by preparing them for dreadful outcomes should they occur; (4) worry, in and of itself, can prevent negative outcomes from occurring (also called magical thinking or thought-action fusion); and (5) worrying about people or situations is evidence of positive personality traits, such as being caring, compassionate, helpful, or organized. Although not all clients with GAD hold every one of these beliefs, our clinical experience has taught us that they typically hold at least some of them.

Before expanding upon ways to address this module of treatment, it should be noted that our position is *not* that positive beliefs about worry are always mistaken or erroneous. Rather, the goal is to help clients determine whether their worries are in fact as helpful as they might think, and if so, whether it is possible to obtain these perceived benefits other than through worry. It is notable that findings from several studies suggest that individuals with GAD hold positive beliefs about the utility of worry to a greater extent than people who do not have GAD (e.g., Dugas, Gagnon et al., 1998; Ladouceur et al., 1999). Furthermore, it appears that the usefulness of worry decreases as worrying becomes excessive, as is the case for individuals with GAD (Pruzinsky & Borkovec, 1990). Stated differently, relative to individuals with moderate levels of worry, clients with GAD not only believe that worrying is *more* useful, but they appear to worry to such an extent that it is actually *less* useful.

Why Address Positive Beliefs about Worry?

The reader might wonder why it is that identifying and reevaluating beliefs about the usefulness of worry is a necessary treatment module. If the ultimate goal of treatment is to assist clients in reducing their worry to a more manageable level (and not to eliminate it altogether), then it might seem relatively benign to hold strong beliefs about the usefulness of worry. However, this is not the case. Although clients present for treatment to reduce their worries and anxiety, this is largely in a "general sense." There is often a paradox present when it comes to clients' relationship to their worries. For example, they may generally wish to feel less anxious and worried, while concurrently believing that it is very important to continue worrying about their children. As such, when faced with the notion of actually worrying less about specific topics (for example, one's children), clients may be ambivalent about change if their beliefs about worry have not been properly addressed. By taking the time to let clients identify their beliefs about the function of specific worries, and ultimately begin to challenge their actual usefulness, treatment motivation and compliance can be enhanced. It is in fact for this reason that this module is introduced prior to initiating the main module of treatment that targets negative beliefs and catastrophic interpretations about uncertainty. Specifically, ambivalence about engaging in treatment, as well as low treatment motivation and compliance, can have a deleterious impact on treatment success. It is therefore of interest to allow clients the opportunity to really consider the actual benefit that they might derive from worry, and whether enduring reductions in worry is a goal worth working toward and striving for.

Relatedly, a second goal of this phase of treatment is to help clients think about what it really means to worry less. This can be a very emotional experience for clients. Most individuals with GAD have difficulty remembering a time when they did not worry. Although they present for treatment in order to reduce their worry and anxiety, many have not given much thought to what their lives would be like without the constant "background" of worry. That is, the notion of a life without excessive worry is largely theoretical for many GAD clients, as they may have no frame of reference or memory of a life before worry became problematic. It is therefore important for the therapist to allow clients to discuss any fears or feelings of loss they might have regarding this potentially significant change.

Identifying and Reevaluating Positive Beliefs about Worry

Returning to the issue of identifying clients' beliefs about the usefulness of worry, any strategy that will facilitate the identification and disclosure of these beliefs can be therapeutically useful. Since clients may hesitate to "admit" they are seeking treatment for something they believe has a positive dimension, it is important that the therapist take the time to explain that it is common for clients to see a positive side to their emotional problems. One of the main treatment strategies that we use to encourage disclosure is the *lawyer-prosecutor role-play*, which is described in Chapter 5. With this method, clients are encouraged to present arguments in favor of the usefulness and value of their worries.

Once clients have identified their positive beliefs about worry, the therapist can proceed to help clients reevaluate these beliefs. In other words, clients are encouraged to begin thinking about whether their worries are as useful as originally thought. This type of reevaluation will set the stage for the next treatment modules. Specifically, if worrying is not as useful as once believed, for example it does not in fact help to solve problems or protect loved ones, then perhaps clients need to learn how to worry less overall, and potentially develop alternate strategies for achieving any perceived benefits derived from worry. The subsequent modules therefore follow naturally from this treatment module. The process of reevaluation of beliefs can be viewed as one of the more purely "cognitive" treatment modules. The primary goal is to help clients to acknowledge that *their beliefs are thoughts and not facts*, and to ultimately develop a more flexible belief system. So rather than adopting a "search and destroy" strategy, where thoughts, assumptions, and beliefs are identified, reevaluated, and replaced by more appropriate or productive ones, this phase of treatment has a much more modest goal. Specifically, cognitive behavioral strategies are used to help clients recognize that their beliefs about the usefulness of worry are interpretations and not facts, to see that other interpretations (or beliefs) also have some merit, and to wonder if perhaps they have overestimated the actual usefulness of their worries. At the same time, clients can begin the process of "imagining a life without constant worry."

Module 3: Reevaluation of Negative Beliefs about Uncertainty

We consider this third module to be the most important component in our protocol, as it forms the backbone of treatment, and is implicated in all subsequent modules. This is because the overarching goal of our treatment is not to target worry content directly, but rather to target what underlies worry. Given the changing nature of daily worry topics that is characteristic of GAD clients, it can be an exercise in futility to focus on specific worries in treatment, as new worries can be expected to crop up each week. Instead, by directing treatment toward changes to negative beliefs about uncertainty—beliefs that in turn fuel the engine of excessive worry—therapists are no longer "chasing a moving target." The therapist should therefore take care not to rush through this phase of treatment in order to ensure that clients are in a position to really benefit from this core module. The primary goals at this stage are the following:

- To understand the concept of intolerance of uncertainty and its relationship to excessive worry and GAD;
- To recognize that achieving complete certainty in daily life is an impossible goal to attain;
- To understand and recognize negative beliefs about uncertainty and how they lead to excessive worry within the worry cycle;
- To recognize uncertainty-driven safety behaviors; and
- To develop and complete behavioral experiments to test out the accuracy of negative beliefs about uncertainty.

Understanding Intolerance of Uncertainty and Its Relationship to Worry and GAD

As described in Chapter 2, a great deal of research has uncovered the close relationship between intolerance of uncertainty and excessive worry. As such, it is a good idea for the therapist to spend a little time telling clients, in a confident manner, about this relationship. For example, clients should know that intolerance of uncertainty is a very strong predictor of excessive worry (see Buhr & Dugas, 2006), and that when people learn to tolerate uncertainty, they tend to worry less (see Ladouceur et al., 2000). That is, once individuals learn to tolerate uncertainty and view uncertain situations as generally less threatening, they will not worry excessively. This is because worry can be construed as an attempt to consider all potential eventualities of a future situation; in other words, it is an attempt to reduce or avoid the uncertainty in novel, unpredictable, and ambiguous situations by thinking about every possible outcome ahead of time. If an individual is no longer intolerant of, or threatened by, uncertainty, there is no experienced need to engage in the prolonged mental activity of excessive worry.

The construct of intolerance of uncertainty is also a helpful tool in explaining the phenomenology of GAD to clients, as it provides a clear "theme of threat" that can account for GAD symptoms. Clients might be unclear as to why they worry excessively about disparate topics, particularly as GAD symptoms are not as naturally cohesive as is often seen in other anxiety disorders. For example, a client with social anxiety disorder might worry about, and avoid, a number of different situations, however they are all tied to an overarching theme of threat—typically a fear of negative evaluation. By contrast, the content of client worries in GAD is highly dynamic, often changing frequently on a daily or weekly basis. Moreover, although GAD worries are experienced as excessive and uncontrollable, the content is typically similar to that seen in normal worry. Although this presentation might seem to be lacking a common thread, it actually makes sense, and can be parsimoniously understood, within the context of uncertainty as the theme of threat.

Specifically, given that life is inherently unpredictable, individuals who are highly intolerant of uncertainty are more likely to feel threatened by daily life situations, and worry as a consequence. Although we all worry on occasion, if an individual's tolerance threshold for uncertainty is quite low, more daily life situations will be construed as threatening, and will therefore provide fodder for worry. Moreover, since each day we are all faced with new and different situations that have some elements of novelty, unpredictability, or ambiguity (e.g., making decisions at work, unexpected traffic, an unusual physical sensation), the content of worry will similarly vary across days and weeks. As such, intolerance of uncertainty accounts for both the dynamic content of GAD worry and its attendant severity.

Because intolerance of uncertainty is such an important concept to the management of worry, clients should have a clear understanding of this information before moving on to other modules (see Chapter 5 for useful analogies for intolerance of uncertainty).

Recognizing That Certainty Is Impossible to Attain

Clients with GAD will often see the goal of treatment quite differently from the one that is truly desirable for GAD symptom reduction. Specifically, they might expect to achieve certainty in their lives as a means of worrying less. This is not, however, an achievable goal. Considering the necessarily unpredictable nature of day-to-day life, seeking out absolute certainty is not only impossible, it also guarantees that one will have to continue striving for certainty on a daily basis as new situations arise. The impossibility of this goal therefore needs to be addressed early on in this stage, and it is important that clients understand and agree with the true goal of therapy (i.e., developing a greater tolerance for uncertainty), as it is more desirable for GAD symptom reduction. A good way to achieve this is to break down the construct of intolerance of uncertainty into its component parts: uncertainty and intolerance. Clients seeking to reduce their worry can either choose to address the first component (i.e., increasing certainty) or the second component (that is, increasing tolerance). In a Socratic fashion, therapists can help clients discover which of these goals is more realistic, more attainable, and more likely to lead to lasting reductions in worry and anxiety levels.

Recognizing the Role of Negative Beliefs about Uncertainty

At this stage of treatment, clients are presented with an expanded model of GAD that incorporates the state of uncertainty and negative beliefs about uncertainty, as well as the role they play in fueling the worry cycle (see Chapter 5 for a description and pictorial illustration of the expanded CBT model for GAD).

Although years of research have consistently identified a strong link between intolerance of uncertainty and excessive worry, clients (and in fact therapists as well) might be unclear as to *why* some individuals might view the uncertainty in daily life situations as threatening and be intolerant to its presence. As with most fears tied to anxiety disorders, it is not the situation per se that is threatening, but rather the expectation of negative consequences or outcomes derived from a particular situation that engenders fear. For example, an individual with a fear of elevators is not afraid of the actual elevator itself, but the potential negative outcomes that might occur in an elevator (e.g., getting stuck, a faulty elevator that crashes). So too with an intolerance to uncertainty, it is the negative expectations, or negative beliefs, about the experience of uncertainty and about potential negative outcomes in novel, unpredictable, and ambiguous situations that are threatening. For example, if a person travels to a country they've never visited before, this is a novel situation with an unknown outcome since one cannot predict how exactly the trip will turn out. Yet travel to an unfamiliar country is certainly not a threatening situation in and of itself; in fact some people might view a vacation somewhere new as exciting. Individuals with GAD however, are more likely to view this situation as threatening because of the uncertainty it generates. Consequently, they will worry about potential negative outcomes, such as bad hotels, high costs, or poor weather while traveling. As such, it is the catastrophic interpretations of uncertainty in novel, ambiguous, or unpredictable situations that fuel worry and foster an intolerance to uncertainty.

There are several negative beliefs, or expectations, about uncertainty that GAD clients can hold, all of which can lead to the perception of situations as threatening (see Chapter 2). The following are directly introduced in treatment:

- *Events with unknown or unclear outcomes will turn out negatively.* This belief involves an overestimation of the likelihood of threat, specifically the expectation that novel, unpredictable, and ambiguous situations are more likely to have a negative outcome than a positive or neutral one. For example, when preparing for a trip, an individual with this belief might expect that they will forget to pack something important.
- *Negative outcomes will be catastrophic.* This belief relates to an overestimation of the severity of threat from an uncertain outcome in a novel, unpredictable, or ambiguous situation. That is, people with this belief assume that if a negative outcome does occur, the outcome will be overwhelming and catastrophic. For example, not only will an individual forget to pack something important, but it will also be a crucial item, such as one's medication or the outfit to wear at an important presentation.
- *Inability to cope with negative outcomes.* In tandem with an expectation of catastrophic negative outcomes, another negative belief involves an underestimation of one's ability to cope with those outcomes. With this belief, there is the expectation of being unable to manage negative outcomes, and of simply being overwhelmed and incapable of effective action. For example, if an individual did forget to pack something for their trip, such as their medication, they might

believe that they will not know how to deal with this situation and the entire trip will likely be ruined as a result.

- *Being uncertain is unacceptable, unpleasant, and unfair.* This is a general negative belief about being in a state of uncertainty. Individuals with this belief tend to view the experience of uncertainty as unacceptable and upsetting, and assume that others do not experience as much uncertainty in their lives. Individuals with this belief also report physical discomfort with the state of uncertainty, and a general unease with "sitting" with feelings of uncertainty; an example of this belief includes the statement, "not knowing drives me crazy."

In addition to providing further psychoeducation about processes involved in the development of excessive worry, clarifying the role of negative beliefs about uncertainty also serves two goals. First, it normalizes the experience of GAD worry. It is clear that if a person believes that novel, unpredictable, or ambiguous situations are likely to yield catastrophically negative outcomes beyond the bounds of one's coping, and are generally unpleasant and unfair, then being intolerant of uncertainty, and worrying to mentally plan and prepare for these situations, is an understandable response. Yet discussing this topic with clients also brings a second goal to the fore, namely the identification of negative beliefs about uncertainty as the primary target of treatment. Specifically, individuals who worry less are more likely to hold balanced beliefs about uncertainty. Therapists will note that a healthy perspective on the actual threat of uncertainty is not to hold positive beliefs, but rather to view these situations in a balanced and more benign manner. That is, people who experience low levels of worry and anxiety tend to expect that uncertainty is a normal part of life (uncertainty can be uncomfortable, but it is not unfair), and that situations with uncertain outcomes will likely turn out all right (realistic estimation of likelihood of threat), and, if not, will likely be manageable and within one's ability to cope (realistic estimation of severity of threat and of coping ability). The challenge for clients will be to learn how to shift their beliefs about the threat of uncertainty by directly testing those beliefs with behavioral experiments.

Recognizing Uncertainty-Driven Safety Behaviors

Although the cardinal feature of GAD is excessive and uncontrollable worry, as is seen with all anxiety-related disorders, there are a number of safety behaviors that clients engage in as well. Another important goal in this treatment module therefore involves helping clients to recognize the different ways in which their intolerance of uncertainty manifests itself in their lives. Generally speaking, intolerance of uncertainty is problematic because clients will expend a great deal of energy using myriad behavioral and cognitive strategies in an attempt to avoid uncertainty-inducing situations. In fact, they typically have been using these strategies for such a long time that they have become automatic. For this reason, it is necessary that clients become *aware* of the various behaviors they engage in as a result of their intolerance of uncertainty, and the impact that they have. This treatment module therefore includes an introduction to safety behaviors and their role in maintaining the cycle of worry, as well as strategies to foster greater recognition of clients' own particular safety behaviors.

Safety behaviors are deliberate acts that individuals engage in as an attempt to avoid anxiety and prevent feared outcomes (Salkovskis, 1991). Using the example of worry about an upcoming trip, an individual might develop a detailed list of items to bring well in advance of their trip and check several times to ensure that all items on the list have been packed. The deliberate actions of list making and double-checking in this case are examples of safety behaviors, as they will reduce the person's anxiety, as well as address worries about the trip ("What if I forget something important?"). The problem is that although safety behaviors serve a functional purpose in the short-term, they actually maintain the worry cycle over the long-term. This is because the nonoccurrence of a negative outcome is directly attributed to the safety behavior. For example, the individual likely thinks that they did not forget to pack important items for their trip because they made a list and double-checked all items in their suitcase. However, this assumption precludes the notion that the negative outcome might not have occurred irrespective of safety behaviors. That is, perhaps they simply would not have forgotten to pack anything important, even without double-checking or making a list of items to pack. As such, safety behaviors reinforce negative beliefs about uncertainty in two ways: They strengthen the assumptions that, (1) negative outcomes would have likely occurred; and (2) safety behaviors directly prevented those negative outcomes.

Safety behaviors across anxiety-related disorders are distinguished by the theme of threat they are attempting to address. For example, safety behaviors in social anxiety can include avoiding eye contact or cutting conversations short, both of which are deliberate actions designed to minimize awkward social interactions, thereby avoiding the overarching threat of negative social evaluation. With respect to GAD, the driving force behind the use of safety behaviors is an overwhelming urge to avoid or minimize the uncertainty in daily life situations, and by extension its anticipated negative outcomes. GAD-related safety behaviors can fall into two general categories: approach and avoidance strategies. Approach strategies refer to the behaviors that involve approaching a given situation in order to eliminate or reduce the uncertainty in the situation as much as possible. Examples of approach strategies include repeatedly seeking reassurance from others before making a decision, obtaining excessive information about a given subject (e.g., going to dozens of stores when buying a gift for someone to ensure that one has the perfect gift), or engaging in excessive preparation (e.g., packing for a short trip at least a week in advance). Avoidance strategies, on the other hand, involve attempts to circumvent uncertainty by avoiding or sidestepping uncertainty-inducing situations altogether. Examples of this strategy include putting off completing a report until the last minute (so that feelings of uncertainty are present for only a short period of time), not accepting a promotion at work (because of the uncertainty involved in taking on new responsibilities), or delegating tasks to others (in order to avoid the uncertainty of potentially completing a task incorrectly). The reader will note that the separation of GAD-related safety behaviors into "approach" and "avoidance" categories is primarily designed to assist clients in better understanding how they cope with their worries, and the function that these behaviors serve. They are therefore not meant to be mutually exclusive or discrete categories, but rather an organizational principle developed to better explain safety behaviors to clients.

It is also important for the reader to understand, and to convey to clients, that safety behaviors are problematic due to their specific purpose, rather than by the details of the actions themselves. That is, *it is not what you do, but why you do it.* There are no safety behaviors that are inherently "bad" actions: making a list before going to the grocery store, double-checking an email before sending it, or asking someone else to choose the restaurant where you will eat, are common—and clearly, normal—behaviors. However, these actions can become safety behaviors when they are deliberately conducted in order to reduce or sidestep uncertainty and avoid an anticipated feared outcome, which, as noted above, reinforces worry in the long run. This stands in contrast to actions that are preference-driven, as there is an assumption of choice motivating the action, rather than anxiety. For example, a person may prefer to reread emails before sending them to ensure that there are no typographical errors, but if they are pressed for time, they are likely able to send unchecked emails with little to no distress. If, however, it is highly anxiety provoking for that person to even consider sending an email without rereading it, then the action of double-checking an email is likely a safety behavior. Since clients will often quite reasonably ask whether certain safety behaviors are normal actions (and therefore not problematic), it is crucial that therapists understand the distinction between choice-driven and anxiety-driven actions, as the perceived "normal" use of many safety behaviors in daily life can serve as a barrier to treatment when targeting these actions.

Developing Behavioral Experiments

At this point, clients should have a good understanding of how negative beliefs about uncertainty contribute to their worries, as well as lead to safety behaviors that ultimately strengthen and maintain the worry cycle. When queried Socratically, most clients will therefore accurately identify the treatment target as a change from negative beliefs to more balanced and flexible beliefs about uncertainty. However, most clients are also typically unsure how this is accomplished. In this component of treatment, emphasis is placed on developing new beliefs through the acquisition of direct evidence about the actual threat of uncertain outcomes in daily life situations through behavioral experiments. That is, belief change occurs through the accrual of compelling evidence about the accuracy of anticipated outcomes in uncertain situations.

Behavioral experiments for GAD involve making a prediction about a feared or anticipated outcome, and then deliberately inducing uncertainty by entering into a novel, unpredictable, or ambiguous situation without the use of safety behaviors. By strategically refraining from using a safety behavior, clients have the opportunity to observe what actually happens in a situation. This allows for the experiential evaluation of negative beliefs about uncertainty, including the expectation that the situation will have a negative and catastrophic outcome (overestimation of likelihood and severity of threat) that will be beyond the client's coping resources (underestimation of coping). For example, an initial behavioral experiment might involve going to a restaurant without first reading a review. The feared outcome might be that the individual will not enjoy the food (anticipated negative outcome), that they have wasted time and money on a ruined evening (catastrophic outcome), and that they won't know how to deal with this terrible restaurant choice and ruined evening (inability to cope).

A notable benefit of behavioral experiments for GAD is that irrespective of the outcome, clients will have the opportunity to test at least one of their negative beliefs about uncertainty. If dinner at the new restaurant was pleasant, this provides direct evidence against the accuracy of an anticipated negative outcome. If instead the client did not enjoy the food at the restaurant, they now have the opportunity to evaluate whether this negative outcome was indeed catastrophic, and how they were able to cope with it (e.g., eating only a part of the meal, and getting something more to eat a little later).

Given that our beliefs about the threat of a situation are unlikely to change without a great deal of evidence, clients will need to engage in a significant number of behavioral experiments across several weeks in order to obtain a preponderance of evidence about the accuracy of their beliefs. As such, the bulk of treatment will involve this module of the protocol. It is not uncommon to spend upwards of six to eight sessions on this component of treatment alone. This is done to ensure that clients have compelling and abundant information about the veracity of anticipated outcomes in situations that provoke feelings of uncertainty. Clients are encouraged to complete at least three behavioral experiments a week for several weeks, recording their (1) feared outcome; (2) the actual outcome; and (3) if the outcome was negative, how they handled the situation. Sessions at this point in treatment involve reviewing the outcome of experiments and brainstorming new experiments for the upcoming week. In addition, after a number of sessions have been devoted to behavioral experiments, it is recommended that therapists aid clients in reviewing the findings of all experiments in order to begin to form overall conclusions. Specifically, clients can be queried about (1) the number of experiments conducted to date; (2) the frequency of negative, neutral, and positive outcomes; (3) the frequency of catastrophic outcomes (when the outcome was negative); (4) their realistic assessment of their coping ability when outcomes were negative; (5) how it felt overall to "sit" with feelings of uncertainty; and (6) whether the feeling of "sitting" with uncertainty was manageable (as opposed to overwhelming).

As clients progress, they are encouraged to develop their own behavioral experiments independently. We have found that some of the best, and most impactful, experiments are those that are devised by the clients themselves. Moreover, in order to ensure that experiments' results are generalizable, it is recommended that therapists guide their clients toward experiments that gradually increase in scope across various areas of life (e.g., work, home and family, social life) and that the "stakes" of experiments are raised, with more challenging experiments being conducted over time.

The primary goal of this treatment module is to encourage clients, through the evidence derived from their experiments, to reevaluate the actual threat of uncertainty, and ultimately develop more balanced beliefs. Specifically, balanced beliefs about the uncertainty in daily life situations include the expectation that, all things being equal, novel, unpredictable, and ambiguous situations are a normal part of life, will likely turn out all right, and if not, are unlikely to be catastrophic or unmanageable. The reader will note that balanced beliefs do not include the expectation of positive outcomes, but rather a more neutral expectation of manageable ones. This is because there are no guarantees that a situation with an uncertain outcome will in fact turn out positively. Rather, through multiple experiments, it is hoped clients will discover that (1) negative outcomes are typically infrequent, rarely catastrophic, and almost always manageable; and (2) the feeling of uncertainty itself is normal and manageable. An ancillary goal of this treatment module is therefore to allow clients to build confidence in their ability to manage adversity through experience, while developing a realistic appraisal of threat that markedly reduces the need to worry. Moreover, given that many novel, unpredictable, and ambiguous situations in daily life can actually have positive outcomes, therapists are also in a position to be able to discuss the notion of *embracing uncertainty* in some situations. Through the actual outcomes derived from behavioral experiments, we have found that clients often discover that the uncertainties in daily life can not only be devoid of threat, but they can also carry the potential for pleasant and enriching experiences.

Module 4: Problem-Solving Training

Up to this point in the treatment protocol, the focus has been on targeting higher-order processes that underlie and maintain excessive worry. Since worries in GAD are varied and dynamic in nature, it is viewed as more effective to target the engine of worry rather than the worries themselves in order to obtain long-term and enduring change. However, the next two modules are a deliberate shift back to worry content. Although we expect that many clients with GAD will experience significant symptom reduction solely through shifting their negative beliefs about uncertainty, it is not uncommon for clients to experience some lingering excessive worries. As such, the next two components of treatment are designed to provide specific strategies for the different types of problematic worries that might remain after working extensively on addressing beliefs about uncertainty.

With respect to worry content, there are two general worry types: (1) worries about current problems; and (2) worries about hypothetical situations. In this module of treatment, the focus is on addressing worries about current problems. For this worry type, we have found that the application of sound problem-solving principles is an extremely helpful treatment strategy. That is, rather than worrying about a problem, it is better to actually solve it through the use of concrete problem-solving skills. As such, following the module on reevaluating beliefs about uncertainty, clients are encouraged to complete a worry monitoring form to determine what, if any, problematic worries remain. For those worries that involve current problems, the treatment then turns to problem-solving training. Obviously, worries about hypothetical situations (for example, worries about situations that have not happened, and in most cases, never will) are not addressed with problem solving. In fact, attempting to solve a problem that may well never exist is not only unproductive, but can actually lead to increased worry. A specific treatment strategy for this type of worry is presented in the next module (see Module 5: Written Exposure). However, for worries about current problems, taking an action-oriented stance such as problem solving is, in our opinion, the most appropriate treatment strategy.

There are two discrete elements involved in this treatment module, improving problem orientation and applying problem-solving skills. As mentioned previously, problem orientation refers to the way in which an individual views problems and problem solving, and is therefore considered a cognitive set. Problem-solving skills, on the other hand, refer to the steps that an individual carries out in order to actually solve a problem. These include: (1) defining the problem and formulating problem-solving goals; (2) generating alternative solutions; (3) choosing a solution; and (4) implementing the chosen solution and assessing its effectiveness (see D'Zurilla & Nezu, 2006, for a detailed description of these steps). In our treatment, we devote as much time to assisting clients in enhancing their orientation toward problems as we do to the application of skills. As such, both of these problem-solving dimensions are treated as separate, albeit complementary, elements.

Given that problem-solving training was not specifically designed for individuals with GAD, it should come as no surprise that it needs to be modified to meet the specific needs of this client population. As a result, we modified "standard" problem-solving training by placing a strong emphasis on the role of uncertainty in both the problematic situation and the problem-solving process, and by consistently distinguishing between the passive process of worry and the active process of problem solving.

Improving Problem Orientation

Uncertainty in the Problem-Solving Process

Daily life problems (that is, problematic situations that occur in the natural environment) have many uncertainty-inducing qualities. For example, the problem itself might be ambiguous or vague, the effects of the chosen solution are unpredictable, and the repercussions of an ineffective solution are difficult to estimate. Not unexpectedly, for a client who holds negative beliefs about uncertainty, the problem-solving process is likely to be construed as threatening and aversive. It should therefore come as no surprise that GAD clients have a negative orientation toward problems and problem solving.

As noted earlier, learning to develop more balanced beliefs about the perceived threat of uncertainty is central to our treatment and is addressed either directly or indirectly in every session. The introduction of problem orientation and problem-solving skills is no exception. The presence of uncertainty in the problem-solving process is therefore discussed in session, as well as any fears that clients might have about the process. The futility of searching for certainty, particularly as it pertains to daily life problems, is also discussed. Rather than worrying about problems, clients are encouraged to "move forward" with problem solving despite the inherent uncertainty of the situation. Not only is this beneficial to clients because they learn how to deal with everyday problems, but they are also given yet another opportunity to directly test out their negative predictions about situations with unknown or unclear outcomes. Thus, in terms of initially addressing problem orientation, it is important to acknowledge the uncertainty of the problem situation, address the client's negative thoughts/emotions in relation to problem solving, and encourage action *toward* the problem.

The Impact of a Negative Problem Orientation

The impact of a negative problem orientation is best seen in the *consequences* of this cognitive set. Specifically, if clients are threatened by problems, doubt their ability to solve them, and anticipate a negative outcome irrespective of effort, then it is likely that they will react negatively on an emotional, cognitive, and behavioral level. In terms of emotions, clients are likely to feel frustrated, irritated, anxious, depressed, or overwhelmed when confronted with problems, given their predisposition to view them as threatening. In terms of cognitions, a negative evaluation of problems is likely to lead GAD clients to worry excessively about problems when they arise. In addition, if problems are left unsolved, they can generate new problems over time, which themselves can become worry topics. Finally, in terms of behavioral consequences, clients might avoid, delay, or impulsively solve problems because they view the problems as threatening, and have a negative outcome expectancy. This final consequence relates directly to the importance of discussing problem orientation prior to addressing problem-solving skills. Specifically, so long as problems are seen as threatening and unlikely to be effectively dealt with irrespective of effort, clients are unlikely to use their problem-solving skills (no matter how good they are). As a consequence, a series of strategies designed to encourage clients to approach problematic situations, rather than avoid them, are used in this treatment (see Chapter 5 for strategies for improving negative problem orientation).

Applying Problem-Solving Skills

In terms of problem-solving skills, the emphasis is placed on two ideas. First, the problem-solving skills component is not presented as "learning about new skills." This is because most people are intuitively aware of the general steps involved in solving problems. Rather, the emphasis is placed on learning how to use the skills *effectively*. Improperly defining a problem, setting unrealistic goals, or being unsure about how to select a potential solution are more likely to be the difficulties that people encounter with problem solving. Focusing on mastering the skills, rather than learning what they are, will be more reflective of the client's experience. Second, clients are encouraged to tolerate uncertainty throughout the problem-solving process. At each step of this process, the goal is to achieve the *best* result for that particular individual, not the *perfect* result. In other words, problem solving is expected to be a deliberate and rational process where clients do the best they can at each step. Once they have completed a problem-solving step, clients need to move forward to the next stage of problem solving, without the certainty that they made the "perfect" or the "right" choice. In essence, the implementation of one's problem-solving skills is an exercise in tolerating uncertainty.

One noteworthy point related to the use of problem solving as a way to tolerate uncertainty is that in reality, things might not turn out as expected. Even when one is highly organized, it is impossible to have complete control (or certainty) over one's environment. Unexpected events can arise, people might not react as planned, and solutions might not work out as well as expected. However, events such as these can promote one's tolerance for uncertainty and allow for the further accrual of evidence against the accuracy of negative beliefs about uncertainty. When clients do not attain their desired goal and come to realize that they can handle unexpected adversity, they greatly benefit from their "mistake." In this way, moving forward with problem solving, despite the uncertainty of the process, represents a "win-win" situation for individuals with GAD. Once they have had some experience in dealing with current problems via problem solving, the therapist can then begin assisting clients in addressing worries about hypothetical situations, assuming that worries of this type remain problematic according to worry monitoring records.

Module 5: Written Exposure

In this treatment module, the therapist introduces clients to a strategy for dealing with worries about hypothetical situations. As noted beforehand, problem solving is not always productive or effective for situations that have not yet occurred (and may never happen). As such, we recommend written exposure to the fears that underlie these types of worries. Examples of worries about hypothetical situations include worrying about a loved one being involved in a serious car accident, potentially becoming seriously ill, or experiencing financial ruin or bankruptcy in the future. Obviously, it is normal to worry on occasion about these types of hypothetical situations, however for most people they can be considered "back of the mind" worries. That is, worries that might emerge on occasion, but are not at the forefront of the mind on a regular basis. Yet GAD clients for whom worry about hypothetical situations is problematic are likely to report experiencing these worries at a high frequency, thereby necessitating a specific treatment intervention.

Written exposure is used to target cognitive avoidance, and allows clients the opportunity to obtain evidence regarding two broad beliefs related to excessive worries about hypothetical situations: (1) believing that one's worst-case scenario is more likely to occur if dwelled upon, and that one would be unable to handle or cope with it if it actually occurred; and (2) being unable to manage the negative emotions elicited by worries about one's worst-case scenario, and becoming overwhelmed or losing control over one's emotions as a result (see Chapter 2 for greater detail about beliefs related to worst fears about hypothetical situations). Given these negative beliefs, clients tend to engage in various cognitive avoidance strategies designed to avoid thinking clearly and vividly about the situations that they fear, or to minimize their negative emotional impact. Common strategies include deliberate attempts at mentally blocking worries and distressing thoughts about feared situations (or replacing them with pleasant thoughts), and distracting oneself in order to avoid thoughts about feared situations. Despite being effortful and time-consuming, these strategies are typically only minimally helpful in dampening thoughts about frightening situations, often leading to an increase in worry and anxiety due to the paradoxical effect of thought suppression (Wegner & Zanakos, 1994). Clients will also typically engage in "worry hopping," that is, switching from one worry topic to another (e.g., switching from worrying about one's health, to worries about the impact that health concerns might have on one's employment, and then switching to financial worries) to avoid thinking too clearly or deeply about any one situation that they fear. Although worry hopping can momentarily reduce anxiety when abandoning one worry topic, there is then a resurgence of distress as the next worry topic is broached.

Cognitive avoidance strategies function as a type of safety behavior. Specifically, by engaging in strategies to avoid or circumnavigate worries and thoughts about feared situations through cognitive avoidance, clients are attempting to reduce anxiety and emotional distress, as well as prevent themselves from thinking about their "worst-case scenario." However, as with all safety behaviors, any benefits derived from their use are short-lived, and actually maintain the problem in the long-term. With respect to cognitive avoidance strategies, the long-term impact resides primarily in the avoidance of thoughts and feelings associated with catastrophic outcomes. So long as clients avoid thinking about their worst fears and experiencing the emotional distress that these fears engender, they are unable to realistically evaluate the likelihood and severity of the hypothetical threat, or their own ability to cope with their emotions and with the feared outcomes if they occurred. As a consequence, worries about hypothetical situations are maintained within the overall cycle of worry.

As with many anxiety-related fears, exposure is an effective strategy for fear reduction, and it provides the opportunity for new learning based on direct experiential evidence. This form of exposure involves asking clients to repeatedly write a detailed, concrete, and vivid description of their worst-case scenario. After each written exposure exercise, clients record their level of distress, their evaluation of the probability of their feared outcome occurring, how catastrophic the outcome would likely be, and their perceived ability to manage their feared outcome.

As with all modules in our protocol, written exposure targets intolerance of uncertainty, albeit indirectly. By writing about their worst-case scenario, clients are directly facing their fear of being overwhelmed by negative emotions as a result of focusing on distressing thoughts (rather than avoiding them), and finding out what actually occurs without knowing with certainty beforehand. Many clients with GAD express the belief that if they focus on their feared outcomes and allow themselves to elaborate on them in a clear and vivid way, they will be overwhelmed by feelings of intense sadness, and anxiety, and that these feelings will never abate. However, one of the goals of written exposure is to allow clients to see that focusing on negative emotions functions more like a dam than a water tap. That is, writing about worst fears in detailed and concrete terms may initially lead to strong negative emotions (like the sudden rush of water after opening a dam), but that these feelings ultimately dissipate over time (like water from a dam eventually slowing to a trickle, unlike opening a water tap that just keeps flowing). Moreover, by repeatedly writing about their worst-case scenario, clients are able to actually think in greater depth about their worst fears, which allows them the opportunity to shift their perspective about feared situations by evaluating the actual likelihood of a negative outcome, and how they would likely cope if it occurred, in a more flexible and balanced manner. In order to better understand the manner in which we present written exposure to clients, please refer to Chapter 5. Once clients have completed a full trial of written exposure, the treatment can progress to the final module, namely relapse prevention.

Module 6: Relapse Prevention

As important as it is for clients to display symptom improvement through the course of treatment, it is of even greater importance that those gains are maintained, and potentially improved upon, over time. This is particularly the case with our CBT protocol for GAD, given that the primary goal of treatment is a shift in beliefs about the perceived threat of uncertainty. Enduring cognitive change requires an abundance of evidence in favor of new and more balanced beliefs, which in this case is obtained through repeated behavioral experiments. Yet it is only time and experience that can provide enough compelling evidence for a true cognitive shift. With this in mind, our final treatment module is designed to help clients maintain their gains following treatment and to continue their progress over time.

Although relapse prevention as a treatment component should include strategies to manage lapses that might occur after treatment ends, it should also leave clients with a sense of confidence in their skills, and a feeling of hope and optimism in their ability to continue improving and building upon their gains over time.

There are several ways in which therapists can foster the maintenance of gains and continued symptom improvement following treatment termination, all of which are expanded upon in Chapter 5. Essentially, the final sessions of therapy should involve a review of the knowledge and skills acquired throughout treatment. Clients should also be encouraged to continue practicing their new skills and prepare for "red flags" or stressors that may indicate a potential lapse in treatment gains. It is worth noting that the therapist can model good habits throughout treatment, which will ultimately aid clients to continue progressing long after therapy has ended. For example, many clients will downplay their treatment gains simply because they are not fully aware of the progress they have made. It is not uncommon for clients to expect treatment success to "look" quite dramatic, with a change in their emotional state taking place from one day to the next. This, of course, does not occur very often, as progress typically takes place in a gradual fashion. As such, many clients might not fully appreciate the progress they have made. The therapist can counteract this by not only frequently praising successes, but also by keeping a written record of progress every week. Clients who see this type of behavior in their therapists are more likely to emulate it once they become their "own therapist." Both in and out of treatment, motivation is vital to continued success; as such, it is extremely important that clients learn to regularly praise and reward themselves for their progress. Clients who stay motivated and confident stand a good chance of experiencing additional symptom reduction and enhanced quality of life after treatment has ended.

Summary and Concluding Remarks

The overall goal of the treatment described in this book is to help clients learn to tolerate, and hopefully even embrace, uncertainty by reevaluating their beliefs about the actual threat of uncertainty in daily life situations. This is accomplished *directly* by helping them to (1) understand the role of negative beliefs about uncertainty in the development and maintenance of worries in GAD; (2) identify the GAD-related safety behaviors that maintain negative uncertainty beliefs by preventing the acquisition of potentially corrective information; and (3) deliberately engage in behavioral experiments in order to directly assess the validity of negative beliefs about uncertainty. Tolerance for uncertainty can also be fostered *indirectly* by helping clients to (1) reevaluate their beliefs about the usefulness of worry; (2) learn to apply effective problem-solving principles to daily problematic situations; and (3) use written exposure to challenge and reevaluate their fears related to hypothetical worries. Throughout treatment, clients are encouraged to seek out and deal with the uncertainty inherent in novel, unpredictable, and ambiguous daily life situations. Ultimately, they are encouraged to view uncertainty as not only unavoidable, but as an opportunity to grow and to develop as a human being. For GAD clients, one of the greatest benefits of dealing with unexpected events (and making mistakes now and then) is that they can begin to see how they are able to cope with adversity when it arises. As a result, clients can gain a sense of empowerment, which can greatly improve their quality of life.

As a final note, it is worth returning to the important role that therapist attitudes play in treatment success. Although our treatment protocol has received considerable empirical support (see Chapter 6), the specific treatment procedures represent only part of the "efficacy picture." Without positive therapist attitudes, such as openness and flexibility, even the best treatment protocol will not prove to be as helpful for clients with GAD. Although one of our main goals in writing this book was to describe a set of theoretically driven treatment procedures, the reader should keep in mind that common therapy factors such as therapist attitudes are at least as important as the specific procedures described herein. Ultimately, increasing our ability to help individuals with GAD will not only depend on perfecting our treatment protocols, but also on focusing on *how* we deliver treatment.

CHAPTER 5

Step-by-Step Treatment

In this chapter, we present a step-by-step illustration of our treatment proto-col. Although the manual we use in our clinical trials has a session-by-session layout, the description presented in this chapter follows a more flexible format. Specifically, as with the treatment overview (see Chapter 4), this chapter is set up according to the different treatment modules. Therapists are encouraged to spend as much time as necessary on any given module before moving on to the next. Guidelines are provided as to when particular modules can be introduced with the ultimate goal of providing a flexible manual that can be tailored to the individual needs of each client. Throughout the chapter, examples of ways of presenting the material are provided. Although these formulations are based on our experience with GAD clients, they remain only examples of how to present the material; ther-apists will undoubtedly want to modify the wording in order to better suit their "clinical style."

Module 1: Psychoeducation and Worry Awareness Training

Presenting the Principles of Cognitive Behavioral Therapy

The first objective in our treatment is to present the principles of cognitive behav-ioral therapy (CBT). Clients are likely to be unsure about what will be involved, so it is important to explain the principles at the outset. This ensures that clients will have some understanding of what is required of them, and the therapist will be in a position to assist them in developing realistic expectations.

It is important that the presentation of CBT principles not be delivered in a rigid or authoritarian manner. Rather, Socratic questioning should be employed whenever possible to encourage the comprehension (and appreciation) of the principles of CBT. For example, when presenting the bi-directional relationship between thoughts, emotions, and behaviors, an illustrative example can be par-ticularly helpful:

THERAPIST: One of the guiding principles of CBT is that there is a strong relationship between the way we think (our thoughts), the way we feel (our emotions), and what we do (our behaviors). We will often represent this relationship with a triangle:

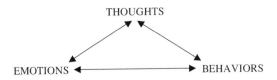

THERAPIST: Each one of these three factors influences the other two. For example, let's say that you are afraid of dogs. If you are walking down the street, and all of a sudden you see a dog, what are you likely to think? (Here, the emphasis is on getting clients to participate, and provide the answers themselves.)

CLIENT: I might think: "Uh-oh, there's a dog. He might attack me!"

THERAPIST: That's right. And how will that influence how you feel and what you do?

CLIENT: Well, I would probably be afraid and anxious, and I would either turn around and walk the other way or cross the street.

THERAPIST: Exactly. Your thought, "he might attack me," can lead you to feeling fearful and anxious, and to avoid the dog.

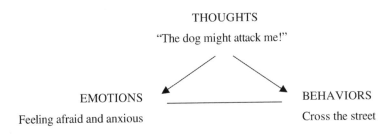

THERAPIST: Now, if you do cross the street and get away from the dog, what might you think and feel?

CLIENT: I would probably feel less anxious. I might say to myself that I got away from the dog, and now he can't bite me, so I'm safe.

THERAPIST: Right. So, just as your thoughts can influence your behaviors and your emotions, so can that relationship go in other directions as well. Your behaviors can influence your thoughts and emotions, and your emotions can have an impact on your thoughts and behaviors. CBT makes use of this relationship to help you understand your problem in a new way, and become less anxious and worried and have a better quality of life. That is, when you have been "living" with your problem for some time, you may have developed ways of understanding and dealing with it that are actually maintaining the problem or even making it worse. CBT will help you to see your problem differently and teach you new ways of dealing with it that are more helpful and effective.

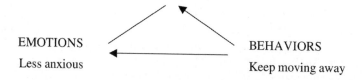

THOUGHTS

"I got away from the dog.
I'm safe."

EMOTIONS

Less anxious

BEHAVIORS

Keep moving away

The active collaboration between client and therapist and the completion of weekly between-session exercises are also important CBT principles to address. Clients need to be aware that they will be expected to participate significantly in their own treatment. If they do not put forth the effort, both in and out of session, they are unlikely to see any notable improvement in their symptoms. Although this information is extremely important, it can sound authoritarian or intimidating to clients, particularly at the start of treatment when they are still unsure about what treatment will involve. Again, by using Socratic questioning, the information can be presented in a nonthreatening manner and can ultimately enhance client motivation. An example of how to present this is as follows:

THERAPIST: One of the major features of CBT is that you and I are both considered experts. You are an expert when it comes to your particular problem, so the knowledge that you have about your problem will be invaluable in treatment. On the other hand, I am an expert at understanding problems in a new way and at teaching skills that people can use to deal with their problems. That means that it is very important that we work together in session. I will need you to participate in sessions because it is the work that you put into dealing with your problem that will lead to real change. I will also be giving you exercises to do between sessions every week to practice new skills or to test out new ideas. Why do you think it's important to do these exercises?

CLIENT: I have no idea. I'm actually a little surprised about all this. I thought that you were going to be fixing my problem.

THERAPIST: Actually, I'm not going to "fix" the problem. I'm going to be inviting you to do that. I'm just going to help you discover ways of dealing with your problem, but it is you who will be responsible for actual change.

This point is a vital one, particularly in CBT. As noted previously, some clients might expect to adopt a passive stance, where almost all the work will be done by the therapist. If clients do not explicitly state their expectations regarding treatment, the therapist might want to take the time to ask them what they think therapy will involve. In this manner, any false preconceptions can be dispelled early on. Returning to our above example, a possible discussion of these issues might be:

THERAPIST: Keeping in mind your role in treatment success, why do you think that between-session exercises are necessary? Before you answer, let me give you an example. Let's say that you decide that you want to learn to play the piano, so you sign up for 12 weekly one-hour lessons. What will happen if you only play the piano during your lessons and not at home?

CLIENT: I'd probably be a pretty mediocre piano player.

THERAPIST: Probably. But why is that? What's the difference between only playing during your lessons and practicing what you have learned in the time between your lessons?

CLIENT: Well, obviously, I would play better if I practiced more.

THERAPIST: That's right. When you learn anything new, whether it is playing the piano, learning how to drive, or acquiring new ways to manage your anxiety, it is only through repeated practice that you improve your skills and feel confident while using them. In other words, it would be a bit of a waste of time if you didn't put your best effort into practicing the skills that you will learn in session. Without repeated practice, you wouldn't have much experience with your skills in the "real world" and you probably wouldn't feel much better.

An alternative method of presenting the rationale for between-session exercises is to present them as "behavioral prescriptions." That is, just as a physician prescribes medication when a patient is not feeling well, the therapist assigns a weekly "prescription" for between-session exercises. As discussed in Chapter 4, the therapist should also take the appropriate steps so that clients are not fearful of what will be required of them in terms of these exercises. It is a good idea to take a few minutes to explain to clients that they will not be asked to do anything unless they understand *why* it is important, have a good idea of *how* to do it, and know *what* to expect. Moreover, clients should always be asked whether they agree with the suggested exercise. Do they clearly see its usefulness? Do they feel capable of doing it? Does it seem too overwhelming? If so, what could they do that would be less anxiety provoking, but would still be worthwhile? When between-session exercises are demystified in this manner, clients are more likely to be motivated and actually carry out their exercises.

Although the discussion of the major principles of CBT might seem to be a lengthy process, it has several notable advantages. First, it allows the therapist to ensure that clients are not holding unrealistic expectations about treatment. Second, client motivation can be enhanced by clearly outlining the reason for its importance and its contribution to treatment success. The discussion of the principles of CBT also allows clients to be fully aware of what treatment will involve and what is expected of them. Since clients must ultimately determine whether CBT is appropriate for them, this information is necessary in order for the client to make an informed decision. Finally, by taking the time to explain these principles, the therapist can also contribute to the establishment of a strong therapeutic alliance, which can make a key contribution to positive treatment outcomes.

Explaining the GAD Diagnosis

One cannot assume that a client who has been given a diagnosis of GAD has received a proper explanation of what that diagnosis entails (unless the treating clinician provided the diagnosis). As such, psychoeducation should also include a detailed description of GAD. This information is provided to ensure that clients understand their disorder and to begin to "normalize" their experience. Among the elements that can be discussed is the fact that GAD is one of the anxiety disorders and that its main feature is excessive worry about multiple daily life events. The chronicity of the disorder can also be underscored by discussing the fact that although the minimum duration is six months for a diagnosis of GAD (by definition), many individuals with GAD cannot recall a time when they did not worry excessively. The associated symptoms of GAD, such as fatigue, irritability, and muscle tension, should also be reviewed. However, in keeping with our objective of targeting excessive worry, these symptoms are best described primarily as the *product* of longstanding worry.

Given that the description of GAD is meant to inform clients about their problem and to begin normalizing their experiences, some time should be taken to discuss the categorical and dimensional models of mental health as they pertain to GAD. Our position is that GAD, like many other mental health disorders, is best viewed from a dimensional perspective. Specifically, we believe that, for the most part, GAD is an excessive manifestation of a set of symptoms that everyone experiences to varying degrees from time to time. One way for the therapist to discuss this is in the following manner:

THERAPIST: One way to think of GAD is as an "all-or-nothing" disorder. In other words, either you have it "completely" or you don't have it at all. This is sometimes referred to a categorical perspective, and it's actually not an accurate way to understand mental health, especially anxiety, since everyone gets anxious sometimes and that's completely normal.

GAD present   GAD absent

THERAPIST: A better way to think about GAD is as a set of symptoms that can be placed on a continuum. Because everyone worries to some degree, we are all on that continuum, albeit at different places.

No worry/anxiety   Extreme worry/anxiety

THERAPIST: Unlike the categorical model, where everyone is placed in one of the two "boxes," the dimensional model places everyone at different points on a continuum, with some people being closer to the "no worry/anxiety" end and some closer to the "extreme worry/anxiety" end. So how do we decide when someone has GAD? Essentially, we draw a line on the continuum that represents our best estimate of clinically significant GAD symptoms; we then assign a diagnosis of GAD to people who surpass this line or threshold.

No worry/anxiety   Extreme worry/anxiety

                                         No GAD   GAD

THERAPIST: Is there a great difference between individuals who fall just a little to the left of the line and those who fall just a little to the right? Of course, the answer is no, but in order for mental health practitioners to have a common language, we need to determine a "clinical threshold" so that we can agree on what constitutes a diagnosis of GAD. When determining a person's place on the GAD continuum, clinicians typically take into consideration the severity of the symptoms as well as the extent to which the symptoms lead to distress or impairment. In other words, in the absence of distress and impairment, a person with high levels of worry and anxiety would probably not receive a diagnosis of GAD.

As can be seen from the description of the dimensional model, emphasis is placed on the universality of anxious symptoms. As a result, assigning a GAD diagnosis becomes a matter of *degree*. For clients who are fearful about entering treatment for a "mental health problem," this type of description can be helpful in and of itself. By thinking of GAD as an extreme form of a normal experience, these clients often feel less threatened by the prospect of receiving help for their worry and anxiety.

Introduction to the Model: The Symptoms of GAD

As discussed in Chapter 4, clients are presented with a clinical model of GAD that reflects the new directions taken from our original treatment protocol. Specifically, the current incarnation of our clinical model emphasizes the bi-directional relationship between thoughts, feelings, and behaviors while giving primacy to the role of negative beliefs, and by extension catastrophic misinterpretations, about uncertainty. It is presented in a stepwise fashion in order to ensure that clients do not become overwhelmed from the outset. The first pictorial illustration is a basic model, where the triggering situations for worry, the "what if"/worry cycle, anxiety, and GAD-associated safety behaviors are presented (see Appendix 5.1 for the first model). Before trying to address GAD symptoms, clients should have a clear idea of how the worry process functions. This is especially important given that the main feature of GAD, excessive and uncontrollable worry, is a covert (or internal) cognitive event that cannot be directly observed. When presenting the initial GAD model, the therapist should walk through each step, eliciting examples from the client along the way. Emphasis should be placed on the cyclical and self-perpetuating nature of the model components. An example of this presentation might be the following:

THERAPIST: There is often a situation or trigger that starts off the chain of symptoms. This situation can be an external event, like reading a news article or getting an unexpected phone call, or an internal thought or feeling, like becoming aware of a physical sensation or thinking about an upcoming meeting with your boss. Although there are many different types of triggers, the common thread between them is that they are typically novel, unpredictable, or ambiguous situations. A novel situation is any type of situation that is new to you in some way, so you don't really know what exactly to expect. Going to a new restaurant might be an example of a novel situation. An unpredictable situation is one where you can't be sure what the outcome is, such as taking an exam at school. An ambiguous situation is one where the situation itself isn't very clear. For example, if your boss asks to speak to you about something related to work, but you don't know whether the conversation will be about something positive, negative, or even neutral. Can you think of some examples of situations in your own life that have made you worry?

CLIENT: Yes, definitely. My wife wants us to travel to Japan together. I have never visited Japan, or any Asian country, so it's entirely new to me. Every time I even think about traveling to a completely different continent, I start worrying.

THERAPIST: So that's a great example of an internal trigger, since you worry when you have thoughts about the trip, and it's also a novel situation because it's new to you.

CLIENT: But it's also an unpredictable situation, isn't it? Since I don't really know how a trip like that would turn out.

THERAPIST: Absolutely! A situation can be both novel and unpredictable, or any combination of the three. It's really just the characteristic of the situation, and there can be more than one. So once you experience a triggering situation, that leads to the next phase, the "What if . . .?" questions, which are thoughts that begin with "What if . . ." or the equivalent (for example, "Wouldn't it be terrible if . . .?"). What might be a "what if" thought you have when thinking about traveling to Japan with your wife?

CLIENT: Well, I have lots of "what if" thoughts about that, but one example is, "What if I go to a restaurant while there and I can't order food because I don't speak Japanese?"

THERAPIST: Great example. However, as I'm sure you know, the cycle does not end there. Once you say that to yourself, do you think about anything else?

CLIENT: I start thinking all sorts of things, such as whether I will end up eating something that I don't like or that makes me sick, and whether I might even have to go to the hospital in a foreign country. I also worry that I'll spend a lot of money on a trip that I won't enjoy.

THERAPIST: Some of those thoughts are *worries*, and they are set in motion by "What if . . .?" questions. Worries often involve a mental attempt to plan and prepare for every eventuality, and they typically include two components. The first involves thinking about all of the negative and catastrophic outcomes that might occur. You gave a couple of examples when you described your thoughts about a potential trip to Japan, including having a hard time communicating since you don't speak Japanese, ordering food that you don't like or that makes you sick, potentially ending up in the hospital, and spending a great deal of money on a trip you don't enjoy. The second component involves a mental attempt to problem solve the negative outcomes that you generated. Do you find that you do that sometimes? Perhaps when you worry about a trip to Japan with your wife?

CLIENT: Sure. I've been thinking that I might try to learn to speak Japanese before I go, perhaps go to some Japanese restaurants to become more accustomed to the food, and maybe talk with a travel agent. But I'm worried that even if I learn Japanese for example, my accent will probably be terrible and people might not understand me. Also, the food in Japan is probably very different from anything I can get at a local restaurant at home, so even if I go to Japanese restaurants here, it won't help me when I need to choose meals in Japan.

THERAPIST: So, you've given some good examples of mental problem solving, but you also described the worry cycle. When you start worrying, that is, thinking about negative outcomes that could happen as well as engaging in mental problem solving, this often leads to more "what if" thoughts, and more worry. In your example, you started to think about going to Japanese restaurants locally as a potential solution to your worry about not liking the food. However, you then started to think, "What if the local Japanese food is different than what they serve in Japan?," which then starts a new series of worries. You might even find that you start with one worry, such as concerns about the food, only to move onto worry topics, such as the financial cost of the trip and the impact this would have on your overall finances.

CLIENT: Yes, that makes sense. I find that my worries spin all over the place, and I might start with worrying about something specific, like the food in another country, and end up worrying about my relationship with my wife or our retirement.

THERAPIST: Exactly! The reason why this happens is because when you worry, you are trying to think about every possible scenario, and how you might deal with it. However, since you are worrying about future events that have not happened yet, there are infinite possibilities about what could happen. As a result, once you start thinking about how you might deal with one situation, for example taking Japanese language courses, you then come up with other "what if" questions that challenge your potential solution, such as "What if my accent is terrible," and "What if people don't understand me when I try to speak Japanese."

In order to avoid any misunderstandings, it is important that the client and therapist agree on a definition of worry. Here we have defined worry as a mental attempt to plan and prepare for any eventuality, which is a straightforward way to explain worry to clients. This definition is then further expanded to include both an elaboration of potential catastrophic outcomes that might occur in the future, as well as a mental attempt to problem solve those negative outcomes. The emphasis at this point in the model is on the cyclical nature of "what if" questions and worries. Specifically, given that the future is inherently uncertain, there are neverending potential "what if" questions, potential catastrophic outcomes, and potential solutions (which themselves lead to more "what if" questions). Unsurprisingly, the ongoing cycle of "what if" questions and worries is time-consuming and mentally exhausting, and it is recommended that the distress or impairment that this worry cycle leads to is validated and discussed with GAD clients.

Once the triggers for worry and the "what if"/worry cycle are introduced, therapists can move forward to the remaining steps in this initial clinical model, which includes anxiety and resultant safety behaviors. Primary goals at this juncture include: (1) the distinction between worry as a cognitive construct and anxiety as a physiological/affective response; and (2) an introduction to safety behaviors and their role in maintaining worry in the long-term. An example of this discussion is as follows:

THERAPIST: Now, let's return to our model. Once you have started a worry cycle, how do you feel physically and emotionally?

CLIENT: Pretty tense. When I'm really worried about something, I can sometimes get knots in my stomach.

THERAPIST: That feeling of physical and emotional discomfort is what we generally refer to as *anxiety*. While worry occurs in the mind, anxiety is felt in the body. There are a number of physical symptoms that you can experience when anxious, including a racing heart, sweating, stomach issues such as the knots in your stomach that you mentioned, and some people experience dizziness, hot flushes, or shortness of breath. In addition to these sensations of anxiety, people who worry chronically also describe feelings of muscle tension, fatigue, and restlessness. Longstanding anxiety and worry can also lead to feelings of irritability, concentration difficulties, and sleep problems. Obviously, these are very unpleasant feelings to be experiencing. Because of the distress and discomfort caused by anxiety, as well as the time and effort spent worrying, you likely try to do something to manage these upsetting thoughts and feelings. If we go back to your worries about a trip to Japan with your wife—what actions have you taken in order to worry less or feel less anxious?

CLIENT: Hmm . . . Well, I've ordered lots of travel books to read, and looked up information online about hotels and restaurants in the major cities. I have to admit I've also talked to my wife about not going to Japan at all, and instead taking a vacation somewhere more familiar, like Hawaii, since we've been there a few times. I've also talked to some friends and family about my concerns involving a trip to Japan. Everyone has told me that I should go, and that I'll have a great time.

THERAPIST: So, it sounds like you have been seeking reassurance from others, gathering more information about the trip, and also attempting to avoid the trip altogether. Do you have any idea why you might be doing these things?

CLIENT: I guess because it makes me feel a bit better, at least for a moment. For example, when my friends and family tell me that the trip will be great and I'll have a good time, I feel less anxious when talking to them, and I'm less worried. But of course, I start worrying again when I think more about it later.

THERAPIST: Exactly. So, all of these actions—reassurance seeking, information seeking, and avoidance—are called safety behaviors. Safety behaviors are any of the things that you do in an attempt to feel less anxious, as well as to try to avoid or minimize some of your feared outcomes. There are all sorts of actions people engage in that can be considered safety behaviors. For example, if you were worried about an upcoming meeting with your boss, you might procrastinate and put off meeting her to a later date and time, or if you were worried about your daughter forgetting to pack something in her soccer bag before going to a game, you might decide to pack her bag yourself. In the case of a trip to Japan with your wife, you might choose to avoid by canceling the trip altogether. By doing this, you would probably feel less anxious, and all of the things you are worried about, such as having a bad time, not liking the food, getting sick, and wasting time and money on a trip that you didn't enjoy, would not happen.

CLIENT: Yes, but I'd feel terrible about canceling the trip, and I'd probably start worrying about where my wife would want to travel to instead.

THERAPIST: That's right. You've actually just identified one of the problems with safety behaviors. Although they can reduce anxiety and prevent or minimize feared outcomes in the short term, they actually maintain worry and anxiety in the long run. There are two reasons for this. First, although your anxiety is reduced when you use safety behaviors, your fears are not. For example, if you avoid going to Japan, you are no longer anxious about taking that trip. But you are still afraid, and likely to worry, about any other trip to a country you are unfamiliar with. Safety behaviors only work in the moment and can actually increase worries in the long run.

CLIENT: That's true! When I talked to my wife about not going to Japan, she suggested that we go somewhere in Europe instead. I've started worrying about everything that could go wrong on a trip to a European country now.

THERAPIST: So that's the first problem with safety behaviors. The second has to do with how you interpret the outcome when you use a safety behavior. As I mentioned before, if you avoided by canceling the trip, all of the negative outcomes you were worried about don't happen. That is, you don't have a bad time in Japan, you don't eat bad food, get sick, or waste your time and money. In your mind, why did you avoid all of these bad outcomes?

CLIENT: Well, I guess if I don't go to Japan, none of those things will happen.

THERAPIST: Exactly. When you engage in safety behaviors, it feels like the negative outcomes that you were anticipating don't happen *because* of the safety behavior. For example, your daughter has all of her soccer equipment in her bag *because* you packed it for her. Or you don't have a bad time in Japan *because* you don't go. But what might be another reason why those negative outcomes didn't occur?

CLIENT: I suppose it's possible that they didn't occur because they weren't going to. I might have a great time if I travel to Japan with my wife.

THERAPIST: That's right. Or your daughter might remember to pack all of her soccer equipment before the game without you packing her bag for her. The problem is that you don't know what actually would have happened, since safety behaviors *prevent* you from finding out. In essence, the very thing that you do to prevent negative outcomes prevents you from finding out whether those negative outcomes would have occurred in the first place. Which means that your worries about potential negative outcomes "feel" true, since the fact that they didn't happen because of what you did seems like evidence that they probably would have happened. So, the whole cycle of worry, anxiety, and safety behaviors continues. And for people with GAD, that cycle has usually been spinning on and off for many years.

Worry Awareness Training

Once the first clinical model has been presented, with an emphasis on the importance of the bi-directional relationship between worries, anxiety, and safety behaviors, the next phase is introduced; namely, worry awareness training. Clients need to be able to clearly "see" their symptoms before attempting to address them. In the case of GAD, it is important that they become experts at recognizing their own worries, as well as begin to recognize and identify the safety behaviors they engage in as a response to worries. Given that some clients feel that they already think too much about their worries, the therapist will occasionally encounter some resistance when asking clients to systematically monitor their worries. However, once clients begin worry awareness training, they typically realize within a short period of time how important and helpful this training can be. Notably, many clients report being surprised about the content of their worries, which highlights the value of tracking thoughts and behaviors of interest in order to obtain a more accurate picture. This is equally true for safety behaviors, which can be tricky for clients to recognize and identify at first. With this in mind, worry awareness training is the first between-session exercise "prescribed" by the therapist.

Clients are asked to record their worries and associated safety behaviors three times a day in their Worry Monitoring Form (see Appendix 5.2 for a copy of the Worry Monitoring Form and a sample of a completed form). Specifically, when feeling anxious, clients are encouraged to record the intensity of their anxiety (on a scale from 0 to 8), and then be observers of their own experience by noting the date and time, the situation that they are in, their initial "what if" thoughts, and any safety behaviors that they were aware of having engaged in.

When clients return to the next session with a completed Worry Monitoring Form, it is important to review the outcome of the exercise in order to both discuss specific findings from the self-monitoring form and to drive home the importance of home exercises at the outset. With respect to client worries, we recommend covering the following points in a Socratic fashion:

- *Clients usually have recurrent worry themes.* Although many will say that they worry about "everything," most clients will have a few worry themes that consistently recur.
- *A worry chain can last a few minutes or a few hours.* Since the goal of treatment is not to eliminate worry, but rather to reduce it to more manageable levels, clients need to see just how much of their time is being consumed by worry. In addition, seeing how one worry can lead to others shows the pernicious cycle of worry.
- *Worries involve future events.* Even when a worry is rooted in a past event (e.g., failing an exam a week ago), it is typically about the future repercussions of the past event (e.g., "How will this affect my grade point average at the end of term?").

In addition, it is a good idea to review the safety behaviors that clients were able to identify, and to begin noting whether there are behaviors that the client engages in consistently, such as avoidance, procrastination, or reassurance-seeking. It is not uncommon for clients to struggle with identifying their safety behaviors, as they are often actions that are woven into their lives seamlessly. It is expected that an awareness of worries and associated safety behaviors is an acquired skill that clients will obtain through consistent self-monitoring.

Module 2: Reevaluation of the Usefulness of Worry

In Chapter 4, we noted that although the most important module in our protocol targets negative beliefs about, and catastrophic interpretations of, uncertainty, it is a good idea to first address positive beliefs about the usefulness of worry. This is because individuals with GAD tend to overestimate the usefulness of their worries, which can ultimately impact upon treatment motivation. Specifically, clients are less likely to want to reduce their worries if they believe that they have a functional purpose. This in turn can serve as a barrier to treatment, wherein clients may show reluctance to reduce their worries and associated safety behaviors. One way to introduce this concept to clients is in the following manner:

THERAPIST: We have already discussed how worries, anxiety, and safety behaviors influence each other to create the worry cycle. However, we also want to start looking at other factors that are involved in keeping the worry cycle going. We will be introducing one of these today. That is, we will be discussing any beliefs you might have about the usefulness of worrying.

When discussing positive beliefs about worry, it is important to take a nonjudgmental stance so that clients can feel at ease about disclosing these beliefs. It is not uncommon for clients to think that their therapist will disapprove of any admission of positive beliefs about worry because of the inherent "contradiction" in such beliefs ("I want to worry less, but I think worrying is useful"). One way to take a nonjudgmental stance is to normalize the experience for clients and to illustrate the commonality of such a belief system:

THERAPIST: Our beliefs about the usefulness of certain actions or behaviors obviously have a strong impact on what we do. It makes sense that we keep doing the things that we believe are useful and let go of the things that we do not find useful. In the same way, the more we feel that worrying is useful, the more likely we are to continue worrying. In fact, research has shown that people with GAD differ from people with moderate levels of worry by their tendency to believe that worrying is particularly useful. Have you ever thought that some of your worries might be useful?
CLIENT: I don't think so. I wouldn't be here if I did.
THERAPIST: Well, that's true in a way. If you weren't bothered by your excessive worry and anxiety, you would not have come for treatment. However, sometimes people with GAD will say that although they dislike their worrying in general, they find that specific worries can be useful. For example, some people will say that although in general they worry too much and would like to worry less, they still believe that it is good that they worry about work because it keeps them motivated. What do you think about that?

We have often found that a good method for drawing clients out when it comes to topics they might be hesitant to disclose (such as admitting to positive beliefs about worry) is to frame the question in a "other people have said" format as illustrated above. In our experience, clients are more likely to disclose if they believe that it is a common phenomenon.

Identifying Positive Beliefs about the Usefulness of Worry

In order to assist clients in identifying their positive beliefs about worry, the therapist will first need to present the most common beliefs typically held by individuals with GAD. As stated previously, our research has shown that positive beliefs typically fall into five categories. Although at this time we encourage therapists to solely present the different belief categories, the following descriptions include an exposition of some of the flaws in logic, or "logic pitfalls," that clients are likely making in terms of these beliefs. During treatment, it is recommended that clients first identify their own beliefs about worry (and generate personal examples from their own worries) before introducing any challenges to those beliefs.

1. **The belief that worrying helps to find solutions to problems.** This category includes beliefs that worry helps to solve problems and find better solutions, that it increases vigilance or preparedness, that it contributes to a more well thought out or efficient reaction, and that it helps to prevent or avoid problems. An example might be: "It is good that I worry about my problems at work because it ensures that I pay attention to them and solve them efficiently." Although there is some truth to this, there are also a few problems with this belief. Although low levels of worry can, at times, be helpful in generating solutions to problems, high levels of worry actually interfere with the problem-solving process. This is because worry makes us see all the ways that our solutions might fail. So, worry, in many cases, actually makes solving problems more difficult.

2. **The belief that worrying serves a motivating function that ensures things will get done.** This is a common belief among GAD clients who often believe that worrying about something that needs to get done will ensure that it does in fact get done. Examples of this include: "If I worry about my grades in school, I'll study harder and do well," and "If I worry about the way my house looks to others, I will be more likely to keep it clean." The main problem with this belief is that worrying is confused with caring. For example, "Worrying about my next exam means that it is important, so worrying will make me study harder." However, if a person worries less about an upcoming exam, this does not mean that they will suddenly become complacent. Rather, it means that they will be less anxious about the exam while preparing for it. In fact, being very worried about something often leads to inactivity because of the negative emotional reactions that are associated with worry. This can particularly be seen with GAD clients, where a common manifestation of intolerance of uncertainty is to procrastinate or avoid. As such, worry might actually have the opposite effect from what was originally intended.

3. **The belief that worrying can protect a person from negative emotions.** This category reflects the notion that by worrying "in advance" about a potential negative event, negative feelings such as disappointment, sadness, or guilt will be prevented should the event actually occur. For example, "If I worry about my husband being injured in a car crash, I will be able to handle it without being overwhelmed by sadness if it occurs." Some individuals with GAD believe that worrying is like "putting money in the bank." They believe that if the feared event takes place, they will have already "invested" in their negative reaction in advance, thereby allowing them to be less affected by the event. Some of our GAD clients have told us "If something happens to someone I love and I haven't

worried about it in advance, I would feel very guilty." This way of thinking puts the person in a position where they must worry constantly, "just in case." One of the problems with this type of thinking is that when negative events do occur, people who have worried about them are unlikely to feel any better than people who have not worried about them. Worry does not protect people from negative feelings because no one feels prepared when an unexpected negative event occurs (e.g., the sudden loss of a loved one, a car accident).

4. **The belief that worrying, in and of itself, can prevent negative outcomes.** This category reflects the belief that the act of worrying can affect the outcome of events; specifically, the belief that one's worries are directly responsible for the nonoccurrence of negative events or the occurrence of positive events. This type of belief is sometimes called *thought-action fusion*. For example, "I have always worried about my child being involved in a serious car accident; it has never happened, so my worrying must be working." This type of thinking is, of course, logically flawed, as the nonoccurrence of an event could be attributed to any number of things. For example, an individual might believe that his plane didn't crash because he worried about it beforehand. However, it is more likely due to the remoteness of the particular event (i.e., planes crash infrequently), the skill of the pilot, or the clear weather during the flight. Another problem with this type of belief is that it usually involves *selective attention*. For example, a client might report that when they worry about presentations at work beforehand, they do well. However, have they ever not worried about a presentation and done well regardless? Conversely, have they ever worried about a presentation and not done well? Individuals with this type of belief will often search out evidence that confirms their beliefs and ignore any disconfirmatory evidence.

5. **The belief that worrying represents a positive personality trait.** This involves the belief that the act of worrying says something positive about the person. For example, worry shows that an individual is caring, loving, or conscientious. An example of this might be "I'm the worrier in my family. If I worried less, my parents would be disappointed in me; they would think that I don't care about them anymore." Implicit in this belief is the assumption that individuals who worry less are less caring, loving, or conscientious. Obviously, this is untrue. In fact, most high worriers likely know someone who holds similar positive character traits in the absence of excessive worry, thereby contradicting their belief.

Once all five of the positive beliefs about worry have been presented, clients are encouraged to begin looking at their own worries and start identifying some of these beliefs. Using the Positive Beliefs about Worry form (see Appendix 5.3 for a copy of the form), which can be completed between sessions, clients are asked to write down examples for each personally relevant belief (they can use their Worry Monitoring Form to assist them in thinking about what purpose specific worries appear to serve). They can also use the form to identify any other beliefs that they might have about the usefulness of worry.

Following the identification of clients' positive beliefs about the function of their worries, the therapist should address why it is important to identify these beliefs and potentially reevaluate them:

THERAPIST: So, why do you think that it is a good idea to identify some of the positive beliefs you have about the usefulness of your worries?

CLIENT: I don't know.

THERAPIST: As I mentioned earlier, we tend to keep doing the things that we feel are useful. So as long as you feel that some of your worries are highly useful, you are unlikely to want to reduce them. It is important that we look at what advantages you receive from worrying and whether it is in fact helpful. I am not saying that there is no usefulness to worry. Instead, I would like us to see if your beliefs are actually true by looking at the evidence and deciding whether worrying less would actually have a negative effect on your life. In addition, we want to make a distinction between worrying occasionally and worrying excessively. This is because when we talk about looking at whether worry is in fact really useful, we are actually talking about the usefulness of excessive worry and all the safety behaviors that go along with it (such as reassurance seeking and procrastination).

Strategies for Reevaluating Positive Beliefs about Worry

In this phase of treatment, the therapist walks a fine line between challenging the client's beliefs in a nonjudgmental manner and allowing the client to express those beliefs. Positive beliefs about worry are sometimes difficult to identify. One reason for this is that clients may not be fully aware of their positive beliefs. Some clients might say that although they know "intellectually" that their worries do not serve a useful purpose, they nevertheless "feel" that they do. Other clients report that although they usually believe that their worries are not helpful, at times they wonder if their worries can help them to deal with life's problems.

A second reason for the difficulty in identifying positive beliefs about worry is that clients might not be willing to acknowledge these beliefs. As mentioned above, many clients are hesitant to discuss their positive beliefs about worry because the beliefs are inconsistent with their consultation motive. Clients sometimes believe that it is unacceptable to be ambivalent or to see a positive side to a behavior they would like to decrease. In fact, some clients have mentioned that they did not think the therapist would be receptive to these ideas and wondered if disclosure of positive beliefs about worry would be interpreted as treatment resistance. Other clients fear that they will "lose face" if they admit to having these paradoxical beliefs. For all these reasons, it is important that the therapist actively encourage the client to become aware of, and acknowledge, their positive beliefs about worry. One method that we have found to be extremely useful in attaining this goal is the lawyer-prosecutor role-play.

Lawyer-Prosecutor Role-Play

In this role-play, the client is first asked to identify a specific worry, for example, "Worrying about my children shows that I am a good parent." The client is then asked to take on the role of a lawyer who must convince the members of a jury that the worry is useful. Once all arguments have been exhausted, the client then plays the role of a prosecutor who must convince the members of the jury that the worry is in fact not useful. We have found that this role-play allows clients to consider "both sides of the coin" in a nonthreatening context. Specifically, because they are taking on different roles, clients are given the opportunity to argue against their previous statements without appearing to be contradicting themselves. Consistent with the principles of motivational interviewing (Miller & Rollnick, 2012), the therapist uses Socratic questioning to help clients reconsider the actual usefulness of worrying when playing the role of the prosecutor. In this case, examples of questions include: "Is there anything else you do that shows you are a caring parent? Do you know any "good" parents who don't worry excessively?" In addition, clients are also encouraged to consider the overall cost of worry to their lives in terms of time and effort and the potential negative impact of worry on their relationships and daily functioning.

By gathering evidence both in defense and in opposition to the usefulness of their specific worries, clients have the opportunity to identify any potential paradoxes in their beliefs about worry. For example, while a client may report that others have told them that they are a good and caring parent, they might also have been chastised by others for "worrying too much" about their children's safety, or been accused by their children of nagging. The paradox between these pieces of evidence can help clients develop a more complete picture of what their worries are actually providing them in daily life. The overall goal of this phase of treatment is to allow clients to begin questioning the actual usefulness of their worries in order to reduce ambivalence and increase motivation for change.

Specific Challenges to the Different Beliefs about Worry

When assisting clients in challenging their positive beliefs, it is important that the therapist address the beliefs regarding a *specific* worry and not the general belief itself. For example, a client might worry excessively about the health of their children because they believe it shows good parenting qualities. In this case, challenges would be to the belief, "Worrying about my children's health shows that I am a good parent," and not to the general belief, "Worry represents a positive personality trait." With that in mind, a list of helpful challenging statements for each of the positive beliefs about worry is presented in Table 5.1.

Reevaluation of Positive Beliefs: A Life without Worry?

One of the by-products of discussing the actual usefulness of worry, and potentially changing clients' perceptions in such a way that they no longer see worry as

Table 5.1 Challenges to Positive Beliefs about the Usefulness of Worry

---

1. *Worry aids with problem solving.* **Example: If I worry about problems that come up at work, I am able to find better solutions for them.**

Possible Challenges:

Do you actually solve your problems by worrying, or are you just going over the problem again and again in your head?

Does worry get you to actually solve your problems, or do you become so anxious that you delay solving your problems or avoid them altogether?

Are you confusing a thought (worry) with an action (problem solving)?

2. *Worry is a motivating force.* **Example: If I worry about my performance at work, then I will be motivated to succeed.**

Possible Challenges:

Do you know anyone who is successful at work and who is not a worrier?

Are you confusing worrying with caring or being conscientious? That is, is it possible to want to succeed at work and not worry about it all the time?

Does your worry really improve your performance? Are there negative repercussions as a result of your excessive worry about work (for example, difficulty concentrating, memory problems, intense anxiety)?

3. *Worry protects against negative emotions.* **Example: If I worry about my son potentially getting a serious disease, I will be better prepared emotionally if it happens.**

Possible Challenges:

Has anything bad ever happened that you had worried about before? How did you feel? Were you buffered from the pain or sadness that it caused?

Does worrying about things that might never happen actually increase your negative emotions in the here and now?

4. *Worry, in and of itself, can prevent negative outcomes.* **Example: When I worry about an upcoming exam at school, I do well; when I don't worry, I don't do well.**

Possible Challenges:

Have you ever done poorly on an exam even though you worried?

Is your rule about worry (that is, worry = good outcome; don't worry = bad outcome) based on real evidence or is it an assumption? For example, is it possible that you only remember the exams you did well on when you worried, and that you forget those you didn't do well on when you worried?

Were you really not worrying when things didn't go well on some exams, or are you just remembering it that way to support your assumption? Could you test this theory? For example, could you track your worry prior to all exams and then look at your performance on each exam?

5. *Worry is a positive personality trait.* **Example: The fact that I worry about my children proves that I am a good and caring parent.**

Possible Challenges:

Is there anything else you do that shows you are a good and caring parent? Is it only worrying about your children that shows caring and love?

Do you know any other parents that you would consider "good and caring" but who do not worry excessively?

Have you suffered any negative consequences from friends or family because of your excessive worry? Has anyone ever considered your excessive worry as a *negative* personality trait? For example, have your children ever said that you smother or nag them too much, or have your friends ever not taken you seriously because you worry so much?

6. The cost of worry: Potential challenges for all worry beliefs.

Has excessive worrying about this topic impacted your relationships with your family or friends?

Has excessive worry impacted your work performance? Do you find that it takes you longer to complete tasks than other people who worry less?

Has your excessive worry led to high levels of stress and fatigue?

How much time and effort do you spend each day worrying about this topic? Do you get better results from your worrying (for example, a better relationship with your children, superior work or school performance) compared to people who worry less?

particularly useful, is that they must now consider alternatives to worrying. Relatedly, many clients report feelings of grief when they realize that they have spent years engaged in the largely fruitless act of worry. As such, therapists might wish to discuss these topics following the reevaluation of positive beliefs about worry.

An important area for discussion involves what the client's life might look like if they worried less. It is important for the therapist to keep in mind that most clients with GAD have suffered from chronic worry and anxiety for the greater part of their lives. Many cannot even conceive of a life without chronic worry. In fact, for those clients who view themselves as "worriers," it can be difficult to determine who they are, and what their personality and character will be like, without worry as a background.

THERAPIST: Obviously you know that the ultimate goal of this treatment is for you to worry less and experience less anxiety both now and in the long term.

CLIENT: I know. It's great. I'm really looking forward to not being so worried and anxious all the time.

THERAPIST: Absolutely! But have you given any thought to what that means? That is, other than feeling relieved that you don't have to spend so much time and energy worrying, what will you do with your days if they aren't filled with worry and anxiety?

CLIENT: I actually hadn't given it much thought. I'm not really sure what I'd do with my time.

THERAPIST: That's not surprising. Most people with GAD have struggled with excessive worry all their lives, so it can be difficult to imagine what life would look like without it. For many people with anxiety disorders, they can remember a time without their symptoms, so they have some idea what a life after excessive anxiety looks like. But that's not the case if you've struggled with a problem all your life. Think of it like someone who breaks a leg. It changes the way they interact with the world: how they sit down or stand up, take a shower, go to sleep, or get dressed. Yet they remember how they did all of these things before they broke their leg. What if instead someone was born with a broken leg (or it was broken at a very young age)? How that person sits or stands up, takes a shower, gets into bed, or gets dressed has always been affected by the broken leg, so even though it's a nuisance, it is also familiar. That person would probably have to learn how to do all of these things differently if their leg was suddenly healed, since they have no memory of two unbroken legs. It's the same for most people with GAD. They don't have a frame of reference for what a life without excessive worry looks like. In fact, you have only known yourself as a "worrier." Who will you be if you are not the person who worries all the time?

Unsurprisingly, this discussion can be extremely emotional, and some clients will be quite tearful, voicing feelings of loss and frustration. Although it is helpful to return to this discussion again near the end of treatment, clients should begin giving some thought to how they would like to occupy their time if they are not spending hours worrying. For example, some alternatives to excessive worry might include taking a class, traveling, or spending more time with family and friends. A helpful exercise to assist clients in giving some thought to what a "life without worry" might entail for them is presented in Appendix 5.4. Clients are encouraged to consider various areas of their lives, and how they might change aspects of their lives if they actually worried less. As with many clients with anxiety disorders, so much time is consumed by GAD symptoms that clients have probably not had the time or the energy to set treatment goals for themselves other than symptom reduction.

As a final note, this treatment module, more than any other, should be applied in a flexible manner. Specifically, although the reevaluation of positive beliefs about worry is an important part of our treatment protocol, our research findings (and clinical experience) show that these beliefs are quite variable among clients with GAD. Despite the fact that the majority of GAD clients believe that worrying is highly useful, therapists can encounter individuals who hold few, if any, of these beliefs. Thus, the therapist should not assume that all clients believe that worrying serves a functional purpose. Nonetheless, given that positive beliefs about worry can interfere with all treatment modules (for example, a client who believes that worrying less is dangerous or risky may avoid fully engaging in treatment), it is crucial that therapists assess worry beliefs at this early stage in treatment.

Module 3: Reevaluation of Negative Beliefs about Uncertainty

Intolerance of uncertainty is both the primary component of our theoretical model of GAD and the foundation upon which our corresponding treatment is built. As such, this module is an extremely important one within our protocol, since it targets the construct that underlies the excessive worry seen in GAD. As discussed in Chapter 4, the central goals for the therapist at this stage are (1) to introduce the concept of intolerance of uncertainty; (2) to present the impact of negative vs. balanced beliefs about uncertainty on the worry cycle; (3) to introduce the concept of uncertainty-driven safety behaviors; (4) to encourage clients to directly test out beliefs about uncertainty through behavioral experiments; and (5) to introduce the notion of embracing uncertainty.

An Introduction to Intolerance of Uncertainty

Because intolerance of uncertainty is a relatively abstract concept that can be challenging for clients to understand, there are several useful analogies that the therapist can use when introducing it to clients, including the following:

THERAPIST: We are now going to begin expanding upon our understanding of GAD by adding "intolerance of uncertainty" to its background. Intolerance of uncertainty can be seen as the fuel for the engine of worry. The more someone is intolerant of uncertainty, the more that person is likely to start asking "what if" questions that lead to worry. So, what is intolerance of uncertainty?

Allergy Analogy

THERAPIST: Obviously, most people dislike uncertainty more or less, but what do we mean when we talk about being intolerant of uncertainty? One way to think about intolerance of uncertainty is as a psychological allergy. People with an allergy, to pollen for example, will have a very strong reaction to even a minute quantity of the substance. That is, they might start sneezing, coughing, and their eyes might redden when exposed to a very small amount of pollen. In the same way, people who are intolerant of uncertainty are "allergic" to uncertainty. Even when there is only a small amount of uncertainty, they will have a strong reaction; in this case, excessive worry and anxiety. For example, someone who is intolerant of uncertainty might worry a great deal about his or her plane crashing because even though it is unlikely, there is still a small chance that it could happen.

Filtered Lenses Analogy

THERAPIST: Another way to think about intolerance of uncertainty is to see it as wearing special filtered glasses. Instead of wearing "rose-colored glasses," people who are intolerant of uncertainty are wearing "uncertainty glasses." These people look at the world through their filtered lenses and see uncertainty more often and faster than other people do. Even when there is only a small amount of uncertainty in a situation (like the possibility of their plane crashing), they will see it immediately and react to it. People who wear these filtered lenses put a great deal of effort into looking for uncertainty in their environment, and if the world is "colored with uncertainty," they often do not see much else. In other words, people who are intolerant of uncertainty are experts at recognizing uncertainty very quickly and thinking about all the potential bad things that could result from it.

For most clients, an important question to answer in treatment is why they experience the symptoms that they do. In the case of GAD, this means explaining why certain individuals worry excessively about daily life events more than others do. Therapists can answer this question using the construct of intolerance of uncertainty to explain the frequency and excessiveness of worry in GAD as well as the dynamic range of worry topics.

THERAPIST: Your intolerance to uncertainty is actually one of the main reasons why you worry excessively. Do you have an idea as to why?

CLIENT: I don't know. Maybe because I want to be more certain?

THERAPIST: That's exactly right! As we have talked about in earlier sessions, worry is a mental attempt to plan and prepare. We tend to worry about situations that have an element of uncertainty to them as a way of thinking ahead of time about all the possible scenarios that might happen, and therefore feel more certain. Everybody does this from time to time, but if you are intolerant, or allergic, to uncertainty, it only takes a small amount of uncertainty in a daily life situation to lead you to worry. It is for this reason that you worry more than others, and that you will often worry excessively about situations that might not worry people who don't have GAD.

CLIENT: So, any situation where I feel uncertain can make me worry because I'm trying to feel more certain.

THERAPIST: Yes. In fact, if we go back to our model, we discussed how new, unpredictable, or ambiguous situations are all potential triggers for worry. Can you see the common element across these types of situations? For example, a trip to Japan with your wife is a situation that is both novel and unpredictable, and it is a trigger for your worries.

CLIENT: Oh, I see! If a situation is new to me, I don't know what will happen. If it's unpredictable or ambiguous, obviously I can't exactly predict what will happen. So, all of those types of situations worry me because they make me feel uncertain. When I don't know for sure what will happen, I worry.

THERAPIST: That's right. Everyone can potentially react to those types of situations with worry, but your *threshold* for uncertainty is lower than it is for people without GAD, so you are triggered more easily by novel, unpredictable, and ambiguous situations. Intolerance of uncertainty also explains why the topics that you worry about can change from day to day: it depends on what type of uncertainty-inducing situations you encounter.

Negative Beliefs about Uncertainty and the Worry Cycle

Once clients have an understanding of the relationship of intolerance of uncertainty to worry, therapists can introduce negative beliefs about uncertainty. The goal at this stage is to further detail the relationship between intolerance of uncertainty and the worry cycle by introducing specific negative beliefs about uncertainty. In addition, an expanded clinical model is presented to clients, with an emphasis on the contrast between negative beliefs and balanced beliefs about uncertainty.

Why are some people more intolerant of uncertainty than others? As with most fears, it is not the situation itself, but the potential consequences of the situation that elicits feelings of danger and threat. As described in Chapters 2 and 4, there are four negative beliefs, or expectations, about uncertainty that account for an intolerance to uncertainty: (1) events with unknown or unclear elements will lead to negative outcomes; (2) negative outcomes will be catastrophic; (3) inability to cope with negative outcomes; and (4) being uncertain is unacceptable, unpleasant, and unfair. Suggestions for how to Socratically introduce negative beliefs about uncertainty are presented below:

THERAPIST: Why do you think that you are intolerant of uncertainty? What is it that you don't like about feeling uncertain?

CLIENT: Well, I think it's because I don't like not knowing what is going to happen, and because I don't know, I'm worried that it will be something bad.

THERAPIST: Exactly! So, what you've just described are beliefs about uncertainty. Research has actually shown that there are many beliefs that people with GAD have about uncertainty, and you just mentioned a couple of them. The first is the belief that events with unknown or unclear outcomes will turn out negatively. Can you think of an example where you thought that?

CLIENT: Absolutely. When I think about taking a trip to Japan with my wife, I am mostly expecting negative things to happen. Also, at work, whenever my boss asks to speak with me, I think that she is unhappy with me about something, and that I might even get fired.

THERAPIST: Great examples. You actually listed a second, related, belief. That is, not only do you expect a negative outcome, but you also expect that outcome to be catastrophic. In your work example, when your boss asks to speak with you, which is an ambiguous situation since you don't know what she wants to talk to you about, you expect that it will be a catastrophic negative outcome— that she will be upset with you, and even fire you. And when you worry about these outcomes, how do you think you would handle them if they occurred?

CLIENT: Really badly, actually. I don't know what I'd do if I were fired. I wouldn't be able to contribute financially to our household, and I can't be sure that I'd even find another job.

THERAPIST: You've just described yet another belief about uncertainty, which is the expectation that you would be unable to cope with a negative outcome if it occurred. A fourth belief, that you mentioned earlier when you said that you don't like not knowing, is that being uncertain is unpleasant, upsetting, and uncomfortable. People with this belief dislike the actual feeling of being uncertain.

CLIENT: Yes, I definitely understand that feeling. It really bothers me when I don't know what's going to happen.

After introducing negative beliefs about uncertainty, therapists can then show a pictorial model to illustrate the role these beliefs have on the worry cycle, as well as provide a contrasting model with balanced beliefs about uncertainty (see Appendices

5.5 and 5.6). As noted in Chapter 4, individuals who do not worry excessively are more likely to hold balanced beliefs about uncertainty and the outcome of unclear or unknown events, including that novel, unpredictable, and ambiguous situations are (1) likely to turn out all right; (2) likely to be manageable even if the outcome is negative; (3) within one's ability to cope; and (4) a normal part of life.

When introducing the clinical models to clients, there are a couple of key points that therapists are encouraged to discuss. First, it is important to normalize the experience of excessive worry given negative beliefs about uncertainty. Specifically, irrespective of the accuracy of one's beliefs, the expectation of unknown negative outcomes beyond one's capacity to cope would necessarily be anxiety-provoking and lead to worry. Second, it is clear that having more balanced expectations about the outcome of novel, unpredictable, and ambiguous events does not lead to the absence of worry. Rather, a noncatastrophic interpretation of these events raises the threshold for perceived threat, such that one is *less* likely to worry. That is, people with balanced beliefs about uncertainty still worry, however the degree of uncertainty and the probability of negative outcomes needs to be higher in order to trigger worry. This highlights the fact that the goal of treatment is not to eliminate worry, as all people worry from time to time. Instead, the goal is to modify clients' beliefs about uncertainty from a catastrophic interpretation of anticipated threat to a more balanced and neutral perspective. The following is a sample discussion of the clinical models and these specific issues:

THERAPIST: You've probably noticed that all of the beliefs that we've just discussed about uncertainty are negative. Specifically, that situations with unknown or unclear outcomes will turn out catastrophically bad, will be beyond your ability to cope, and are unfair, unpleasant, and uncomfortable. Is it fair to say that anyone who has these thoughts about these kinds of situations would probably worry?

CLIENT: Yes. I never thought about it like that, but yes, thinking like that would make anyone worried about what could happen.

THERAPIST: That's right. But obviously not everyone worries as much as you do. So how do you think people who worry less look at situations with unknown or unclear outcomes?

CLIENT: Maybe they like uncertainty? Or they think that the outcome will always be positive?

THERAPIST: Not necessarily. After all, sometimes negative things can happen. So, it's probably not realistic to expect to believe that the outcome will always be positive. Think about people you know who worry less. If we go back to your worry about your boss asking to speak with you—what might your friends, family, or coworkers say to you about your concerns?

CLIENT: Well, actually a good friend of mine said that I don't know what my boss wants to talk to me about, but that I've always done a good job and received positive feedback, so she probably just wants to talk about details about the job. My friend also said that even if my boss was upset about a mistake I made, he was confident that I could handle whatever the problem was. He said that

if he were in my shoes, he wouldn't be worried. That actually n
lot better.

THERAPIST: It sounds like your friend approached the situation
with more neutral, or balanced, beliefs about uncertainty. Is it ... --,
if you approached these types of situations in a more balanced way that you
might feel differently about them? In other words, do you think you would
be less likely to worry if you saw uncertainty as a normal part of life, and you
expected situations with unknown outcomes to probably turn out all right
and to be largely manageable if any difficulties arose?

CLIENT: Yes, I think so. If I saw situations with unknown outcomes in that way,
I would probably view them as less scary overall.

THERAPIST: Exactly. In other words, you wouldn't feel as threatened by novel,
unpredictable, or ambiguous situations, and you wouldn't feel the need to mentally prepare for them by worrying. If we compare these two sets of beliefs about
uncertainty, negative vs. balanced (see Appendices 5.5 and 5.6), in a model, we
can see that the uncertainty in a given situation is very threatening when you
hold negative beliefs, which then leads to a worry cycle of "what if" thoughts,
worries, anxiety, and safety behaviors. However, if you hold balanced beliefs
about uncertainty, situations with unknown or unclear outcomes are less likely
to be threatening, and the cycle never even begins. This of course doesn't mean
that people with balanced beliefs never worry, rather that their threshold for
tolerating uncertainty is much higher, so they simply worry less as a result.

CLIENT: That makes sense! So, I guess I need to change how I think about uncertainty. Unfortunately, I have no idea how I'm supposed to do that.

When questioned Socratically, most clients will come to the conclusion that
developing more balanced beliefs about uncertainty will ultimately reduce their
overall worry level and is therefore the primary goal of treatment. However, they
will also frequently note confusion about how to develop such beliefs. At this stage
of the module, discussion returns to safety behaviors, both in terms of the problems with their use, and the specific types of behaviors seen among GAD clients.

Uncertainty-Driven Safety Behaviors

As discussed in Chapter 4, the safety behaviors seen among GAD clients involve
deliberate attempts to avoid, reduce, or otherwise sidestep the uncertainty experienced in daily life situations. For the sake of clarity, uncertainty-driven safety
behaviors are described as either "approach" actions designed to reduce uncertainty by acquiring more information in a given situation, or "avoidance" actions
designed to bypass uncertainty-inducing situations altogether. It is good to keep
in mind that although safety behaviors are discussed in "approach" and "avoidance" terms, this is largely to better explain to clients the function of these behaviors, namely to attempt to circumnavigate the uncertainty experienced in daily
life situations. However, as noted in Chapter 4, these are not empirically derived
categories.

At this point in treatment, therapists are encouraged to briefly review both the rationale behind the use of safety behaviors and the problems that ensue from their use, as well as introduce the uncertainty-driven nature of safety behaviors in GAD. This discussion will set the stage for the implementation of behavioral experiments, which involve having clients test out the accuracy of their beliefs about uncertainty by deliberately refraining from engaging in safety behaviors.

THERAPIST: Earlier you said that although you would like to change your beliefs about uncertainty to a more balanced perspective, you didn't know how. That's a very important point, but before we can answer how you change your beliefs, we need to add a final piece to the worry puzzle. As you know, one part of the worry cycle involves the safety behaviors that you engage in to both reduce your anxiety and prevent the feared outcomes that you generated through worry. Early on, I asked you to monitor your safety behaviors along with your worries. Can you recall some of the safety behaviors that you engage in?

CLIENT: Yes. I noticed that I often seek reassurance from friends and family and look up lots of information online, particularly when I have to make a decision about something. I also avoid situations that make me anxious, like trying to avoid taking a trip to Japan with my wife.

THERAPIST: Great examples. You might not have noticed, but all of those safety behaviors serve a similar function. They are designed to help you reduce, avoid, or otherwise get around uncertainty. So, while worry is a mental attempt to reduce uncertainty, safety behaviors are a physical attempt to reduce or avoid uncertainty through deliberate action. Some GAD safety behaviors involve approaching a situation and trying to reduce the uncertainty by acquiring more information, and some involve avoiding the situation altogether. For example, when you ask other people their opinion before you make a decision, you are trying to reduce your uncertainty about whether or not you are making the right decision. If you put off or avoid a meeting with your boss that is worrying you, you are attempting to avoid the uncertain situation altogether. You might also find that you sometimes do a "GAD dance," where you go back and forth between approaching a situation to reduce the uncertainty and avoiding it completely. For example, you might look up information online before making a purchase, but then find that you take a step back and put off buying anything.

It can be helpful to provide clients with a list of common safety behaviors (see Table 5.2), as it is not uncommon for clients to be unaware of some of the actions they engage in to reduce or avoid feelings of uncertainty. This is unsurprising given that the primary theme of threat within this treatment for GAD is not a tangible object or situation, such as a fear of elevators or social interactions. Rather, it is the presence of an unknown or unclear quality of a given situation that elicits distress. As such, it can be difficult for clients to recognize the actions conducted to subvert situations that trigger uncertainty.

Table 5.2 Examples of Uncertainty-Driven Safety Behaviors

"Approach" Strategies

1. *Wanting to do everything yourself and not delegating tasks to anyone else.*
   Example: Doing all the housework yourself because otherwise you cannot be certain that it will be done right.

2. *Looking for a lot of information before proceeding with something.*
   Examples: Reading a lot of documentation on a topic; asking for the same information from a number of people; and shopping for a very long time before choosing a present for someone.

3. *Second-guessing or going back multiple times and changing a decision you have already made because you are no longer certain that it was the best decision.*
   Example: Buying an item, such as a new pair of shoes, and going back to the store several times to exchange them or return them.

4. *Looking for reassurance (asking questions or seeking out opinions from others about an action or decision).*
   Examples: Asking family or friends what you should wear when going out; telling others about a decision you made or action you took and asking them to tell you whether they thought it was the right action or decision.

5. *Rechecking and doing things over because you are no longer sure you did them correctly.*
   Example: Rereading emails several times before sending them to make sure that there are absolutely no mistakes.

6. *Overprotecting others (e.g., family members and children), doing things for them in order to make sure that they are completed and/or done correctly.*
   Example: Packing your children's schoolbags, lunches, or sports equipment bags to ensure nothing is forgotten.

7. *Engaging in excessive preparation or planning.*
   Example: Packing for a trip weeks in advance; going through all of your recipes and picking a large number of courses in advance of a dinner party.

"Avoidance" Strategies

1. *Avoiding fully committing to certain things.*
   Examples: Not fully committing to a friendship or romantic relationship because the outcome is uncertain; not fully engaging in therapy because there is no "guarantee" that it will work.

2. *Avoiding situations altogether.*
   Examples: Not going out to social events when you aren't sure who will be there; avoiding trying new things, such as new sports or leisure activities that you haven't done before.

3. *Finding "imaginary" reasons for not doing certain things.*
   Examples: Finding excuses to not move out of the family home; not doing exercise that you know is good for you by telling yourself that you might not be able to stand the discomfort of exercising.

4. *Procrastinating (putting off until later what you could do right away).*
   Examples: Putting off a phone call because you are not certain how the person receiving the call will react; delaying making a decision because you are not certain that it is the right decision.

5. *Impulsive decision making (deliberately making a quick and careless decision, like a coin toss, in order to avoid thinking about making the wrong decision).*
   Example: When unsure about what movie to go see, showing up at the theater and seeing the first movie that is playing at that time.

Once uncertainty-driven safety behaviors have been presented, discussion can then turn to a brief review of the problems with the use of safety behaviors, and their impact on negative beliefs about uncertainty and the worry cycle. Although safety behaviors can provide the short-term benefit of anxiety reduction and perceived prevention of feared outcomes, the long-term effects of safety behaviors are considerable, as safety behaviors maintain the worry cycle in several ways. First, the nonoccurrence of negative outcomes following the use of safety behaviors is taken as evidence that those outcomes would have occurred in the absence of the behaviors. Second, safety behaviors prevent the acquisition of potential corrective information about the actual likelihood of a feared outcome. For example, let's say that an individual makes a detailed to-do list for themselves every day to ensure that they don't forget to do everything that needs to be completed for that day. When they complete everything on the list, they are assured with complete certainty that they did not forget to do anything. The list therefore feels necessary. However, they are unable to determine whether they would have in fact forgotten to complete any of the listed tasks, as they do not have the opportunity to engage in daily tasks without the list for guidance. Moreover, attempts to avoid or minimize the uncertainty in triggering situations prevent clients from learning whether they are able to sit with and tolerate the feeling of uncertainty without being overwhelmed.

These inherent problems with safety behaviors maintain the worry cycle by preventing clients from testing out whether their negative beliefs about the outcome of unknown or unclear events are in fact accurate. They are therefore unable to obtain potentially disconfirming evidence that might instead favor more balanced beliefs about uncertainty. It is these problems associated with safety behavior use that therapists will need to underscore to clients in order to pave the way for behavioral experiments.

Testing Out Beliefs About Uncertainty: Behavioral Experiments

Once clients have an understanding about (1) the significant impact that negative beliefs about uncertainty have in fueling the worry cycle, and (2) the role that safety behaviors play in preventing the acquisition of potentially corrective disconfirmatory information, behavioral experiments can be introduced. The initial emphasis is on providing a rationale for enduring cognitive change through the accrual of evidence about the accuracy of negative beliefs about uncertainty. It is expected that if clients consistently obtain evidence in favor of balanced beliefs about uncertainty, their interpretation about the threat of the uncertainty present in novel, unpredictable, and ambiguous situations will shift. This in turn will lead to reduced worry and anxiety, as situations with unknown or unclear outcomes are perceived as less threatening overall.

Because this rationale could potentially appear complex to clients, suggestions for presenting this material are described below.

THERAPIST: Earlier you mentioned that you didn't know how you would go about changing your beliefs about uncertainty. It's actually an important point to consider. How do we change a belief, that is, change our minds, about anything? Let's say that I drove to work every day and you wanted to convince me to ride my bike to work instead, how would you try to change my mind?

CLIENT: I would probably tell you that it is much healthier to ride a bike every day than to sit in a car, that it's better for the environment, and that you would save a lot of money on gas.

THERAPIST: So, you would give me lots of reasons for why bike riding is better than driving a car when going to and from work. But what if I still thought it was better to drive in to work?

CLIENT: I guess I would ask you why you prefer driving to work. For example, if you tell me that it's quicker and easier, I would ask you about the traffic that you deal with every day, and maybe how long it actually takes you to get to work by car. You might find it takes only a bit more time getting to work by bike, and it is certainly less stressful than being caught in traffic.

THERAPIST: That's excellent! So basically, you would give me lots of evidence in defense of bike riding. You would also ask me for my reasons in support of driving to work, and try to challenge them. In essence, you would try to build a case *for* your position, bike riding to work, and *against* my position, driving to work.

CLIENT: Yes, that sounds right.

THERAPIST: Well that's basically how we change our minds, or in the case of our work together here, change or shift a belief. That is, we need evidence in favor of one belief and against another, and if that evidence is compelling and meaningful, we are likely to change our minds. The same holds true for negative beliefs about uncertainty. If you want to be able to potentially hold more balanced beliefs about uncertainty, and view novel, unpredictable, and ambiguous situations as less threatening overall, you will need evidence that these situations are not in fact threatening.

CLIENT: That makes sense. So how am I going to get that evidence?

THERAPIST: Great question. In order to determine whether situations with unknown or unclear outcomes are actually threatening, you will need to be scientific about it. You are actually going to gather your evidence through experiments, which we call behavioral experiments. We use behavioral experiments to make predictions and test them out. As we discussed earlier, one of the problems in the worry cycle is that when you use safety behaviors, you assume that there will be a negative outcome in an uncertain situation, so you act to prevent or reduce it before ever finding out what would actually happen. Basically, safety behaviors prevent you from getting the evidence you need to determine whether your negative beliefs about uncertainty are accurate. Because of this, behavioral experiments will involve deliberately entering into novel, unpredictable, and ambiguous situations without using safety behaviors. In this way, you will be able to make a prediction about what you are afraid will happen and test out whether your prediction is correct.

Once clients understand the rationale behind behavioral experiments, it is important that the specific beliefs targeted for testing are highlighted. Specifically, the three negative beliefs about uncertainty that relate to outcomes are most amenable to direct testing and are therefore the initial focus; these include: (1) situations with uncertain outcomes will turn out negatively; (2) negative outcomes will be catastrophic; and (3) inability to cope with negative outcomes.

Behavioral experiments targeting negative uncertainty beliefs involve identifying at the outset both a specific situation where clients have the opportunity to refrain from engaging in safety behaviors, and the feared or predicted outcome. After clients have completed an experiment, they are asked to record the actual outcome, and if the outcome was negative, how they handled the situation. In this manner, they are directly testing whether a situation with an uncertain outcome did in fact have a negative outcome, and if it did, whether that outcome was catastrophic or beyond their ability to cope. For example, a client might choose to allow their friend to decide which restaurant and film to go to during an evening out. In this case, the typical safety behavior might involve refusing to delegate any tasks to others in order to be completely certain about the evening's activities. The client might initially record the following:

Experiment: Letting my friend pick which restaurant we eat at and which movie we see (typical safety behavior: not delegating decisions to others).

Feared outcome: I won't like the food at the restaurant or the movie that my friend chose. I will have a terrible evening, waste time and money, and my friend will be upset that I didn't like her choices.

One of the benefits of these types of behavioral experiments is that irrespective of the outcome, clients will have the opportunity to test out some of the negative beliefs about uncertainty. For example, the outcome of this experiment might be as follows:

Actual outcome: I had a great time out with my friend! The food at the restaurant she chose was delicious, and we both really enjoyed the movie.

This positive outcome allows for testing of the first belief, namely that events with unknown or unclear outcomes will turn out negative. The results of this experiment provide some initial evidence that the anticipation of a negative outcome may be incorrect.

If on the other hand the outcome of the experiment was negative, the results might be as follows:

Actual outcome: The restaurant that my friend chose was very nice, but I thought that most of the food was too spicy for me, so I couldn't eat very much. The movie was pretty good, but there were lots of people, so it was a bit noisy in the theater.

Coping: Because I was still a bit hungry after I left the restaurant, I decided to get some popcorn at the movies. I was going to pick up something else afterward, but I was full after the popcorn.

In this case, because the outcome was negative, the client has the opportunity to test out whether the negative outcome was catastrophic, and how they were able to cope. A debrief of this experiment is likely to yield that although some of the feared outcomes did occur (i.e., the individual did not like the food at the restaurant chosen by their friend), it was certainly not catastrophic, as they liked the restaurant and the movie, so they probably would not state that the evening was a waste of time and money. Moreover, the client's coping was appropriate to the situation (having some popcorn at the movies), and in fact they had developed an alternate strategy (pick up some food after the movie) if the first option was not effective.

Constructing Behavioral Experiments

It can be initially challenging for clients to identify specific novel, unpredictable, or ambiguous situations that they can seek out without the use of an accompanying safety behavior. With this in mind, the first behavioral experiments that clients conduct should be relatively structured. When experiments are first presented, the following elements should be considered:

- *Set specific experiments.* Before leaving session, clients should have a clear idea of exactly what behavioral experiments they will be conducting. It is not recommended to ask them to simply seek out uncertainty-driven situations and attempt to refrain from engaging in safety behaviors. Initial experiments can include:
  - Going to a new restaurant without looking up the menu or any online reviews beforehand (addressing information seeking safety behavior);
  - Calling a friend you have lost touch with, without planning the conversation beforehand, and inviting them out for a social outing, such as lunch or a coffee date (addressing excessive preparation safety behavior);
  - Not looking at your cell phone for one or two hours (addressing double-checking safety behavior).
- *Three experiments a week.* In order to assist clients in obtaining a preponderance of evidence from their behavioral experiments, it is important that they are completed regularly, and on a weekly basis. We recommend that clients complete three experiments each week. Some clients initially state the ambitious intention to complete one experiment each day, however in order to ensure success, we will typically tell our clients to set only three experiments as their goal for the week. That is, although they can complete more, the expectation is only for three experiments. In this manner, clients are less likely to be disappointed in themselves if they are unable to complete the challenge of completing one experiment a day.

- *Recording the outcome.* As is standard in CBT, we strongly emphasize the importance of always recording the outcome of behavioral experiments. With a physical record of their experiment results, clients are able to draw conclusions about their findings across a number of experiments without having to rely on memory. With this in mind, a Behavioral Experiment Record Form is available for use in Appendix 5.7. Clients are encouraged to record the specific task and their feared outcome prior to conducting the experiment, and to subsequently record the actual outcome, and how they coped with the situation (if the outcome was negative).

- *Experiments should have an observable outcome.* When first devising behavioral experiments with clients, the therapist should take care to ensure that an observable outcome could be realistically expected prior to the next session. Although later experiments can include feared outcomes that are not immediately observable, first experiments should be clear and observable in order to allow for debriefing in session. For example, a good first experiment might involve not checking one's cell phone for an hour, with the feared outcome being that the individual will miss an important call or text during that time. Because of the specificity of this experiment, the client will be able to determine whether their feared outcome was accurate after the experiment has ended, and report on the actual outcome as a result. By contrast, a less beneficial experiment might involve writing an email without checking for spelling or grammatical errors. In this case, the feared outcome might be that there would be a mistake in the email, and that the recipient would notice and think poorly of them. However, although a sent email can be viewed afterward to investigate the feared outcome of making a mistake, the client will be unable to know whether the recipient noticed any mistakes or held a negative impression of them as a result (unless specifically mentioned by the recipient).

- *Experiments can be repeated.* Although clients are encouraged to complete three behavioral experiments a week, they do not all need to be different. Clients can choose to repeat the same experiment multiple times a week, or the same experiment across weeks. For example, experiments involving delegating household tasks to family members (such as allowing one's children to pack their own schoolbag), not checking one's cell phone, or picking clothes for work without asking for reassurance, are all amenable to repeated testing. In fact, conducting these experiments multiple times allows clients to make more compelling observations about the frequency and severity of negative outcomes, and their coping ability.

As noted earlier, behavioral experiments are a powerful tool for shifting negative beliefs precisely because they allow clients to form their own observations and conclusions about outcomes without the interfering effect of safety behaviors. However, a compelling case for balanced beliefs about uncertainty is best made when there is a great deal of evidence generated by clients. Otherwise there is the danger of clients attributing outcomes to luck or happenstance. For example, if, as a behavioral experiment, a client allows their child to pack their schoolbag, the outcome might be positive; that is, their child might not forget to pack any-thing important. Yet the client is more likely to interpret this finding as a fortunate occurrence if the experiment was only conducted once or twice, as opposed to a more compelling and enduring finding about their child's ability to manage their own schoolbag if the same experiment was conducted numerous times across several weeks. With this in mind, we therefore recommend spending upwards of six to eight sessions solely on behavioral experiments in order to allow clients to properly test out their fears related to uncertainty-inducing situations, and to ulti-mately build a compelling case in favor of balanced beliefs about uncertainty.

Debriefing Behavioral Experiments

The review and debriefing of clients' behavioral experiments takes two forms in session. First, once clients have begun completing experiments, the next session should focus on a discussion of the outcomes from the past week's specific experi-ments. We recommend reviewing each experiment individually and discussing (1) whether the actual outcome matched the feared outcome; (2) whether the actual outcome was positive, neutral, or negative; (3) if the outcome was nega-tive, was it perceived as catastrophic; and (4) how the client views their coping strategies when negative outcomes occurred. We have found that it is important to frame the initial conclusions from these experiments, irrespective of outcome, as tentative findings that will likely benefit from further investigation. That is, the therapist should take care not to discuss these results as clear evidence against negative beliefs and catastrophic interpretations of uncertainty, but rather small pieces of a larger puzzle that is yet to be completed. This allows clients to form their own conclusions without feeling that their therapist is pushing them toward a particular way of thinking. A sample discussion for debriefing behavioral experi-ments is provided below:

THERAPIST: I thought we would start by reviewing how you did with your behavioral experiments this week. I believe that one of your experiments was to let your daughter pack her own soccer bag, without reminding her or tell-ing her not to forget anything. Since your daughter plays soccer twice a week, you were going to do that experiment twice. You were also going to try a new restaurant in your neighborhood without looking up their menu, or any reviews, online. So how did it go?

CLIENT: Well it was an interesting week. It was harder than expected for me to leave my daughter alone when she packed her sports bag, but I was able to do it both times. I was also able to go to a new restaurant with my wife, and I didn't look up anything about the place beforehand.

THERAPIST: That's great! OK, let's go through each experiment one at a time. Let's start with dinner at the new restaurant. What was your feared outcome, and what was the actual outcome?

CLIENT: My feared outcome was that the food at the restaurant would be very expensive, and that neither my wife nor I would like anything on the menu, and that it would be a completely wasted evening. As for what actually happened, my wife and I loved the food! It was a wonderful restaurant, but the meal was pretty expensive. We were going to have dessert there, but given how much the meal cost we decided to just have coffee instead and have dessert when we got home.

THERAPIST: So, looking at the actual outcome, would you say that it was a positive, a neutral, or a negative outcome?

CLIENT: Oh, definitely positive! Even though it was a bit more expensive than I expected, it was a great place for us to go, and I think we will probably go again for a special occasion.

THERAPIST: Based on the outcome you described, it sounds like it definitely had some positive elements, since you and your wife both enjoyed your meal, but the price of the food was high, which was one of your feared outcomes, and that is a bit of a negative outcome.

CLIENT: Yes, I guess that's true.

THERAPIST: If we look at that negative outcome, how bad, or catastrophic, was it?

CLIENT: Honestly, not that bad at all. Our dinner was more expensive than places we usually go to, but I think it was worth it. We also adjusted by not having dessert, and by ordering the house wine instead of buying a bottle of wine.

THERAPIST: That was the next thing I was going to bring up. Based on what you described, you coped with the negative aspect of this experiment by ordering slightly less (no dessert) and substituting a bottle of wine with the house wine. How do you think you managed that situation?

CLIENT: I hadn't really thought of those actions as coping, but you're right, I did manage the cost issue while at the restaurant. When I look at it, I think I handled that situation really well. My wife and I had a great evening, and I wasn't too bothered by the increased cost of everything.

THERAPIST: Great. Now let's look at your other two experiments involving letting your daughter pack her own sports bag. Last time you told me that your feared outcome was that she would forget something important, that her coach would be furious, and that she could even get kicked off the team. So, what actually happened?

CLIENT: Well the first time she packed her own bag, she didn't forget anything. So that was a positive outcome. The second time however, she forgot to pack her kneepads, and she didn't realize until she got to the field.

THERAPIST: That's interesting! The first experiment had a positive outcome, but the second one had a negative outcome that included a part of your feared outcome. How bad would you say that outcome was, and how did you handle it?

CLIENT: I actually didn't handle the situation; my daughter did. She told her coach that she forgot her kneepads, and he told her to get a spare pair in the equipment room, which she did. She didn't like wearing old kneepads, but I think it was actually a good lesson for her. I'm actually pretty glad that I did that experiment, and I think I'm going to keep doing it. So even though the outcome was technically negative, I think it was still positive overall.

THERAPIST: It sounds like you didn't see the actual outcome of the second experiment involving your daughter as negative at all, so I'm assuming that you didn't see it as catastrophic. It also sounds like you coped pretty well with the outcome, as you saw it as a good lesson for your daughter even though she did in fact forget something. So, these experiments were your first foray into deliberately entering into situations with unknown outcomes and observing what actually happens. Any tentative conclusions so far?

CLIENT: I think they went really well, so I'm curious to try different experiments and see how they turn out. I'm definitely not sure whether things will turn out so well with bigger experiments.

THERAPIST: That's a great point. I guess you will have to keep doing behavioral experiments and see what happens. Being curious about the outcome of future experiments is actually a great way to put it. Rather than just assuming a negative outcome, you can learn to be curious about what the actual outcome will be. The only way to find out what happens in uncertainty-inducing situations, and how you will handle them, is to deliberately face the situation and test out your predictions.

The second form of debriefing of behavioral experiments in session involves an analysis of all experiments completed to date, with the goal of drawing larger conclusions. This can be repeated every few sessions, as the total number of experiments increases. The following points are some recommendations for topics to review and expand upon with clients when discussing behavioral experiments as a whole:

- How many experiments have been conducted to date?
- How many were positive? Neutral? Negative?
- When outcomes were negative, how often were they catastrophic?
- When outcomes were negative, how did you handle the negative outcomes?
- What do you think about your ability to manage negative outcomes when they arise?
- What conclusions can you draw so far about the accuracy of your negative beliefs about uncertainty?

Although we have not discussed any specific behavioral experiments related to the negative belief that uncertainty is unacceptable, unpleasant, and unfair, this belief can be targeted both directly and indirectly. For clients who express significant distress at the notion of "sitting" with uncertainty, or describe a fear of being overwhelmed while in an unresolved uncertainty-inducing situation, some behavioral experiments can be adjusted to test out the impact of sitting with a state of uncertainty directly. An experiment of this type might involve delaying one day prior to addressing an uncertainty-inducing situation, such as not verifying for a day whether a task delegated to another person was completed. Sitting with the feeling of uncertainty can also be addressed indirectly by asking clients about it when debriefing behavioral experiments and discussing overall conclusions. Questions can include: (1) "How did you feel when deliberately entering into a situation with an unknown or unclear outcome (e.g., anxious, uncomfortable)?" and (2) "Were you able to manage any uncomfortable feelings, or was it overwhelming to sit with the feeling of uncertainty?" Clients are often able to alter their perspective on the unpleasantness and unfairness of uncertainty following the direct experience obtained through behavioral experiments.

Expanding the Range of Behavioral Experiments

As noted previously, the ultimate goal of behavioral experiments within our protocol is to shift clients' perception of novel, unpredictable, and ambiguous situations as inherently threatening to a nonthreatening, more balanced perception. This objective necessarily involves a shift in perspective across most areas of life, and as such it is important that conclusions drawn from behavioral experiments be generalizable, and not construed as simply situation-specific. With this in mind, there are several ways to widen the net of behavioral experiments, such that clients are generally more tolerant of uncertainty irrespective of the situation.

INCREASING THE STAKES

Although initial behavioral experiments should be small and structured, as clients become more comfortable with engaging in experiments, they can begin completing more challenging experiments. For example, an early behavioral experiment might involve allowing friends to make the plans for a social gathering (that is, not engaging in the safety behavior of refusing to delegate tasks to others). A more challenging experiment might involve not planning an entire day's activities while away on vacation (not engaging in excessive preparation). The second behavioral experiment example is more challenging, as the stakes are higher than in the first one. Specifically, potential negative outcomes for the first experiment are likely minimal, such as not enjoying a social gathering with friends, whereas the potential negative outcome of having a bad time for an entire day during a vacation is more significant, given the cost, and the limited time typically available for vacations.

Therapists are encouraged to keep in mind that low-stakes experiments are recommended at first in order to minimize the likelihood of a more impactful negative outcome should it occur. Negative outcomes are expected to occur on occasion when clients engage in behavioral experiments, however, it is best for clients to have had some experience managing mild negative outcomes before attempting more challenging experiments.

EXPANDING EXPERIMENTS ACROSS LIFE AREAS

It is not uncommon for clients to largely focus on experiments within only one or two particular domains of their life, such as work/school, home, or leisure activities. However, in order to maximize the generalizability of experiment findings, we recommend encouraging clients to incorporate behavioral experiments across all areas of life, such as social interactions and relationships with family and friends, in addition to those listed above. This can typically be accomplished by identifying common safety behaviors, and subsequently brainstorming with clients how these behaviors can be targeted in other areas of life. For example, if a client has completed a number of experiments involving delegating household tasks to family members, they might try to extend experiments involving delegation of tasks to work situations or to social outings with friends.

The above guidelines can be used to assist clients in broadening the depth and range of their behavioral experiments. However, we have found that as clients become more comfortable with experiments, they are increasingly able to identify on their own what experiments would be most beneficial to them in their quest for evidence about the accuracy of their beliefs. In fact, often the most original and impactful experiments that clients conduct are self-generated. In this case, the therapist's role shifts primarily to reviewing findings, praising clients for their efforts, and ultimately assisting clients to contemplate the place that uncertainty can have in their lives.

Embracing Uncertainty

As discussed extensively in Chapter 2, intolerance of uncertainty is a central process driving the worry cycle in GAD. It is therefore logical that treatment focuses on increasing tolerance to uncertainty in order to ultimately reduce worry and anxiety. Yet the word "tolerance" does not have positive connotations. Rather, it reflects acceptance of a particular state, perhaps with slight annoyance. For example, an individual can tolerate a few ants while enjoying a picnic, but they are certainly not enjoying their presence. However, this begrudging acceptance of uncertainty ignores the fact that many situations with uncertain outcomes can actually be positive or carry heretofore unknown benefits. As such, we feel that it is of value to discuss with clients the notion of occasionally embracing uncertainty, instead of simply tolerating it. We have found that although clients are quite skeptical initially of the idea that being uncertain could have benefits, they are nevertheless able to recognize aspects of uncertainty worthy of being embraced as treatment progresses and their perspective shifts over time. The following are positive aspects of uncertainty that can be discussed with clients.

The Benefits of Surprise and Spontaneity

People with GAD exert a great deal of energy, through both their thoughts (worries) and their actions (safety behaviors), attempting to be prepared for any situation. As such, unexpected situations are invariably experienced as aversive. Yet there can be great joy and pleasure derived from unexpected surprises in life, such as opening a wrapped gift, receiving an unexpected call from an old friend, or finding money in an old pair of jeans. In fact, many of the pleasant surprises we experience in life occur at unexpected or unplanned times. It is through spontaneity, and allowing one's self to try new things without a concrete plan, that these experiences are most likely to occur.

In a similar vein, because of the tendency to avoid being in a state of uncertainty, the feeling of "not knowing" is experienced as unpleasant and uncomfortable. Yet for those who do not view uncertainty as threatening, "not knowing" can be experienced as excitement. In this case, butterflies in the stomach can feel like they foreshadow pleasant future events, rather than simply a feeling of discomfort. As clients engage in behavioral experiments that involve experiencing novel situations, the positive elements of the situation can be highlighted, over and above the absence of negative outcomes.

Building Confidence

One of the great benefits of behavioral experiments for GAD clients is the opportunity it affords them to learn about their own ability to cope with adversity. Not only is it exhausting and time-consuming to attempt to avoid or reduce the uncertainty in most daily life situations, it deprives individuals of the chance to see how they manage negative outcomes without advance preparation. When individuals are constantly mentally planning for potential calamities ahead of time, they are essentially telling themselves that they are incapable of thinking on their feet, a belief that does not foster a sense of self-confidence. However, through direct experience acquired from behavioral experiments, clients are able to see how they actually fare when unexpected negative outcomes occur. As a result, they can become less fearful of situations with uncertain outcomes overall, because they are more confident in their ability to manage adversity should it arise.

It has been our clinical experience that working on this module with clients across a number of sessions frequently leads to substantive changes in their relationship to the state of uncertainty, such that it is viewed as markedly less threatening overall. This is turn leads to the report of significantly reduced worry and anxiety. However, despite the benefits of targeting negative beliefs about uncertainty, some clients continue to experience ongoing and lingering problematic worry. With this in mind, the next two modules are designed to address the excessive worries that might remain.

Module 4: Problem-Solving Training

Up to now, the primary treatment focus has been on addressing what underlies excessive worry, rather than directly targeting worries themselves. Although addressing clients' negative beliefs about uncertainty is expected to shift their interpretations about the danger of uncertainty-inducing situations and thereby reduce worry, some clients nevertheless report significant ongoing lingering worries. As such, it is a good idea for therapists to provide worry monitoring forms in order to identify what specific worries remain excessive. From there, clients are encouraged to identify whether particular worries involve current problems or future hypothetical situations, as excessive worries falling within each of these worry types is addressed with a specific treatment intervention.

This module targets worries about current problems over which clients have some degree of control. The emphasis is on developing a more neutral and accepting perspective toward problem solving and implementing problem-solving skills to address problematic situations rather than simply worrying about them. With this in mind, the problem-solving training module is split into two phases: (1) improving problem orientation; and (2) applying problem-solving skills. In the following sections, each one of these phases is presented separately; however, the reader should keep in mind that both phases are inexorably linked. For example, until clients recognize that their problems are not entirely aversive and threatening, they are unlikely to implement their problem-solving skills no matter how good they might be.

Improving Problem Orientation

Problem solving is introduced as a practical alternative to worry if we can agree that worrying about problems is not especially useful. This idea, that clients can "replace" excessive worry with actual problem solving, should be underscored repeatedly throughout this module. Excessive worry about problems is not an active strategy, although clients might initially view it as such. On the other hand, the active process of problem solving can actually lead to change in a problematic situation.

THERAPIST: Early on in treatment, we had spent some time talking about whether excessive worry is actually beneficial. In some instances, we found that worrying excessively can have the opposite effect to what you previously believed. For example, worrying excessively about projects at work can make you so anxious that rather than motivating you to work on them, you procrastinate instead. So, if worry is not that useful, what do you think you could do instead?

CLIENT: I don't know. I have been thinking a lot about that, and I assume that I should just stop worrying, but that's easier said than done. I definitely worry less now, but I still have some worries that bother me and I'm not sure how to deal with them. How can I just stop worrying?

THERAPIST: You are absolutely right. It would be great if you could just shut off worry like a light switch, but it's not that simple, is it? We've recently been talking about classifying your remaining worries as either being about current problems or hypothetical situations. We are now going to start working on specific strategies for these different worry types. The first one I will be introducing today is problem solving as a way to deal with your worries about current problems. So, you are not simply going to "stop worrying," but start replacing worry with a more productive strategy.

CLIENT: Well, I'm really not very good at solving my problems.

THERAPIST: Well, if that's true, then it is even more important to start working on this. But what you just said about your ability to solve problems relates exactly to what we will be discussing today: negative problem orientation.

Negative problem orientation is a factor that contributes to excessive worry, and it interferes with your problem-solving ability on many levels.

Prior to beginning a discussion on negative problem orientation and its impact on both problem solving and the worry cycle, it is a good idea for therapists to briefly discuss with clients some of the research findings in the area. For example, it is helpful for clients to know that the research to date suggests that excessive worriers are just as skilled at problem solving as people who worry less. However, people who are prone to worry have a more negative problem orientation. In other words, they have more negative attitudes and beliefs about problems and problem solving. The following is a suggestion for the presentation of negative problem orientation:

THERAPIST: What is negative problem orientation? It refers to the way we view problems, and the way we view ourselves as problem solvers. People who have a negative problem orientation tend to (1) view problems as threatening; (2) doubt their ability to solve problems; and (3) believe that problem solving will turn out badly no matter what. In other words, people with a negative problem orientation will say to themselves: "I don't like problems, I'm not good at solving them, and when I try to solve them, it doesn't work out well." Have you ever thought like that?

CLIENT: Absolutely. I hate dealing with problems and I do think that I'm not good at solving them. I usually ask other people for advice on how to deal with them.

THERAPIST: If you remember, when we talked about negative beliefs about uncertainty, I told you that they have a number of effects on your thoughts (worry), your feelings (anxiety), and your behaviors (safety behaviors like reassurance-seeking or avoidance). Negative problem orientation works in the same way. When you have negative beliefs about problems and your ability to deal with them, this has a strong impact on your emotions, your thoughts, and your behaviors.

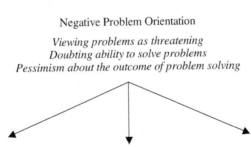

Negative Problem Orientation

Viewing problems as threatening
Doubting ability to solve problems
Pessimism about the outcome of problem solving

Emotional Consequences	Cognitive Consequences	Behavioral Consequences
Frustration, irritation, anxiety, and depression	*Worries about problem, new problems, new worries*	*Avoidance, procrastination, impulsive problem solving*

When presenting the consequences of negative problem orientation, it is best for therapists to encourage clients to generate examples through Socratic questioning. This can be achieved by logically linking the beliefs underlying negative problem orientation to the expected impact. For example:

THERAPIST: So, if a person saw problems as entirely threatening and believed that they were a poor problem solver, how do you think they are likely to feel when a problem comes up?

CLIENT: Probably pretty annoyed. I hate it when there is a problem. I also get anxious.

THERAPIST: Exactly, so the emotional effect for you is that you have lots of negative feelings like irritation, annoyance, and anxiety whenever you encounter a problem.

When discussing the consequences of a negative orientation, there are several possibilities that can be considered. In terms of behavioral consequences, clients have a tendency to avoid or delay solving problems for as long as possible. However, if left unsolved for long enough, one problem can create new problems over time. Other behavioral consequences include asking others to solve the problem rather than dealing with it personally, or solving it impulsively in order to worry about it for the least amount of time. The cognitive consequences of a negative problem orientation, however, are what makes this construct such a central factor in the worry cycle. This can be discussed with clients in the following manner:

THERAPIST: So, what do you think the impact of your negative orientation toward problems has on your thoughts? Do you think it makes you worry less or more?

CLIENT: It makes me worry more.

THERAPIST: Why do you think that is?

CLIENT: Well, if I'm not solving a problem, I am going to continue to worry about it.

THERAPIST: That's right. So long as you are not using an active strategy to deal with your problems, you are likely to continue to worry about them. In fact, if you leave problems unsolved for long enough, they can create new problems. On the other hand, have you ever tried to not think about your problems, that is, to ignore them instead of worry about them?

CLIENT: Absolutely. I think I go back and forth between worrying about problems and ignoring them.

THERAPIST: That leads to another consequence of negative problem orientation, which involves not being very good at recognizing problems when they come up. If you ignore problems, you are less likely to see them early on and deal with them. Are you starting to see how your attitude toward problems is having a huge impact on your life?

At this stage in treatment, we recommend that therapists incorporate the role of intolerance of uncertainty into the discussion. This will not only highlight the consistency of intolerance of uncertainty throughout treatment, but will also allow therapists to normalize negative problem orientation with respect to GAD. It is important that clients realize that when they hold negative beliefs about uncertainty, having negative beliefs about problems and problem solving is a natural consequence.

THERAPIST: Why do you think that people with GAD have such a negative problem orientation? Why would you be more likely to have negative beliefs about problems and problem solving than someone who worries less?

CLIENT: I don't know.

THERAPIST: A major reason for the relationship between GAD and negative problem orientation has to do with intolerance of uncertainty. As we have discussed before, intolerance of uncertainty and negative beliefs about uncertainty are the fuel for worry. Even a little bit of uncertainty causes people with GAD to worry, and they tend to view the world through a filter where they are constantly searching out uncertainty-inducing situations. Let's see how this relates to problems. First of all, how would you define a problem?

CLIENT: I would say that a problem is something that does not have an obvious solution and that could turn out badly.

THERAPIST: So, a problem is a situation that has no obvious solution and that could have a negative effect in the future. In other words, the outcome of problem solving is unpredictable.

CLIENT: I see. . . . Problems set off my negative beliefs about uncertainty. That explains why I tend to avoid solving problems or ask for advice from others when I'm faced with a problem. Those are uncertainty-related safety behaviors.

THERAPIST: That's right. When we look at it this way, it makes sense that you would find problems threatening. At the same time though, you have been working on testing out your negative beliefs about uncertainty by conducting behavioral experiments. A good way to see problem solving is as just another one of those experiments.

CLIENT: But how am I supposed to change my negative problem orientation? Will I just have to use positive thinking?

THERAPIST: That's a great question. The answer to that is no. We are now going to start discussing ways to change your negative problem orientation, but that does not mean just "thinking positive." Instead, it means learning to be more realistic, flexible, and balanced in your thinking by acknowledging both the negative and the positive sides of problematic situations.

Strategies for Improving Problem Orientation

Although there are a number of different strategies that can be used to help clients improve their problem orientation, we typically focus on three of these strategies. Specifically, we believe that it is beneficial to assist clients in (1) recognizing problems before it is too late; (2) seeing that problems are a normal part of life; and

(3) seeing problems as opportunities rather than threats. For additional therapeutic strategies, the reader is referred to the work of D'Zurilla and Nezu (2006) on problem-solving therapy.

Recognizing Problems Before It Is Too Late

One of the consequences of finding problems aversive is the tendency to avoid recognizing problems as they come up in daily life. Often, problems can start out small and it is only when they are ignored that they begin to grow and become more serious and complex. For example, a client might have had a misunderstanding with a colleague at work. If left unsolved, the colleague might begin to hold a grudge and believe that the client is an uncaring or selfish person. The colleague might then begin to tell other coworkers about the problem, thereby making the problem more complex as other people are brought into the situation. From this example, it is evident that if the problem had been dealt with immediately, it probably would have been easily resolved. Instead, by ignoring or failing to see the problem, it developed into a "minor crisis" at work, with many people involved. This example clearly shows the importance of dealing with problems as soon as they arise. In order to assist clients in improving their ability to recognize problems when they arise, we recommend using two strategies: (1) using one's emotions as cues; and (2) developing a list of recurrent problems.

In terms of the first strategy, a common obstacle to identifying problems is the tendency that many people have to interpret their negative emotions as the problem. For example, many clients identify their problem as frustration or stress. However, these emotions are not the problem (in terms of problem-solving theory). Rather, they are likely to be the byproduct of the actual problematic situation. For example, if a person has many reports to do at work and he is very anxious and stressed about it, the problem is not that he is stressed. Instead, the problem is that he has to complete the reports; his anxiety and stress are due to the fact that he has this particular problem. With this in mind, clients can begin to use their emotions as a cue that there is a problem in their environment:

THERAPIST: The first strategy is to use your emotions as cues. Your negative feelings can be used to let you know that there might be a problem. When you are feeling anxious, stressed out, or demoralized, you can ask yourself: "Is there a problem I am not seeing that is leading to these emotions?" Our emotions, when we are attentive to them, can be very useful in helping us to recognize problems. This strategy has two advantages. First, it will allow you to recognize your problems more quickly and potentially avoid having a small problem become a big problem. Second, it will help you to see your negative emotions in a more "positive" light. In this case, they serve an important function as an early detection system.

The second strategy is to encourage the client to write a list of recurrent problems. It is common to almost everyone that certain problems keep coming up again and again. Examples of recurrent problems include difficulties with a work colleague and end-of-the-month financial problems. However, every time problems recur, most of us have a tendency to react to them with surprise and disappointment, as if they were occurring for the first time. By writing out a list of recurrent problems, clients will be better able to recognize them quickly when they arise. In addition, the accompanying feelings of surprise and disappointment are less likely to develop simply because the problem is expected. This second strategy can be incorporated into a between-session exercise whereby clients are asked to keep the list accessible at all times in order to be better able to recognize problems quickly and react to them with less anger and disappointment.

Seeing Problems as a Normal Part of Life

It should come as no surprise that individuals with a negative problem orientation have a tendency to feel resentful when problems develop. One of the reasons for this is that they will often view problems as abnormal ("If I plan for everything and reduce all uncertainty in my life, no problems should ever arise. It is not normal for me to have unexpected problems come up."). However, one of the difficulties with believing that problems are abnormal is that the individual will expend a great deal of energy trying to avoid problems rather than dealing with them. As with attempting to eliminate uncertainty, this is an exercise in futility. Having to deal with problems is a normal and unavoidable part of life. As such, therapists should spend some time discussing this issue with clients. The goal is to allow them to see that everyone has problems to varying degrees in their lives:

THERAPIST: Having to deal with problems is a normal and inescapable part of life. Try to find someone who has no problems and you will come to the same conclusion. If a person believes that it is abnormal to have problems, that person will spend more time feeling annoyed by the problem than trying to solve it. It is much more useful to put that energy into solving the problem, getting it over with, and not worrying about it anymore. For some people, the reason why they feel that problems are abnormal is because they attribute their problem to personal incompetence or deficiencies. For example, if you believe that you have problems because you are flawed in some way ("I just don't have it when it comes to getting along with people"), you will tend to see your problems as being abnormal. However, it is important to remember that all of us have problems no matter how intelligent, sociable, attractive, or skillful we may be. It might seem that some people do not have problems, but this is probably because they deal with them quickly and efficiently. By not attributing your problems to "who you are," but instead to the fact that you are a human being (and all of us have problems from time to time), you will be better able to see your problems as a normal part of life and to start dealing with them more efficiently.

Seeing Problems as Opportunities Rather Than Threats

This final strategy for addressing a negative problem orientation is extremely important in getting clients to take action *toward* their problems. It is no secret that when a situation is viewed as entirely aversive, one is unlikely to approach it. In our daily lives, we have a tendency to avoid threats and approach opportunities. The goal of this treatment strategy is to assist clients in becoming more flexible in thinking about problems. Specifically, clients are encouraged to see some of the opportunities that exist in solving problems rather than focusing entirely on the negative aspects. It is important to note, however, that this does not mean that the threatening components of a problem are ignored. No one enjoys dealing with problems, but if there is a challenge or opportunity in a problematic situation, then clients are more likely to attempt to deal with it. As such, therapists should assist clients in starting to view problems as situations that can carry an opportunity, while at the same time remaining aware of the threat. This is accomplished by helping clients to see that problems do not need to be slotted into the following categories:

Seeing a problem as either completely negative or completely positive is an extreme way of viewing the problem. In reality, there are a multitude of points between those two extremes. Rather, clients can be encouraged to see both of these extremes as lying on a continuum:

It is unrealistic to expect clients to see their problems as only representing an opportunity, but this continuum can allow them to view their problems as not 100% threatening either. By looking at problems and trying to extract the opportunities from the situation, clients can perhaps shift a little from the "threat" extreme and move closer to the "opportunity" extreme. This can be accomplished by getting clients to ask themselves: "What is the opportunity for me in this situation?" Opportunities that can be found in problematic situations include acquiring new skills or sharpening existing ones, and improving relationships with coworkers, friends, and family. The following are a few examples of how perceptions of threat can be shifted on the continuum toward perceptions of opportunity:

Example 1: A Job Interview.

The initial reaction to this situation might be: "I hate interviews. Why do I have to go through this agony? I never do well in these types of situations. I will make a fool of myself just like the last time. I just wish it was over." A more flexible way of thinking might be:

I'm really nervous before going to an interview. What is the threat in this situation? Well, I might not do well during the interview and not get the job. Who knows, I might even make a real fool of myself. What is the opportunity for me in this situation? Maybe I need to learn to show others just what I am capable of doing. Interviews are not easy, but it would be great if I could learn to sell myself. That is a skill that I will need many times in my life. I guess I could try to look at this as an opportunity to get experience interviewing and to get better each time.

Example 2: The Illness of a Loved One.

The initial reaction to this situation might be: "Someone who I am close to is suffering from a serious illness that requires expensive treatment. Why does this have to happen to our family? It's awful to have to spend so much money on this medication. One day we won't be able to afford it any longer. This is so unfair." A more flexible way of thinking might be:

I feel sad and frustrated about this whole thing. What is the threat in this situation? Well, the illness could get worse and who knows where that could lead? Even if the medication works, we could not be able to afford it for much longer. What is the opportunity for me in this situation? It is certainly difficult to see how illness can be an opportunity. I guess I could see this situation as an opportunity to show that I really care. I could help out as much as possible and try to be a model of hope and strength. Although I am definitely very upset, I see this as an opportunity to be strong for someone I love.

Therapists can use the two previous examples to help clients identify opportunities within varied problematic situations. Again, it is important that clients not be under the impression that they simply need to "think positive." Instead, the goal is to try to find a challenge or opportunity in a situation that was previously seen as altogether threatening.

A between-session exercise can be implemented here to help clients identify opportunities in problem situations. For example, clients can be asked to look through their Worry Monitoring Form and identify any current unsolved problems that are leading to worry, then try to think about (and record) the challenges or opportunities present in at least one problem with the ultimate goal of perceiving it as less threatening. Once clients have integrated some flexibility in thinking about their problems, therapists can move to the next phase of problem-solving training.

Applying Problem-Solving Skills

In Chapter 4 we discussed how problem-solving *skills* appear to be mostly unrelated to GAD, since clients are aware of, and understand, all the steps involved in problem solving. However, this does not mean that they display good problem-solving *ability*. As mentioned previously, it is clear that negative problem orientation can interfere with the proper use of problem-solving skills, which considerably decreases an individual's ability to solve problems. In other words, although GAD clients have the requisite skills to solve daily life problems, they either do not apply those skills effectively, or they avoid problem solving altogether. Furthermore, although the problem-solving skills of GAD clients do not seem to be extremely poor, they are not particularly strong either. That is, even though their skills are similar to those of people from the general population, it appears that most people are not especially skilled at effectively working through the problem-solving steps. Thus, although our theoretical model identifies negative problem orientation as the main problem-solving factor of interest in GAD, our treatment includes comprehensive problem-solving training, which includes the review and practice of each problem-solving skill.

One thing that we have consistently noticed in treatment is that although GAD clients are willing to work on each step of the problem-solving process, they often have difficulty completing a stage and moving on to the next. This is likely to be due to their desire for certainty and for the "perfect" solution. As such, the goal of this phase of treatment is not only to help clients to refine their problem-solving skills, but also to encourage them to tolerate uncertainty by moving forward in the process despite the uncertainty inherent in each step (that is, problem definition and goal formulation, generation of alternative solutions, decision making, and solution implementation and verification).

Problem Definition and Goal Formulation

Before trying to solve a problem, one must first properly define it. Although this might seem obvious, our clinical experience has taught us that many people define their problems in vague or confused terms. In addition, we have observed that many of our clients do not "separate" their problems, so that their problem definition actually includes several problems at once. In many ways, this is the most important step in effective problem solving, since a poorly defined problem can have a negative impact on all the remaining steps. For example, if a person is being given more files to work on at his job than they can handle, an ill-defined problem definition might be: "My boss is a selfish person who takes advantage of me." If the problem is defined in this way, it becomes difficult to think of a goal for problem solving ("How can I make my boss more sensitive and caring?") and the remaining steps become impaired as well. In this case, a more appropriate problem definition might be: "My boss gives me more files to work on than I can handle." When the problem is defined in this way, the resultant goals and potential solutions are clearer and more achievable (for example, "My goal is to have my workload lightened.").

In order to effectively define a problem, the following guidelines can be considered. A good problem definition should:

- Be clear and use concrete language.
- Comprise facts, not assumptions.
- Answer three questions:
  - What is the situation?
  - What would I like the situation to be?
  - What is the obstacle that is interfering with the attainment of the desired situation?
- Focus on the central conflict, namely, the discrepancy between the actual and the ideal situation. When a problem is under one's direct control, emotional consequences should not be considered the main problem. In situations where one has little or no control, emotion management can be the central problem (for example, "How do I cope with the illness of my spouse?").
- Not be overly narrow in its scope. For example, a problem defined as "How can I write five reports in one hour?" is quite narrow in scope and, as such, only allows for one or two solutions. Alternatively, a problem defined as "How can I complete my reports more efficiently?" allows for a broader array of solutions.

One point to note about problem definition is that it can often require readjustments throughout the problem-solving process. For example, a problem definition provided by the client may initially include more than one problem. This type of error is quite common and will occasionally go unnoticed by the therapist upon first glance at the problem definition. However, if difficulties arise in subsequent steps of the problem-solving process as a result of a poor problem definition, the therapist and client should return to this initial step and adjust the definition as necessary.

When formulating goals, it is important to keep the following three guidelines in mind. First, goals should be *clear, concise, and formulated in concrete terms*. When goals are formulated in vague or unclear terms, it can be difficult to know not only how to achieve them, but also if they have been achieved. For example, if my goal is "to be happy," it is difficult to know if I have achieved it (that is, "How often do I want to be happy? How happy should I be?"). The second guideline is that goals should be *realistic and attainable*. Problem solving is most effective when the likelihood of achieving a goal (and resolving the problem) is high. If goals are unrealistic, clients will tend to become frustrated or disappointed. The final guideline is to *be aware of the timeline* for achievement of a particular goal. Depending upon the problem, clients might develop short- or long-term goals. While it is not surprising that some goals take longer to achieve than others, it is important that clients expect this so as not to experience feelings of disappointment. In addition, it can be helpful to set short-term goals even when the final goal is a long-term one. It can be quite demotivating to invest effort in a situation when no return is expected for an extended period of time. For example, if someone has decided to change their level of fitness and has set a certain weight and body fat percentage as their ultimate goal, it would be a good idea to set intermediary targets in order to remain motivated and driven toward the final goal.

Unlike the problem definition step, where clients are encouraged to ensure that only one problem is included in the definition, it is acceptable at this stage to have more than one goal. However, this is specifically in reference to the time in which the goal is expected to be accomplished, meaning that one can have both short- and long-term goals for a particular problem.

Generation of Alternative Solutions

This stage of problem solving is often referred to as the "brainstorming stage." The idea is to generate as many potential solutions to the problem as possible, in order to increase the chances of finding the best solution. Although this may appear to be an easy thing to do, very few people actually take the time to generate multiple solutions before making a decision. In fact, most people will think of only one solution, and then apply it without considering other possibilities. Alternatively, some people will come up with several solutions; however, they are the same solutions that they came up with in the past that were either ineffective or only worked in the short term. Why does this occur? There are two primary obstacles to the development of numerous and varied solutions. The first obstacle is *habit*. As noted previously, we tend to return to "tried and true" solutions when solving problems in our daily lives. Although this can be beneficial for many of our problems, sticking with the same strategies out of habit can, at times, prevent us from finding a better solution. The second obstacle to the generation of alternative solutions is *convention*. By doing things in a conventional manner, we might have the impression that we are doing "the right thing," even when this is not the case.

At this stage, the most effective way to generate multiple creative solutions is to use the following three principles of brainstorming:

1. **Deferment of Judgment Principle.** According to this principle, clients need to suspend any judgment or evaluation of solutions when trying to generate them. In order to come up with varied solutions, it is important not to censor oneself from the outset (e.g., "Oh, that's just a silly solution; I won't consider that one"). During the subsequent decision-making step, inappropriate solutions will be eliminated, so there is no need to screen or remove any solutions during this step. With this in mind, clients are encouraged to come up with solutions that might even be considered "crazy," since these types of solutions can facilitate the generation of other original and unconventional solutions that might be more appropriate.
2. **Quantity Principle.** From a logical standpoint, clients are more likely to come up with a good solution for a particular problem if they have many potential

solutions from which to choose. As such, the second principle of brainstorming states that the more solutions that an individual can think of, the better. Therapists should encourage the generation of at least 10 or 12 solutions for a particular problem.

3. **Variety Principle.** This principle states that more good quality solutions are available when there is variety in the types of solutions generated. A mistake that many people make is to generate multiple solutions that all reflect the same general idea. For example, for a "weight" problem, solutions such as taking up jogging, swimming, or hiking are all solutions that fall within the same set: they all involve physical activity. If clients only generate potential solutions that fall within one set, there is little actual variety of choice. Varied solutions for a weight problem might include taking up jogging, changing one's diet, and spending a weekend at a health spa. Although all these solutions address the problem, they do not reflect the same set.

Although the therapist should keep in mind the "deferment of judgment" principle at all times (and not negatively evaluate a solution), once clients have completed their list of solutions, it is a good idea to initially run through the list and discuss ways to improve it. For example, the therapist and client should discuss ways of formulating as many of the solutions as possible in concrete behavioral terms. "Taking up jogging" is a good example of a concrete solution in that it is clear what would be required of the individual should this solution be chosen. However, a solution such as "develop a more positive self-esteem" is a much less concrete strategy. If a client chose this solution, they might have a new problem, namely, figuring out how to go about enhancing self-esteem!

As a final note, creative and practical solutions can sometimes be found by combining two or more solutions. We have often found that the combination of two mediocre solutions can create one excellent solution. Such modifications can also help clients to consider every solution generated, even those that initially seem "crazy," unrealistic, or silly.

Decision Making

This stage involves going over the list of alternative solutions and ultimately choosing the *best* solution for the problem. This stage can be particularly difficult for GAD clients, as they will often try to find the *perfect* solution. The problem with this type of thinking is that it can prevent clients from moving forward in the problem-solving process. It is therefore important that therapists remind their clients that this stage is just another step of the problem-solving process and that it should not become another topic for excessive worry. Rather, it can be viewed as yet another way to test out their beliefs about uncertainty.

In order to effectively complete this stage of problem solving, clients need to look at the available solutions and pick the best one for their particular problem. This is achieved by asking clients to evaluate each solution and determine which one has the most advantages and the fewest disadvantages. Therapists can guide clients through this process by asking them to consider four questions for each alternative solution:

1. **Will this solution solve my problem?** A solution that does not address the problem or the stated goals is probably not the best one to choose.
2. **How much time and effort are involved in this solution?** From a practical point of view, a solution is probably not ideal if it involves an excessive amount of time and effort to complete.
3. **How will I feel if I choose this solution?** When picking a solution, the emotional consequence of a particular solution is certainly a factor for consideration. Some options might make clients feel anxious or nervous, and others might leave clients feeling bad about themselves.
4. **What are the consequences of this solution for myself and others in both the short- and long-term?** A good solution should have more positive than negative consequences, for oneself and others, both now and in the future.

Although all four of these questions are important, the therapist should be mindful that clients are not using them to eliminate all *imperfect* solutions. That is, every solution will have some advantages and disadvantages, simply because if there existed a solution that solved the problem, required little time and effort, made the client feel good, and had no negative personal or social consequences, it would have already been found. As such, clients need to ask all four questions for each potential solution, and then decide which one *best* fits the problem.

Solution Implementation and Verification

Solution implementation involves planning how to carry out a chosen solution, and then actually implementing it. This can be a very difficult stage for GAD clients because it tends to "activate" their intolerance for uncertainty. Specifically, there are no guarantees whether a chosen solution will work as expected, and that can be quite difficult for many clients. However, because clients will have had previous experience with tolerating uncertainty, they should have developed some "momentum," such that implementing a chosen solution can be seen as just another exercise in tolerating uncertainty.

Prior to carrying out a solution, clients should plan the steps involved. This will not only ensure that they will know what to do, but will also increase the likelihood that they will actually carry out the solution. The steps involved should be concrete and specific, and depending upon the complexity of a solution, a timeline for the execution of each step can also be established. However, the therapist needs to keep in mind that the goal involves not only knowing what to do, but *actually doing it!* In other words, GAD clients should not be overly meticulous or seek excessive information when devising their plan, as this could be a way of avoiding the actual implementation of the solution. In most cases, however, by taking the time to plan the major steps involved in implementing the solution, clients are more likely to carry it out. Therapists should praise their clients for any movement toward implementing their solutions, and remind them that they are not only working toward solving their problems in an active manner, but also testing their beliefs about uncertainty and increasing their overall tolerance for uncertainty.

The second part of this final step involves the important task of verifying if the solution that was carried out is working as planned. As noted previously, one of the reasons that problems are so stressful is that it is impossible to predict exactly what will happen once a solution is implemented. As such, it is necessary to assess whether or not the solution is actually working, and this can be accomplished by setting up "markers" along the way. Clients are encouraged to think of some index that will let them know if the solution is working as planned. These indices can be observable information, such as higher grades if the problem was poor performance at school, or a check of one's mood following implementation of the solution (for example, "Am I feeling better since I put my solution into action?").

One of the major reasons why it is important to establish checks is to spot whether the solution is *not* working early on. Even with the best-laid plans, a chosen solution might not solve the problem. Clients should be able to identify this as soon as possible in order to begin taking steps toward correcting the situation. If a solution is in fact ineffective, clients can begin troubleshooting the source of the problem by returning to earlier steps. Was the solution carried out effectively? Did it best answer the decision-making questions? Was the problem correctly identified? Was the goal realistic and achievable? By walking through the various steps, clients can usually identify where problem solving went astray. If, on the other hand, a solution is working, then clients should be encouraged to reward themselves for a job well done.

One Final Note about Problem Solving

Perhaps the greatest challenge when introducing problem solving to clients is the tolerance for uncertainty required by *therapists*. There is no perfect answer for any of the problem-solving steps, and therapists themselves might initially feel unsure throughout the process. However, this can be highly beneficial in session, as there is the opportunity for therapists to model comfort with the uncertainty at various steps. Our suggestion for the ideal method of presentation in this phase of treatment is to initially use a working example to illustrate the effective use of all the problem-solving steps. This can then be followed by collaboratively working through the client's problem in session, and then having the client carry out the chosen solution. Although this will likely be difficult for clients because it involves solving their own problem, the assistance of the therapist allows this to be an intermediary stage that is less anxiety provoking (see Table 5.3 for a list of helpful questions that the therapist can ask clients when working through the problem). Finally, as a between-session exercise, clients should be encouraged to walk through the steps alone and record the results of each step on the Resolution of a Problem form (see Appendix 5.8 for a copy of the form). Once clients have

Table 5.3 Steps to Effective Problem Resolution

---

1. What is the problem? That is, what is the current situation, what would you like it to be, and what is the obstacle that is keeping you from achieving your ideal situation?

2. What goal would you like to achieve? Is it realistic and achievable?

3. What are all the possible solutions to this problem? Keep in mind to: (a) defer judgment ("crazy" solutions are all right); (b) come up with at least 10 solutions; and (c) generate varied solutions.

4. Which is the best (not the perfect!) solution? Specifically, which solution best answers the following questions: (a) Will this solve your problem? (b) How much time and effort are involved in this solution? (c) How would you feel if you use this solution? (d) What are the consequences of this solution to yourself and others in both the short and long term?

5. How will you carry out this solution? That is, what steps do you need to take to actually start implementing this solution?

6. How will you know if this solution is working? What checks or markers will you use that will tell you whether your solution is going as planned?

---

developed some confidence in their problem-solving ability, treatment can move to the next module.

Module 5: Written Exposure

In this treatment module, clients learn a specific strategy for dealing with worries about hypothetical situations. Examples of these types of worries include worrying about developing a serious illness, experiencing a natural disaster (for example, an earthquake, a hurricane, a tornado), or not being financially able to retire once retirement age is reached. These types of worries are typically not effectively managed through problem solving because the feared situation has not happened (and may never happen); therefore, most attempts at problem solving are largely unproductive. As discussed in Chapter 4, everyone worries about these types of topics on occasion, however they are typically experienced as "back of the mind," that is, they are not frequent, excessive, and uncontrollable worries that are easily triggered by uncertainty-inducing situations. These "front of the mind" worries are addressed through written exposure, wherein clients learn how to expose themselves to vivid and concrete mental images of their fears in order to address their tendency to engage in cognitive (and affective) avoidance. Written exposure allows clients the opportunity to test the accuracy of two broad beliefs: (1) thinking about worst-case scenarios is dangerous, as it increases the possibility of their occurrence; and (2) the negative emotions that worst-case scenarios elicit are dangerous, as they would be overwhelming, unmanageable, and result in loss of control over emotions. This treatment module can be very difficult for clients because it involves facing significant fears by focusing on thoughts and images that they have tried very hard to avoid for a long time. It is therefore extremely important that therapists take the time to properly explain the rationale behind this treatment module. The rationale for the use of written exposure is somewhat complex, and as with any treatment strategy, clients must fully understand why they are being asked to do something before they actually do it.

The Futility of Cognitive Avoidance

Prior to introducing written exposure, it is important to illustrate to clients how attempts at avoiding or blocking distressing thoughts and worries can be counter-productive. Research on thought suppression has shown that trying to suppress a thought is not only ineffective, it can result in a paradoxical increase in that thought. As most clients are unaware of this phenomenon, an effective way to illustrate the effects of thought suppression is to ask them to engage in the white bear experiment.

Instructions for the White Bear Experiment

THERAPIST: Today we are going to talk about cognitive avoidance, which include various efforts that people engage in to try to avoid certain distressing thoughts. However, before we do, I would like you to try a little experiment with me. For 60 seconds, I am going to ask you to close your eyes and think of anything that you like. Anything at all, there are no restrictions, except for one small thing: I want you to absolutely *not* think about a white bear. I don't want you to picture a white bear or even think the words *white bear*. But other than that, you can think of anything else. I am going to keep time while you do this, and I will simply ask you to raise your hand every time, if any, the thought crosses your mind. Are you ready? Go. (The therapist then records how many times the client raises their hand.) So, how did it go? Do you remember how many times the thought of a white bear came up?

CLIENT: Almost the entire time; at least 10 times.

THERAPIST: That's interesting. How many times did you think of a white bear on your way over to my office today?

CLIENT: None.

THERAPIST: How about yesterday? How many times did the "white bear" thought come up?

CLIENT: None, again.

THERAPIST: Interesting. So, all day yesterday and today you did not have a single thought about a white bear. And yet, when I specifically asked you not to think of one for one minute, you were unable to. Why do you think that is?

CLIENT: I have no idea.

THERAPIST: Well, research shows that trying *not* to think about something doesn't work. In fact, it can produce two types of opposite effects. One is the *enhancement effect*, which you just experienced. That is, trying to deliberately suppress a thought can bring on that very thought while we are trying to avoid it. The second effect is the *rebound effect*. In this case, after trying to suppress a thought, it might tend to pop up in your mind. In the case of our experiment, you might find that you will think about a white bear on the way home or this evening. So, what does all this say about your worries?

CLIENT: I guess it means that if I try not to think about something unpleasant, like my children getting injured or killed in a car accident, I'll actually end up thinking about it even more.

THERAPIST: That's right. Trying to block or avoid upsetting worries can actually lead to more worries popping up in your mind.

Cognitive Avoidance and Neutralization

In order to clearly illustrate the importance of exposure in reducing fears, the therapist can initially discuss the concepts of avoidance and neutralization in terms of behavioral rather than cognitive avoidance. That is, it is easier to discuss these abstract concepts in reference to a specific observable fear before relating them to the cognitive construct of worry. A useful example is elaborated upon below, using a dog phobia analogy:

THERAPIST: Why do you think that we tend to avoid the things that we fear? Very simply, we do it because avoidance works. If I am afraid of something, once I avoid it, I feel less anxious. For example, if I am afraid of dogs, and I see someone approaching with a dog while am walking down the street, I will probably become very anxious. However, what will happen once I cross the street?

CLIENT: You'll feel better.

THERAPIST: That's right. Once I avoid the dog, I'll probably feel less anxious. Let's look at this using a graph, where the horizontal line represents time and the vertical line represents anxiety.

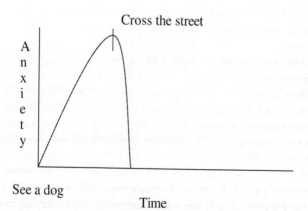

THERAPIST: Using this graph, we can see that once I see the dog my anxiety goes up, but the moment that I cross the street (and avoid the dog), my anxiety goes down. What is the problem with this? What do you think will happen to my fear of dogs so long as I avoid them?

CLIENT: You'll probably continue to be afraid of them.

THERAPIST: That's right. In fact, I might become even more afraid of them over time, because I might say to myself: "Good thing I avoided those dogs; who knows what would have happened?" If we look at this continued avoidance on a graph, it would look like this (see below), with a dip in anxiety every time I avoid and an increase in anxiety every time I see a dog. We call this the avoidance curve, and we can see that avoidance decreases anxiety in the short term but maintains the fear in the long term.

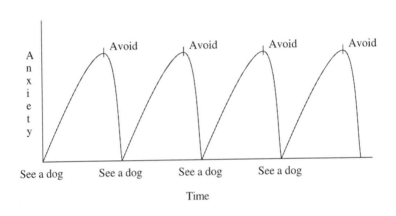

THERAPIST: Unfortunately, avoidance is not the only way that we maintain our fears. Neutralization can have a similarly negative effect. Neutralization refers to a deliberate attempt to reduce the experience of anxiety while in a fearful situation. For example, if I am afraid of dogs, I might decide that I need to confront my fear and stop avoiding them. With that in mind, I go to visit my friend at his house, since he has a dog. Once there, I get very anxious, so I decide to look out the window and think of something else. What will happen to my anxiety?

CLIENT: It will probably go down.

THERAPIST: That's right. It will probably go down, but not all the way since I'm still in the same room with the dog. Also, once I look back at the dog, my anxiety goes back up. This time, I try to lower my anxiety by looking at the dog's tail instead of his teeth, which again makes me feel a bit less uncomfortable. These behaviors are examples of neutralization, and if we were to draw this on a graph, it would look like this:

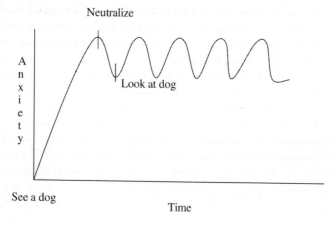

THERAPIST: This graph, which illustrates the neutralization curve, shows how each time I neutralize, my anxiety goes down a little bit. The problem with this behavior is that, like avoidance, it maintains anxiety in the long term, even though it decreases it somewhat in the short term.

THERAPIST: So how are avoidance and neutralization used in relation to worries? Well, the same logic applies to our thoughts. For example, if a person is very afraid of one day being injured or trapped in their home if there was an earthquake, they might try very hard not to think about that possibility. This avoidance of scary thoughts is referred to as cognitive avoidance. So, by trying not to think about your fears, you are in fact maintaining them. Neutralization also contributes to maintaining your fears. When you are worried about a potential problem, you might try to reassure yourself by thinking: "It won't happen" or "It won't be that bad if it does." You might also find that you "worry hop," that is, once you start worrying about one feared situation, you switch to different, but related, topics. For example, you might start worrying about developing a serious illness, and then switch to how your family would cope, and what the impact would be on the family finances. Do you ever find yourself coping with your worries through cognitive avoidance or neutralization?

CLIENT: Yes, definitely. I worry a lot about people in my family being hurt or killed in an accident. The thoughts are so upsetting that I try to push them out of my mind or think of other things. I don't want to dwell on horrible thoughts like that.

Cognitive Avoidance as a Safety Behavior

As noted earlier, cognitive avoidance involves the avoidance of both distressing thoughts associated with the worst-case scenarios about hypothetical situations, and the negative emotions they engender. Cognitive avoidance therefore serves a similar function as safety behaviors, since GAD clients attempt to dampen their negative emotions and avoid feared thoughts. However, the attempt to avoid or neutralize upsetting thoughts not only leads to a resurgence of thoughts over the long term, it prevents clients from learning what would actually happen if they allowed themselves to see, in their mind's eye, the situations that they most fear. Specifically, they are unable to learn that upsetting thoughts and feelings are not dangerous, that thinking about worst-case scenarios does not increase their likelihood of occurrence, and that the intensity of negative emotions naturally abates over time. Moreover, clients are prevented from observing, or even giving thought to, their actual coping ability should a worst-case scenario occur, as well as how they might manage themselves and their distress in the face of strong negative emotions. As such, the thoughts and feelings associated with worries about hypothetical situations remain threatening and anxiety-provoking, such that the worry cycle is maintained. Accordingly, written exposure is designed to address worries about hypothetical situations by targeting client fears associated with thinking or dwelling upon upsetting thoughts and emotions.

Prior to introducing written exposure and the mechanics of its execution, the role of cognitive avoidance as a form of safety behavior, and its impact upon the worry cycle, should first be discussed with clients.

THERAPIST: When we first introduced the worry cycle and negative beliefs about uncertainty, we talked about the significant impact that safety behaviors have in both maintaining the worry cycle and preventing you from obtaining evidence about the truthfulness of your beliefs. Yet cognitive avoidance functions very much like a safety behavior because although you might reduce your anxiety and avoid upsetting thoughts in the short term, the thoughts and negative feelings always come back. In addition, you never get to find out what happens when you face upsetting thoughts and feelings rather than trying to push them away. Let's say that we take your worry about a family member being injured in an accident; what are you worried might happen if you focused on those thoughts, in clear, vivid, and concrete terms, instead of trying to avoid them?

CLIENT: Well, I know this is probably silly, but it really feels like thinking about that stuff is tempting fate. It feels as if something bad might actually happen if I were to focus on those thoughts. But beyond that, it's just so upsetting. I don't know what I'd do if anything happened to the people I love and care about. I can't stand even thinking about it!

THERAPIST: So, you've described some pretty negative beliefs associated with thinking about that particular scenario. You mentioned that it might be more likely to happen, that you don't think you could cope with it if it did, and you also described great distress at sitting with the negative feelings that the thoughts cause. It's easy to see why you would want to avoid thinking about that worry if all of those beliefs are true. Have you ever tested out any of these beliefs?

CLIENT: You mean deliberately think about upsetting things? No, I haven't.

THERAPIST: Well, the problem with that is similar to the problem we encountered with negative beliefs about uncertainty. Unless you test out negative beliefs, they continue to "feel" true. This is because your safety behaviors, in this case, cognitive avoidance, prevent you from finding out whether your feared negative outcomes are actually true. And in this case, avoiding distressing thoughts and feelings keeps your worries at the front of your mind, where they continually pop up.

Introducing Written Exposure

Given the severity of the feared outcomes, it is not surprising that clients with GAD would attempt to avoid dwelling and elaborating upon upsetting thoughts and emotions, as well as show reluctance toward reversing this strategy and focusing on them instead. Yet this is exactly what is required of clients when engaging in written exposure. Specifically, clients are asked to write about their worst-case scenario related to a feared hypothetical situation for at least 20 minutes. This process is repeated every day, with clients being encouraged to go further into depth about their fears across sessions. Although we have found written exposure to be a very powerful strategy that allows clients to shift their perspective on their worries and move them to the back of their mind, it is nonetheless a daunting task for clients. As such, it is crucial that therapists take the time to discuss the rationale presented above, and of course empathize with any concerns clients might voice. However, in tandem with this, it is also extremely important that therapists not apologize for asking clients to engage in written exposure, but rather display confidence in the benefits of this therapeutic tool. Negative thoughts and emotions, while distressing, are nothing to fear, and are not dangerous in and of themselves. It is important to remember that the goal of written exposure is to allow clients the opportunity to learn that (1) they will not be overwhelmed, lose control, or "go crazy" by experiencing and focusing on their negative emotions; (2) feared outcomes are not more likely to occur by virtue of thinking about them; and (3) they are more capable of managing adversity, should it arise, than they expect. It is only by experiencing and processing their negative thoughts and feelings that clients will be able to shift perspective about the actual threat of their feared scenarios.

Identifying the Worst-Case Scenario

Although written exposure targets excessive worries about hypothetical situations, the primary goal is to access clients' worst fears that underlie hypothetical worries. As such, it is important to identify the worst-case scenario driving these worries. Therapists can assist clients with this through the use of the downward arrow, or catastrophizing, technique (Provencher, Freeston, Dugas, & Ladouceur, 2000; Vasey & Borkovec, 1992). The following steps are recommended to help clients access their worst fears:

1. Therapists begin by asking clients to formulate their worry in simple terms. For example, "What if my flight runs into turbulence?"
2. Clients are then asked the following question: "If your worry came true, what might happen next?" or "If your worry actually happened, what could that lead to?"

3. Once the client has identified the next link in the worry chain (e.g., "The plane could crash"), therapists can then ask the same question a second time, with the goal of moving progressively toward the worst-case scenario fear.

4. Once clients respond to this second prompt, therapists repeat the question until the client is no longer able to provide an answer to the prompt, suggesting that the core fear has been identified (e.g., "I could die, and my children would be left to fend for themselves").

An example of a client's responses to the downward arrow technique is provided below for a work-related worry:

"I will not be able to make a deadline at work."

"My boss will be upset."

"I will lose my job."

"I won't be able to find another job."

"I won't be able to pay my bills."

"I will have to move back home and be financially dependent on my parents."

"My family will see me as an embarrassment."

"I will be a failure."

When using the downward arrow technique, it is important that therapists not direct clients in their answers, but simply follow their lead. Furthermore, it is important to strike a balance between accessing an important fear while not going so far that the client is unable to fully engage in the exposure process. Specifically, if a client mentions that the scenario is too "far-fetched," this can indicate that an outcome identified earlier in the downward arrow would be a more appropriate exposure theme for that particular client. For instance, using the work example presented above, a client might eventually come up with the fear "I could end up on the street, homeless and penniless, with all my friends becoming disgusted with me." Most likely, clients will say that this scenario is in fact "ridiculous" because they know that it will not happen. It is therefore not appropriate for the exposure scenario.

Conducting Written Exposure

As noted above, written exposure involves identifying the worst-case scenario tied to a worry about a hypothetical situation and writing about it for 20 minutes every day for approximately one week. The following are guidelines for the successful completion of written exposure:

- *Find a quiet place and time to write.* Because clients are being asked to deliberately focus and write about avoided thought content, it is not uncommon for them to want to avoid this exercise or seek out distractions while completing it. With this in mind, we find it helpful to remind clients about the goals of the task, and to emphasize that they are more likely to complete it if they have a specific time and place, devoid of distractions, where they can carry out their written exposure. It is also helpful to remind clients to turn off their cell phones, as well as other distractions such as music or television in the background.
- *Write for 20 minutes every day.* It is important to ensure that clients understand that written exposure should be completed in one session, that is, 20 consecutive minutes a day, rather than writing a few minutes throughout the day. Unless clients allow themselves to fully experience the distress that their thoughts and feelings elicit within the limited time frame, they will be unable to form any conclusions about the consequences of their thoughts and feelings.
- *Write a coherent first-person story keeping with the same theme.* Clients are encouraged to write a coherent story, from a first-person perspective, in the present tense. In this manner, clients are most likely to vividly access their worst fears. Although clients write about the same topic for each exposure session, they are encouraged to delve deeper into the narrative of their worst-case scenario over time. Specifically, as written exposure sessions progress across days, clients can intensify the experience by increasingly describing their deepest thoughts and feelings related to their fear.
- *Focus on the worst-case scenario in vivid and concrete detail.* One of the problems with the way clients with GAD think about their catastrophic hypothetical situations is that, in an attempt to avoid being distressed or overwhelmed, their

thoughts about these situations are vague, abstract, and lack concreteness. This prevents clients from thinking about their worst fears in any depth, and potentially reevaluating how dangerous they actually are, before hopping to other worries or otherwise attempting to engage in thought replacement, distraction, or suppression. As such, an important component of written exposure is not only writing about one's worst-case scenario, but doing so in a vivid, detailed, and concrete way that is likely to elicit negative emotions.

- *Record observations after each writing session.* Similar to behavioral experiments, clients are encouraged to record their observations about the impact and the perceived threat of focusing on their worst-case scenario after each session. This allows clients to directly observe changes to their negative beliefs across successive repetitions. To assist with this, we have provided a Written Exposure Summary Form in Appendix 5.9 that can be used by clients following exposure. The evolution of clients' reactions to written exposure over successive repetitions can then be discussed and debriefed in session. In particular, clients are asked about their specific feared outcomes (for example, "What if I become overwhelmed by negative emotions?" or "What if these negative feelings never go away?"). After having completed a week of written exposure between sessions, we recommend that therapists take the time to review each specific fear identified by clients, and discuss the direct experiential observations that clients made as a result of having conducted exposure.
- *Expect to be upset.* Although this will likely be unsurprising, clients can expect to experience a general increase in their distress when engaged in exposure. This is of course due to the focus on long-avoided fears, and although this distress will dissipate, it can be disconcerting to clients if unexpected. As such, we recommend normalizing the initial increase in anxiety, and occasionally a brief increase in overall worry, when engaged in exposure. However, it is important to ensure that clients are aware that this is a temporary effect of exposure, and not a cue to discontinue the exercise.

For the majority of clients, three to five days in a row of written exposure is sufficient to see a marked shift in negative beliefs about the consequences of distressing thoughts and emotions. However, in our clinical experience, we have found that many clients report preferring to continue engaging in written exposure for an additional few days or a week in order to thoroughly process their thoughts and emotions about their worst-case scenario. The reader might be surprised to discover that it is typically clients themselves who request extending their exposure exercises. However, it can be very powerful for clients to directly experience how negative thoughts and feelings, while upsetting, will not bowl them over. As discussed in Chapter 4, engaging in written exposure is similar to opening a dam; there is a strong and intense rush of thoughts and emotions initially, but it gradually abates to a trickle.

Once clients have completed written exposure, therapists are encouraged to debrief the exercise with clients, with an emphasis on negative beliefs about distressing thoughts and emotions, and any changes that clients have noted. It is not surprising to find, at this end stage of treatment, that clients report significant reductions in overall worry, in addition to reduced worry about the hypothetical situation initially targeted with written exposure. It can be helpful to remind clients that this therapeutic tool does not eliminate worries about one's most feared worst-case scenarios, but rather brings them to the "back of the mind." As such, it is normal to worry about hypothetical situations on occasion, as we all do sometimes. Once this treatment module has been completed and the therapist and client feel that termination of treatment is imminent, they can then move to the final treatment module, relapse prevention.

Module 6: Relapse Prevention

The final treatment module deals with maintaining gains and preventing relapse following treatment termination. Although we refer to this stage as relapse prevention, data from our clinical trials show that many clients actually continue improving following treatment termination (see Chapter 6). As such, the goal at this stage is to help clients continue using the skills acquired in treatment with the hope that progress will be maintained long after the final session is over. We break down this module into three components: (1) daily maintenance; (2) check-ups for good mental health hygiene; (3) identification of at-risk situations; and (4) preparation for at-risk situations.

Daily Maintenance

Daily maintenance is based on a very simple idea; namely, that strategies that helped clients to get better will also help them to stay better. In other words, if clients stop using the skills acquired in therapy, it is unlikely that they will maintain their treatment gains in the long term. This means that it is in the clients' best interest to continue engaging in behavioral experiments targeting negative beliefs about uncertainty, reevaluating their positive beliefs about worry, and if covered in treatment, addressing life's problems by using effective problem-solving strategies, and engaging in written exposure for excessive worries about hypothetical situations. Most importantly, however, clients should continue deliberately inviting uncertainty into their lives, and hopefully begin to weave behavioral experiments into daily life as a new habit. The best way for clients to take charge of their own symptom maintenance is by learning to become their own therapist:

THERAPIST: Now that treatment is coming to an end, it is important that you learn to become your own therapist. What I mean by this is that you will start to take on the role that I have been assuming in treatment. In addition to teaching you the necessary skills you need to manage your symptoms, I monitored your progress on between-session exercises and helped you to troubleshoot any problems that came up. It is this role that you will need to fill now. Once treatment ends, you will need to assign yourself exercises, carry them out, and monitor your progress. For example, you can work on challenging your positive beliefs about worry, or assign yourself new behavioral experiments involving facing uncertainty. Being your own therapist also implies regularly evaluating your method of reacting to worries, encouraging yourself to persevere even when it's difficult, and congratulating yourself for both your large and small successes.

Some clients enter treatment with the belief that when therapy ends, they will no longer be worried or anxious. This is obviously not the case. In our treatment, as with most other CBT protocols, clients do not typically end treatment entirely symptom-free. Rather, a successful treatment experience will see clients leaving with a significant reduction in symptoms, an array of new tools and strategies for dealing with their symptoms, and a number of successes using those skills under their belt. Considering how long most clients have suffered with GAD, it is unrealistic to expect to be symptom-free after only a few months. However, if clients continue working with the skills acquired during treatment, there is no reason to believe that further improvement will not occur. The ultimate goal of daily maintenance is that the skills learned in therapy become automatic, and that clients use these skills without being fully conscious of each decisional step. This goal, however, will only be attained if clients regularly use the strategies over extended periods of time.

Check-Ups for Good Mental Health Hygiene

When it comes to our dental health or our physical health, most everyone knows that some basic care and attention is needed on an ongoing basis. For example, beyond going to the dentist or the family doctor for formal check-ups, it is generally understood that we all need to brush and floss our teeth and try to avoid sweets for the ongoing health of our teeth and gums, and we need to exercise and eat healthy nutritious foods for the ongoing health of our bodies. Unfortunately, while these basic acts of dental and physical hygiene are widely accepted in society, the equivalent is not yet the case for mental health. As such, it can come as a surprise to some clients that their mental health will require some basic care and maintenance, and that ideally this would be the case for everyone: just as our teeth and our bodies require some care and attention to stay healthy, so do our minds.

With this in mind, a good habit for all clients to adopt as treatment moves toward termination is the self-assignment of check-ups. That is, on a regular basis, it is a good idea for clients to set aside 20 to 30 minutes to review their overall mental health. The frequency of mental health check-ups is dependent upon the client, but it is recommended that immediately after treatment termination, client check-ups should occur on a weekly basis. As their confidence grows, check-ups can take place once a month or once every two to three months. In our clinical experience, clients are most likely to engage in mental health check-ups if they set a specific date and time, and record the findings from their check-up in a notebook or electronic device. As check-ups are meant to be maximally beneficial for clients, topics to cover can vary according to the individual, however common points for review include clients' current level of worry and anxiety, their progress with behavioral experiments, a review of ongoing exercises and assignment of new ones, and evaluation of personal goals in both the short and long term. When clients view the ongoing management of their worry and anxiety as a normal part of a healthy life, they are more likely to incorporate good habits learned from CBT into their lives and build upon and maintain their gains for years to come.

Identifying At-Risk Situations

The identification of at-risk situations is important because it helps clients adopt realistic expectations about how their worry and anxiety will fluctuate following the termination of treatment. Therapists will want to help their clients become aware that everyone experiences decreases in their quality of life during periods of high stress or negative mood. For GAD clients, stressors such as moving, changing employment, or experiencing interpersonal difficulties, as well as times when they are feeling more tired or "down" than usual, can serve as triggers to increase worry and anxiety. These types of fluctuations in symptoms are perfectly normal. They only become a problem when clients interpret them catastrophically (i.e., "I am so worried and anxious again! I undid all the progress I made in treatment!"). As such, it is important that clients learn to identify these periods of stress so that they will not be caught off guard when they are feeling more worried and anxious. In fact, clients can use increases in their symptoms as a "red flag" that alerts them to apply their newly acquired skills and work on them in a structured manner.

It is also equally important that clients have realistic expectations for themselves. Progress in therapy does not mean that clients will experience a smooth and regular decrease in worry and anxiety. For all clients, there are weeks where their symptoms are higher, other weeks where worry and anxiety might drop sharply, and still other weeks where there is little or no change. This intermittent fluctuation in worry and anxiety can also be expected following treatment. Experiencing a period of greater worry and anxiety should not be viewed as a failure or a relapse. Rather, it is an opportunity to continue working on the skills that will ultimately give clients a better chance at long-term protection against excessive worry and anxiety.

Preparing for At-Risk Situations

One of the best ways that therapists can assist clients in preparing for difficult situations in the future is to clearly distinguish between a lapse and a relapse. The key difference between both events is the reaction that clients have to a rise in their symptoms:

THERAPIST: It is important to keep in mind that there is a significant difference between a lapse and a relapse. A lapse can be understood as the result of normal fluctuations in worry and anxiety levels. A relapse, on the other hand, is more or less a return to the state you were in before treatment began. Therefore, to experience an increase in worry and anxiety from time to time is unavoidable and is not necessarily a relapse. However, your reaction to an increase in worry and anxiety is an important factor in determining whether a lapse will become a relapse. For example, let us suppose that two individuals worry a lot during a three-day period. In the middle of the week one of the two realizes that an accumulation of work has been causing their stress and worry. They tell themselves that they will try to finish the excess workload as soon as possible, within reason, and will relax on the weekend. They can always work for two hours Sunday morning if it isn't finished by Friday. By the end of the week, they have finished their work and are satisfied and relaxed. The other individual is also stressed and worried because of an accumulation of work. They do all that they can to finish, but are not very optimistic about finishing by Friday. By 5 p.m. on Friday the individual has finished their work and says, "What a crazy week! I am never able to get through a surplus of work without worrying about it all week! It took all my energy! What will it be like next time? I probably won't be able to handle it . . ." We can see from this example that the second person is on their way to a full-blown relapse simply because they reacted to the situation catastrophically.

One way that clients can prepare themselves for both treatment termination and any at-risk situations that might occur is to develop a plan of action before the end of therapy. Since one of the goals of treatment is to teach clients how to become their own therapists, they should be encouraged to set goals for future progress without the therapist's help. For example, a client with continuing worries about their job might decide to plan additional uncertainty-driven behavioral experiments and to use effective problem-solving strategies for any work-related difficulties that arise. In this manner, clients can continue working regularly with their acquired skills and develop a greater sense of control over their worry and anxiety.

One Final Point

As treatment comes to an end, it may be important to return to an issue that was discussed right at the start of treatment: the distinction between normal and excessive worry. Paradoxically, if clients have made great strides during treatment, the therapist may have to encourage them to accept a certain level of worry in response to life's daily problems. We have found that some clients forget that moderate levels of worry and anxiety are unavoidable and a normal part of life. These clients may have unrealistic expectations and may be at risk for relapse. As such, they may need to be reminded that everyone has moments where they are more anxious and stressed. This is certainly not a sign that treatment was unsuccessful. In fact, clients who leave treatment feeling that their worry and anxiety are manageable and their quality of life is improved have made wonderful progress. As such, they should be heartily congratulated.

Preliminary CBT Model of Generalized Anxiety Disorder

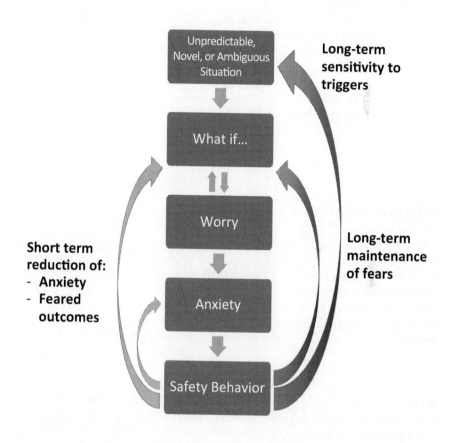

Worry Monitoring Form

Worry Monitoring Sample

Date/Time	Situation	Worry ("What if?")	Anxiety (0 to 8) (none to extreme)	Safety Behavior ("What did I do to cope with worry and anxiety?")
Wednesday 9am	Thinking about what to wear for a meeting at work	What if I pick something that is inappropriate? I could look foolish	4	Went through my closet and tried on lots of different outfits. Asked my partner what they thought I should wear
Wednesday noon	Colleagues invited me out to lunch with them, but I was planning to catch up on my work at my desk	What if I say no to the lunch invitation and my colleagues are upset with me? What if they tell my boss that I am a difficult co-worker?	6	Went out to lunch with coworkers (avoided saying no)
Wednesday 8pm	Received a text from a friend asking me to call her	What if something's wrong? What if she's mad at me? She might yell at me on the phone	6	Asked my partner what I should do. Avoided phoning (texted her and asked what she wanted to talk about)

Worry Monitoring Form

Date/ Time	Situation	Worry ("What if?")	Anxiety (0 to 8) (none to extreme)	Safety Behavior ("What did I do to cope with worry and anxiety?")

Positive Beliefs about Worry Form

Below are a number of beliefs that people can have about worry. They have been grouped into different categories. Please indicate by checking off "YES" or "NO" whether you have experienced each type of belief about worry; if "YES," write down a personal example for each.

1. Beliefs about worry as something that can help you to resolve problems. This means all beliefs that convey the idea that worrying helps to fix problems, find better solutions, become more aware of problems, be better prepared to face them, react better when problems occur, and avoid potential problems.

   YES: _____ NO: _____
   Personal example:

2. Beliefs that worry is a good way to motivate yourself. This means all beliefs that convey the idea that worrying will motivate you to do things you would otherwise avoid. These beliefs can relate to responsibilities at work, household tasks, social activities, or leisure activities.

   YES: _____ NO: _____
   Personal example:

3. Beliefs about worry as a way to protect yourself from negative emotions. This means all beliefs that convey the idea that by worrying about something beforehand, you can protect yourself from subsequent despair, disappointment, or guilt if the event actually occurs.

   YES: _____ NO: _____
   Personal example:

4. Beliefs that the act of worrying can have an effect on events. This means all beliefs that convey the idea that the act of worrying itself can have an effect on events, that worries have power over the occurrence or nonoccurrence of events.

YES: _____ NO: _____
Personal example:

5. Beliefs about worry as a positive personality trait. This means all beliefs that convey the idea that a person who worries is considerate, prudent, and cares about the well-being of others. These beliefs also imply that worrying about someone is proof of love or caring.

YES: _____ NO: _____
Personal example:

Can you think of any other examples of beliefs about worry, that don't fit into the preceding categories?

YES: _____ NO: _____
If YES, please describe:

Goals for the Future: A Life without Worry

Below are a number of different life domains. Give some thought to how you might wish to change or add to each life area if you worried less. Take some time to consider tasks or activities that you might not have thought of in the past because they seemed a bit too scary or could lead to worry. Keep in mind that you don't need to complete this sheet at one time. Rather, you can come back and add to it over time as you think about how you might see what your life without worry could look like.

Relationships with Family and Friends (for example, spending more time with old friends, organizing family outings, allowing your children more independence, reconnecting with old friends)

_____

_____

_____

_____

Hobbies, Leisure, and Social Activities (for example, taking up a new hobby or interest that you were hesitant to try in the past, such as taking dancing lessons or learning to swim)

_____

_____

_____

_____

Work/School Performance and Activities (for example, taking on new work responsibilities, looking for other employment opportunities, taking a class, working more independently at school or work)

_____

_____

_____

_____

Daily Tasks or Chores (for example, allowing your children to take on more household chores unsupervised, making fewer to-do lists)

_____

_____

_____

_____

Your Personality or Character Traits (for example, being more spontaneous by planning last-minute activities, or being more carefree and easygoing by reducing some of the structure in your daily schedule)

_____

_____

_____

_____

The Impact of Negative Beliefs about Uncertainty on the Worry Cycle

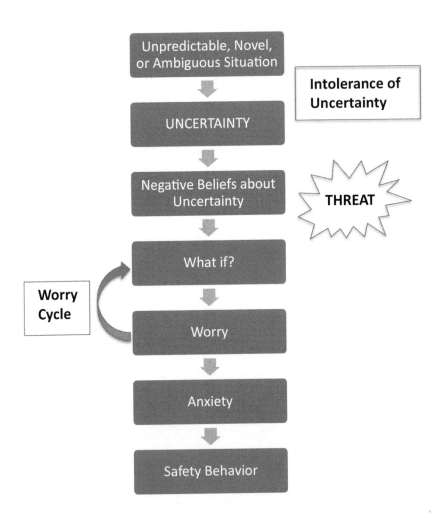

The Impact of Balanced Beliefs about Uncertainty on the Worry Cycle

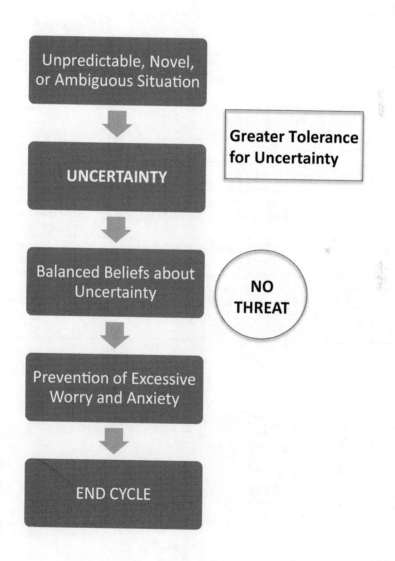

Behavioral Experiment Record Form

Behavioral Experiment Examples

Experiment	Feared Outcome	Actual Outcome	Coping (if actual outcome was negative)
Left cell phone unattended for one hour (no checking)	What if I miss an important call or text? The person could be mad at me or something bad could happen and I wouldn't know.	I didn't get any calls or texts during the time I didn't check my phone.	No coping needed.
Left cell phone unattended for one hour (no checking)	What if I miss an important call or text? The person could be mad at me or something bad could happen and I wouldn't know.	My friend texted me to ask whether we could change the time that we were supposed to meet for dinner.	I texted my friend back once I got his message. We changed our meeting time. He didn't even mention that I hadn't texted him back right away.
Went to the grocery store without a list to buy items for dinner (no list making)	What if I forget something important? I'll have to go back to the store and waste a lot of time and effort. My dinner will be late and my evening will be ruined.	I did forget one item that I wanted to use to make dinner.	I ended up changing the recipe a little bit and made dinner without the missing ingredient. It was still pretty good.

Behavioral Experiment Record Form

Experiment	Feared Outcome	Actual Outcome	Coping (if actual outcome was negative)

Resolution of a Problem Form

Step 1A: Problem Definition (*What is the situation? What would you like the situation to be? What is the obstacle keeping you from your ideal situation?*)

Step 1B: Goal Formulation (remember to keep your goals realistic, achievable, and related to your definition of the problem)
   Short-term goals:

   Long-term goals:

Step 2: Generation of Alternative Solutions
   Keep in mind the rules of brainstorming: (1) deferment of judgment; (2) quantity of solutions (at least 10 to 12 possibilities); and (3) variety of solutions

Step 3: Decision Making
   Consider the following criteria:
   - Will this solution solve the problem?
   - How will I feel if I choose this solution?
   - How much time and effort are involved?
   - What are the consequences to me and to others in the short and long term?

   Chosen solution:

Step 4A: Solution Implementation
   Write out the steps that you need to take to carry out your chosen solution

Step 4B: Solution Verification
   Write out what checks or markers you will use to determine whether your chosen solution is solving the problem

Written Exposure Summary Form

Before starting written exposure, take the time to think about and answer the following questions:

In writing about your worst-case scenario, what are your feared outcomes (that is, what are you afraid might happen if you allow yourself to imagine and write about your worst fear)?

What is the likelihood that you will be completely overwhelmed by negative emotions (sadness, despair) if you allow yourself to really think about, and focus on, your worst-case scenario (from 0 to 100%)?

The following questions are to be answered after each written exposure session:

- How anxious/upset were you *before* you completed exposure (from 0 to 10)?
- How anxious/upset were you *after* you completed exposure (from 0 to 10)?
- What do you think is the likelihood that your feared worst-case scenario will actually occur (from 0 to 100%)?
- How catastrophic do you think it would be if your worst-case scenario actually occurred (from 0 to 100%)?
- If your worst-case scenario did actually occur, what is the likelihood that you would be able to manage the situation (from 0 to 100%)?

Looking back on your predictions when you first started this exercise, what did you learn by writing about your worst fear?

CHAPTER 6

Treatment Efficacy

In Chapters 4 and 5, we presented our cognitive behavioral treatment for generalized anxiety disorder (GAD). In the current chapter, we will review the research on the treatment. We will begin with a discussion of the advantages and disadvantages of different criteria for establishing a treatment's efficacy. Next, we will review the main findings from clinical trials conducted by both our research team and others, as well as discuss what we have learned so far about predictors of treatment outcome. Most recently we have developed a more streamlined version of our treatment that consists of just one strategy—behavioral experiments targeting intolerance of uncertainty, as described in Module 3 of Chapters 4 and 5. We will discuss some of the ideas that led us to develop this new treatment, and we will summarize the key findings from a preliminary study we conducted to assess its therapeutic potential.

Criteria for Establishing Treatment Efficacy

There are many ways of assessing treatment efficacy in clinical trials. As mentioned previously, the comprehensive assessment of GAD offers several advantages, the most important being that each assessment method provides different information on clients' state and progress. In the following sections, we discuss three of the most widely used criteria/methods for assessing treatment efficacy in clinical trials: diagnostic remission, statistical comparisons of mean effects, and clinically significant improvement. Whereas the criteria for diagnostic remission and clinically significant improvement are applied to each participant, statistical comparisons of mean effects are assessed for entire groups or subgroups of participants.

Diagnostic Remission

In many clinical trials, diagnostic remission (that is, not meeting GAD diagnostic criteria following treatment) is used as one of the main criteria for treatment success. The assessment of diagnostic remission is an attractive success criterion for many reasons. First, it is nonambiguous; clients are either in remission or not in remission. Second, it is based on criteria contained in diagnostic systems such as the *Diagnostic and Statistical Manual of Mental Disorders, Fifth Edition* (*DSM-5;* American Psychiatric Association, 2013). Third, the assessment of diagnostic remission facilitates communication with clients, their families, other health professionals, and third-party payers such as insurance companies. For example, insurance company representatives will not want to know if treatment led to reliable changes in standardized measures of worry and anxiety; they will want to know if clients no longer meet GAD diagnostic criteria following treatment.

Although the assessment of diagnostic remission is attractive for the aforementioned reasons, it is an incomplete (and at times, inaccurate) way of evaluating client progress. One of the problems with using diagnostic remission as a treatment success criterion resides in its either-or quality; clients either meet GAD diagnostic criteria or they do not. Like any measurement technique based on a yes/no answer, the assessment of diagnostic remission can be an unreliable method of appraising client progress. To illustrate this point, imagine a client who continues to be a very high worrier following treatment, but has only two of the six GAD associated symptoms (for example, restlessness and difficulty concentrating). This client would meet the conditions for diagnostic remission (three associated symptoms are required to meet GAD criteria), but the remaining GAD symptoms would likely continue to lead to important interference or distress in the client's life. In this case, therefore, the answer to the either-or diagnostic question would not capture the interference and distress that result from the client's residual symptoms. As another illustration, consider the example of a client presenting at the outset of treatment with markedly severe GAD. The client shows a very large reduction in symptoms and reports a dramatic improvement in quality life following treatment, yet continues to surpass the diagnostic threshold for GAD. According to the diagnostic remission criterion, the client still has the disorder, leading to the conclusion that treatment was not successful. However, given the client's major improvement, both therapist and client are likely to conclude that treatment *was* successful. In this case, the binary, either-or approach fails to capture meaningful improvement in the client's condition.

Another notable problem with the remission criterion is that GAD has relatively low diagnostic reliability; even experienced clinicians often have difficulty agreeing on the presence or absence of GAD. This problem is further complicated by the fact that therapists tend to underestimate GAD symptoms following treatment because they "want" their clients to be in remission. This is why treatment studies typically call upon an independent evaluator (someone not involved in other aspects of the study) to assess diagnostic remission. For these reasons, the assessment of diagnostic remission is insufficient as a sole marker of treatment efficacy. Combined with the methods described in the following paragraphs, however, diagnostic remission may provide the answer to one part of the important question of treatment efficacy.

Statistical Comparisons of Mean Effects

In addition to assessing diagnostic remission, clinical trials typically submit data to statistical comparisons of mean effects. These analyses can be used to examine within-group effects (e.g., to compare post-treatment scores to pre-treatment scores in one treatment condition); between-group effects (e.g., to compare post-treatment scores in two treatment conditions); and within-between group effects (e.g., to compare pre- to post-treatment changes in two treatment conditions). Generally speaking, differences are considered "real" when there is less than a 5% probability that they are the result of chance fluctuations. Thus, in most cases, the expression "statistically significant effect" means that there is a 95% probability that the observed effect is real and not due to random variations.

Statistical significance testing, which is also referred to as probability testing, has come under intense criticism. The main critique of probability testing is that it addresses a dichotomous question (much like diagnostic remission). Obviously, the "5% principle" should not be applied in a rigid fashion, but clear guidelines on how to carry out probability testing in a flexible and justifiable way are lacking. Given these (and other) limitations of probability testing, it is now widely recommended that researchers also report the size of the observed effects. Roughly speaking, an effect size can be conceptualized as a standardized measure of the magnitude of an effect. Thus, by combining the calculation of effect size (magnitude of effect) with probability testing ("realness" of the effect), statistical comparisons of mean effects can provide a considerable amount of information about treatment efficacy.

Statistical comparisons of mean effects have many advantages. First, they are firmly grounded in scientific theory and research and are widely acknowledged to be the most important means of assessing treatment efficacy. Second, as mentioned above, they allow researchers to compute the magnitude of effects as well as the probability that the observed effects are true effects and not the result of chance variations. Third, statistical comparisons of mean effects allow researchers to arrive at general conclusions about the treatment under study (for example, that on average, the treatment leads to significant change for individuals with a particular disorder).

Although statistical comparisons of mean effects have many advantages, they also have some serious limitations, not the least of which is that they do not provide information on the outcomes of *individual* participants in a clinical trial. By focusing on changes within a group and on differences between groups, these tests do not offer information about treatment progress for individual clients. Further, statistical tests do not tell us if the observed changes are *clinically significant*. It may be that a group of individuals has statistically improved following treatment, but this does not necessarily imply that the individuals have made changes that translate into real improvements in their daily lives. Only tests of clinical significance directly address this question.

Clinically Significant Improvement

In addition to the assessment of diagnostic remission and statistical significance, treatment studies now tend to include the evaluation of clinically significant improvement. Simply stated, clinically significant change is attained when a client returns to normal functioning following treatment. In a landmark article, Neil Jacobson and Paula Truax (1991) reviewed a rationale and a methodology for calculating clinically significant change. Although there exist more sophisticated methods for calculating the clinical significance of change, the methods described by Jacobson and Truax have the benefit of being both relatively simple and informative. Furthermore, a study of the accuracy of different methods of calculating clinical significance suggests that those described by Jacobson and Truax are equivalent to more complex methods (Atkins, Bedics, McGlinchey, & Beauchaine, 2005). Basically, the authors argue that two questions should be addressed when assessing the clinical significance of each client's change. First, is the client's progress reliable? In other words, is the client's *treatment response* most likely real or due to chance variations? Second, following therapy, does the client display greater similarity to people with GAD or to those without GAD? From a statistical perspective, this can be formulated in the following way: do the client's post-treatment scores on measures of GAD fall closer to those of untreated GAD clients or to those of individuals from the general population? The question being posed here is whether a client has attained *high end state functioning*. According to Jacobson and Truax, the answers to these two questions will provide key information about the clinical significance of client progress.

The assessment of the clinical significance of change is helpful in a number of ways. First, it allows one to evaluate treatment gains for each individual client. Thus, clinical significance testing provides idiosyncratic information that can ultimately help us to understand *why* some clients benefit from treatment more than others do. The measurement of clinical significance also offers information that is meaningful to clients. For example, many GAD clients want to know if they have "really" changed over the course of treatment, and if they are now "normal" in terms of their worry and anxiety. Although group analyses cannot directly answer these questions, clinical significance testing makes this type of information available to clients. Finally, the methods described by Jacobson and Truax can be easily modified for the purposes of a given study. For example, in our own treatment studies, we have typically defined treatment response (or reliable change) as a 20% reduction in pre-treatment scores.

Although the assessment of clinically significant change offers many advantages, it is not without limitations. One of the problems with the assessment of clinical significance is that treatment response and end state functioning are ultimately questions requiring a yes/no answer, and as such, are prone to the limitations inherent in the evaluation of dichotomous responses. Another limitation of clinical significance testing relates to the reliability of the calculations. For example, when calculating a "cut score" that best distinguishes the GAD population from the general population on a given measure, one must rely on the available normative data for that particular measure. Obviously, the validity of the chosen cut score will be the direct result of the quality of the available normative data.

As with the other measurement methods described herein, the assessment of clinically significant change is insufficient in and of itself for the assessment of treatment efficacy. However, by combining it with the evaluation of diagnostic remission and statistical comparisons of mean effects, researchers can present a fairly comprehensive and accurate picture of the efficacy of a given treatment. In the following sections, we focus mainly on these assessment strategies in presenting the findings from our clinical trials. Readers should also know that post-treatment results presented in this chapter are based on all clients entering treatment. For clients not completing treatment (and thus, not attending post-treatment assessments), pre-treatment scores were carried forward to post-treatment. In other words, in the absence of post-treatment data, we assume that clients made no progress. Although this is a conservative approach, it is the most appropriate way of evaluating a treatment's efficacy because one simply should not assume that a client made progress in the absence of data. Therefore, the post-treatment data presented in the following sections are based on all clients entering treatment or what is often referred to as the "intent-to-treat" sample.

Studies of Treatment Efficacy

Since developing our cognitive behavioral treatment (CBT) for GAD, we have tested its efficacy in different ways. We have compared our treatment to a passive control condition (waiting list) and to an active control condition (applied relaxation). We have also compared our treatment to a nonspecific active control condition (active listening) in terms of its ability to facilitate medication discontinuation.

CBT and Wait-List Control

In our initial controlled clinical trial, we assessed the efficacy of our CBT protocol by comparing it to a wait-list control condition (Ladouceur, Dugas, Freeston et al., 2000). The treatment, which was administered over 16 weekly sessions, targeted intolerance of uncertainty, positive beliefs about worry, negative problem orientation, and cognitive avoidance. The sample consisted of 26 adults with a mean age of 40 years. All participants had a primary diagnosis of GAD. In an effort to have a clinically representative sample, we did not exclude clients taking psychotropic medication or having other psychological conditions. We did require, however, that medication use be stable and that comorbid conditions be less severe than the GAD diagnosis. Most participants had comorbid anxiety disorders and one third of them were taking medication for their anxiety.

Study participants were assessed with the Anxiety Disorders Interview Schedule for *DSM-IV* (ADIS-IV), which was used to diagnose and establish the overall severity of GAD and comorbid conditions. Participants also completed questionnaires, which were used to assess the study's main outcome variables: pathological worry, GAD associated symptoms, state anxiety, and severity of depressive symptoms. In addition, participants were asked to complete a measure of intolerance of uncertainty so that we could assess the impact of treatment on underlying cognitive processes (although most measures used in our treatment studies are described in Chapter 3, the reader may want to consult the original treatment articles (Ladouceur et al., 2000; Dugas et al., 2003; Gosselin et al., 2006; Dugas et al., 2010) for a full description of all measures used in each study). Although participants completed other questionnaires (such as measures of common therapy factors), we will focus our discussion on the variables mentioned above because they represent the study's main outcomes and processes.

In the first phase of the study, participants were randomly selected to receive treatment ($n = 14$) or to be placed on a 16-week waiting list ($n = 12$). As expected, we found that relative to participants in the wait-list condition, treated participants had higher rates of GAD diagnostic remission and showed greater statistical and clinical change on overall GAD severity, pathological worry, GAD associated symptoms, state anxiety, and severity of depressive symptoms. Although these results were encouraging, they were not surprising given that the treatment condition was being compared to a wait-list control condition. Although waiting lists typically lead to some improvement in symptoms (mostly because clients have positive expectations about the treatment they will soon be receiving), they nonetheless represent the least stringent of control conditions. Therefore, in this type of study, one must take a close look at the magnitude of change (or effect size) that results from receiving the treatment (see below).

In the second phase of the study, the 12 participants in the wait-list condition were offered the same 16-week treatment. Once wait-listed participants had received treatment, we examined treatment effects for the entire sample of 26 participants and found that 20 of 26 participants (77%) no longer met GAD diagnostic criteria at post-treatment. We also noted statistically significant decreases on all outcomes from pre- to post-treatment. More importantly, effect sizes were large (by convention, $d = 0.8$ or greater is considered a large effect size) for all outcome variables: $d = 3.2$ for overall GAD severity, $d = 2.4$ for pathological worry, $d = 1.6$ for GAD associated symptoms, $d = 0.9$ for state anxiety, and $d = 1.1$ for depressive severity. When we examined the clinical significance of change, we found that 65% of participants were high responders (20% change on at least two-thirds of outcome measures) and that 62% met criteria for high end state functioning (that is, their scores were within nonclinical range on at least two-thirds of outcome measures).

In the final phase of the study, we examined the maintenance of treatment gains during the year following treatment termination. Remarkably, all participants were available for follow-up assessments as none had dropped out during the treatment or follow-up phases of the study. Overall, we found that participants maintained their treatment gains over the follow-up period, and 77% of participants continued to be in diagnostic remission at 6-month and 1-year follow-ups. Moreover, statistical comparisons of post-treatment and follow-up means showed that treatment gains were maintained on all measures of outcome. Finally, at 1-year follow-up, there was a slight and nonsignificant decrease in the percentage of participants who were high responders (62% as opposed to 65% at post-treatment) and who met criteria for high end state functioning (58% compared to 62% immediately following treatment).

Of interest, we found that changes in intolerance of uncertainty closely paralleled changes in symptoms during treatment and follow-up. The treatment led to statistically significant decreases in intolerance of uncertainty, and these changes were maintained at 6-month and 1-year follow-ups. Furthermore, for most clients, changes in intolerance of uncertainty preceded changes in time spent worrying over the course of therapy, further supporting the notion that intolerance of uncertainty is an important treatment target (Dugas, Langlois, Rhéaume, & Ladouceur, 1998). In fact, the latter finding suggests that the treatment may exert its effects on pathological worry by first leading to changes in intolerance of uncertainty.

Overall, the results from our first randomized controlled trial indicated that approximately three out of four participants were GAD-free following treatment and at 1-year follow-up. Moreover, about 60% of participants met conditions for high end state functioning immediately following treatment and at 1-year follow-up. Although the treatment did not lead to ideal outcomes, the results indicated that most clients benefited greatly in the short term and long term.

Group CBT and Wait-List Control

In our second clinical trial, we tested the efficacy of our treatment when offered in a group format (Dugas, Ladouceur, Léger, Freeston et al., 2003). We hypothesized that therapeutic factors unique to group therapy such as altruism, vicarious learning, interpersonal learning, role flexibility, and group cohesiveness might be advantageous for many clients with GAD. We also wondered if the group therapy format might help reduce client demoralization, which is a common complication of GAD, especially when chronic. In addition, we noted that research had shown impressive gains with group treatment for other anxiety disorders—another good reason to test the group format with people with GAD.

As in our first trial, we assessed the efficacy of the treatment using a wait-list control condition. The sample consisted of 52 adults with a mean age of 41 years. All study participants had a primary diagnosis of GAD. Again, we did not exclude clients with comorbid conditions (if these conditions were less severe than the primary diagnosis of GAD) or taking psychotropic medication for their anxiety (if the medication use was stable). Most participants had at least one additional disorder and about 20% of them were taking anxiolytic or antidepressant medication. The study's main outcome variables were overall GAD severity, pathological worry, GAD associated symptoms, state anxiety, and depressive severity. Participants also completed a measure of adaptive functioning within various social contexts, as well as the Intolerance of Uncertainty Scale.

In the first phase of the study, the participants either received treatment immediately ($n = 25$) or were placed on a waiting list ($n = 27$). Those in the immediate treatment condition were divided into five groups, with four to six participants per group. The treatment, which targeted intolerance of uncertainty, positive beliefs about worry, negative problem orientation, and cognitive avoidance was administered over 14 weekly 2-hour sessions by two clinical psychologists. As anticipated, results from the first study phase showed that compared to those on the waiting list, treated participants had higher rates of remission and showed greater statistical and clinical change on all measures of outcome. Again, these results are not surprising given that the treatment was compared to a waiting list, which is a non-stringent control condition.

During the second phase of the study, which began after the 14-week waiting period, wait-listed participants were divided into five treatment groups, with four to six participants per group. Once all participants had received treatment, we examined post-treatment outcomes for the entire sample. The percentage of participants no longer meeting GAD diagnostic criteria was 60%. Not surprisingly, we found statistically significant decreases on all study measures. Pre- to post-treatment effect sizes were medium to large for all outcomes: $d = 1.8$ for overall GAD severity, $d = 1.6$ for pathological worry, $d = 1.2$ for GAD associated symptoms, $d = 0.9$ for state anxiety, $d = 1.0$ for severity of depressive symptoms, and $d = 0.7$ for social adjustment. Although the effects sizes obtained with group treatment were considerable, they were nonetheless not as large as those obtained in the previous study of individual treatment.

The clinical significance of pre- to post-treatment change was again assessed according to treatment response and end state functioning. Consistent with our previous study, treatment response was defined as a 20% change in pre-treatment scores, and end state functioning was defined as a score that was within one standard deviation of the mean of normative nonclinical samples. Following group treatment, 60% of participants were high responders (20% change on at least two-thirds of outcome measures) and 65% of participants met criteria for high end state functioning (within nonclinical range on at least two-thirds of outcome measures).

In the study's final phase, we assessed all available participants at 6 months, 1 year, and 2 years following treatment. The percentage of participants no longer meeting diagnostic criteria was 88% at 6-month follow-up, 83% at 1-year follow-up, and 95% at 2-year follow-up. When we looked at the question of change in various outcomes from post-treatment to follow-up assessments, we found no evidence of deterioration on any of the outcome measures over the two-year period. In fact, we found that worry scores actually decreased during the two-year follow-up. Thus, in terms of pathological worry, participants were doing better 2 years after treatment than immediately after the end of treatment. Finally, we examined clinically significant improvement over the 2-year follow-up period and found an increase in the percentage of high responders (72% at 2-year follow-up as opposed to 60% at post-treatment) as well as in the percentage of participants meeting criteria for high end state functioning (72% at 2-year follow-up compared to 65% at post-treatment).

Although the follow-up data are impressive, they may represent an overestimation of continued progress as the number of participants available for each assessment steadily decreased over time, with only 39 participants being available for the 2-year follow-up evaluation. It may be that participants not doing as well over the follow-up phase of the study were less motivated to attend all assessments, thus leading to an overestimation of remission rates during follow-up. Nonetheless, at the very least, it appears that clients typically maintained their treatment gains in the two years following treatment termination.

With the goal of investigating treatment mechanisms, we subsequently examined the relationship between intolerance of uncertainty and the various treatment outcomes (Dugas, Ladouceur, Léger, Langlois et al., 2003). When examining pre- to post-treatment changes, we found that changes in intolerance of uncertainty predicted changes in pathological worry and GAD associated symptoms, above and beyond common therapy factors such as therapist characteristics, treatment credibility, and client motivation. In terms of pre-treatment to follow-up changes, the results indicated that only client motivation and pre- to post-treatment changes in intolerance of uncertainty predicted changes in pathological worry and GAD-associated symptoms at 2-year follow-up. Thus, it appears that the extent to which clients become more tolerant of uncertainty over the course of treatment predicts their GAD symptoms immediately after treatment, as well as up to two years following treatment termination. These findings further add to the evidence indicating that intolerance of uncertainty is an important target when treating individuals with GAD.

Overall, the findings from the individual and group treatment studies suggest that both treatment formats are efficacious. Individual treatment, however, appears to be more effective than group treatment in terms of short-term progress, as evidenced by higher GAD remission rates and larger effect sizes on most outcome measures. Interestingly, the follow-up data suggest that individual and group treatment provide clients with similar long-term gains. As a case in point, when remission rates were calculated in the most conservative way possible for the group treatment study (by assuming that clients unavailable for follow-up assessments had relapsed), the percentage of participants in remission was 71% at 1-year follow-up and 77% at 2-year follow-up. A final notable comparison of the individual and group treatment studies concerns dropout rates. None of the participants in the individual treatment study dropped out of treatment, whereas 10% of those in the group treatment study did not complete the full treatment. Thus, it may be that individual treatment is an acceptable format to a greater proportion of clients with GAD. This, in turn, may be the result of the greater flexibility of individual treatment, which provides the therapist with more "room" to adapt treatment to the specific needs of each client. In summary, although the findings of the group treatment study are very encouraging, the data suggest that individual treatment is the optimal treatment format for those who suffer from GAD.

CBT, Applied Relaxation, and Wait-List Control

In this trial, we compared our CBT protocol to applied relaxation and a wait-list control (Dugas et al., 2010). Given that our previous treatment studies had shown that our CBT protocol leads to statistically and clinically significant change, our main objective in carrying out this study was to test our treatment against a well-established intervention, namely applied relaxation. We chose applied relaxation as an active control condition for a number of reasons. First, applied relaxation has received empirical support for the treatment of GAD (Chambless et al., 1998; American Psychological Association, Division 12, Society of Clinical Psychology).

Thus, we reasoned that it would allow for a relatively stringent test of our treatment's comparative efficacy. Second, applied relaxation is widely used in clinical settings. In fact, it is included in practice guidelines for the treatment of GAD (for example, the guidelines of the National Institute for Health and Care Excellence [NICE]). Finally, the therapeutic procedures involved in applied relaxation are very different from those involved in our treatment. We wanted the comparison condition to be distinct from our treatment so that we could draw firm conclusions about treatment differences in terms of both outcomes and treatment mechanisms. We also included a wait-list condition in order to replicate the finding that both treatments were superior to being placed on a waiting list.

One of the main challenges we faced in designing this study was dealing with potential allegiance effects. In simple terms, allegiance effects may occur when researchers wittingly or unwittingly favor a condition in an experiment to which they feel a certain loyalty. This can occur when researchers compare a treatment they have developed with other treatments. To counter potential allegiance effects, we took a series of steps. First, independent assessors (senior doctoral students not involved with other aspects of the study) administered diagnostic interviews and other assessment procedures at all measurement times. Most importantly, the assessors were not involved in treatment delivery and were unaware of participants' experimental condition. Second, we hired a psychologist who was not trained in CBT to be the main therapist for both treatment conditions. In this way, we hoped to limit biases concerning one type of therapy over the other. We also reasoned that by employing a therapist who had not trained in CBT, the study's results would generalize to more therapists, not only those who had extensive training in cognitive behavioral theory and treatment. Finally, weekly clinical supervision was offered by one "expert" in each treatment condition. In the applied relaxation condition, clinical supervision was provided by an experienced psychologist who was not previously involved in the development and validation of our cognitive behavioral treatment.

For this study, we recruited 65 adults with a primary diagnosis of GAD with a mean age of 39 years. Once again, comorbid diagnoses and medication use were allowed, but within the limits described in the previous treatment studies (59% had comorbid conditions and 55% were taking medication for their anxiety). The treatment outcome variables were similar to those of our previous treatment studies; participants completed measures of overall GAD severity, pathological worry, and GAD associated symptoms, as well as measures of anxiety proneness (often referred to as trait anxiety), and depressive severity.

After completing baseline measures, participants were randomly allocated to the experimental conditions: 23 were assigned to CBT, 22 to applied relaxation, and 20 to the waiting list. Participants in the treatment conditions received 12 weekly individual sessions of CBT or applied relaxation, with all sessions lasting 50 to 60 minutes. We decided to offer our CBT protocol in a slightly "condensed" format (12 sessions as opposed to 16 sessions in our previous individual treatment study) because we felt that 12 sessions might prove sufficient to cover all treatment modules. In hindsight, it appears we were somewhat overly optimistic, as is discussed below. The applied relaxation condition, which was also offered over 12 weekly sessions, included training in: (1) psychoeducation and tension awareness; (2) tension-release for 16, 7, and 4 muscle groups; (3) relaxation by recall; (4) relaxation by counting; (5) conditioned relaxation; and (6) relapse prevention. The treatment conditions were matched on a number of important features such as duration of treatment, use of a clearly articulated theoretical model, and number of between-session exercises. We re-administered all outcome measures at post-test, 6-month follow-up, 1-year follow-up, and 2-year follow-up.

Analyses within the treatment conditions showed that at post-treatment, CBT and applied relaxation both led to significant improvements in all outcome measures. We then compared each treatment condition to the waitlist condition. We found that CBT and applied relaxation led to significant decreases in overall GAD severity when compared to the waitlist condition. However, only CBT led to significant improvements in pathological worry and GAD associated symptoms. Neither treatment led to significant improvement in anxiety proneness or severity of depressive symptoms relative to the waitlist condition. It is worth noting that the wait-listed participants showed improvements that were unusually large relative to observations in previous studies, which may have attenuated the ability to detect the true therapeutic effects of CBT and applied relaxation.

As noted earlier, those assigned to the waitlist condition were randomly allocated to CBT or applied relaxation following the waiting phase. In a second set of analyses, we did a head-to-head comparison of the CBT and applied relaxation conditions on short-term outcomes (pre-treatment to post-treatment) and long-term outcomes (up to 2 years post-treatment). Given that CBT and applied relaxation are grounded in different rationales we had expected that improvements in pathological worry would be greater for those who received CBT and that improvements in GAD-associated symptoms (e.g., muscle tension, sleep disturbance) would be greater for those who received applied relaxation. However, *both* treatments produced significant and comparable improvements in nearly all outcomes. In retrospect, this makes good sense given that cognition, emotion, physiology, and behavior are interconnected systems. So, even when a treatment seems to focus more heavily on a subset of these systems (e.g., cognitive activity versus somatic symptoms), those that are not explicitly targeted will still show corresponding improvements. Having said this, CBT did emerge superior to applied relaxation on one outcome: the Clinical Global Impression Improvement scale, which was the independent assessors' rating of each person's improvement in *overall* well-being.

With respect to long-term outcomes over the 2-year follow-up, CBT participants continued to show improvements in pathological worry, anxiety proneness, and overall well-being after treatment ended. Those who received applied relaxation remained stable after treatment; they neither deteriorated nor improved. However, when the treatments were compared head to head, any differences between them were not statistically significant. We also examined rates of diagnostic remission. CBT and applied relaxation were comparable to one another in rates of remission at every assessment point throughout the follow-up period, with the majority of participants in each treatment condition achieving remission status.

On balance, this particular clinical trial showed that CBT and applied relaxation led to significant improvements that were fairly similar. It should be noted that effect sizes for the CBT condition were generally smaller in this trial than in the previous trial in which we tested the 16-session version of the treatment. Our clinical experience in offering the 12-session treatment was that most clients would have benefited from a few additional sessions to more fully integrate the implications of the treatment's underlying principles. We have thus come to the conclusion that in this particular case, more is better and that 14 to 16 regular 50-minute sessions are generally required to fully cover all treatment modules and their various applications.

CBT and Medication Discontinuation

It is well established that many individuals with GAD struggle with long-term medication use (Ashton, 2001). In particular, the use of benzodiazepines over extended periods of time can lead to a number of problems. First, their long-term use is associated with both physical dependency and tolerance effects. Second, their extended use sometimes leads to important side effects such as nausea and difficulty concentrating. And finally, many long-term benzodiazepine users report high levels of psychological dependency and are unable to cease their medication use. Given these considerations, we were interested in knowing if our treatment could help GAD sufferers who are long-term benzodiazepine users to discontinue their medication.

In this study (Gosselin, Ladouceur, Morin, Dugas, & Baillargeon, 2006), we recruited 61 individuals with a primary diagnosis of GAD. The sample consisted of 36 women and 25 men, with a mean age of 50 years. All participants had been taking benzodiazepines for at least one year, with a mean duration of use of over seven years. All participants reported a desire to discontinue their medication use, and 59% reported having already unsuccessfully tried to cease taking benzodiazepines. In line with our previous treatment studies, comorbid diagnoses were allowed. Eighty percent of participants had at least one secondary disorder, with social anxiety disorder being the most frequently diagnosed condition. Participants were randomly assigned to CBT plus medication taper ($n = 31$) or active listening plus medication taper ($n = 30$). Those in the CBT condition received the treatment modules targeting intolerance of uncertainty, positive beliefs about worry, negative problem orientation, and cognitive avoidance. Those in the active listening condition explored their life experiences with the goal of facilitating both self-awareness and understanding of their anxiety. The therapist's role was to provide an empathetic and nonjudgmental environment within which clients could talk about themselves. By using a nonspecific psychotherapy condition such as active listening, we hoped to determine if the specific modules of our treatment were responsible for group differences, as opposed to common therapy factors such as the therapist–client working alliance and the change expectations that come with working with a competent health care provider. As for the medication taper procedure, it aimed for a decrease of the daily dose of benzodiazepines by 25% every two to three weeks over the course of treatment.

Each participant received 12 combined sessions of medication taper and psychotherapy (either CBT or active listening), with each combined session lasting 90 minutes. In the first part of the session, the participant met with a physician for about 20 minutes to review progress, assess withdrawal symptoms, and determine the following week's dose. In the second part of the session, the participant met with a clinical psychologist to receive either CBT or the nonspecific active listening intervention. Participants were assessed at pre-treatment, post-treatment, and at follow-ups of 3 months, 6 months, and 1 year after treatment termination. The assessment instruments and procedures were similar to those used in the previously described studies, with the addition of a medication self-monitoring agenda (and the use of urine tests to confirm the validity of the self-reports of medication intake).

Overall, the results showed that in combination with medication taper, CBT was more efficacious than active listening in producing benzodiazepine discontinuation. At post-treatment, 74% of participants in the CBT condition had attained complete benzodiazepine cessation, whereas only 37% of those in the active listening condition had attained a similar result. Furthermore, these findings remained fairly stable during the year following treatment termination, with significantly more participants in the CBT condition having attained complete cessation of their benzodiazepines at all follow-up times. It should be noted, however, that we found no between-group differences in the quantity of benzodiazepines taken. Although this latter finding stands in sharp contrast to the rates of complete discontinuation, it is nonetheless consistent with the findings of other studies involving medication taper procedures. Specifically, many studies suggest that the final stage of medication tapering (complete cessation) is the most difficult for long-term users. Consequently, it may be that one of the main benefits of CBT is to provide clients with "tools" that allow them to successfully navigate the challenges involved in the final stage of medication tapering, namely complete cessation.

We were also interested in comparing CBT and active listening in terms of their respective impacts on the presence and severity of GAD. We first looked at diagnostic remission at post-treatment and found that 65% of participants in the CBT condition no longer met GAD criteria whereas only 20% of participants in the active listening condition achieved similar results. Over the follow-up phase of the study, the rates of diagnostic remission increased in both conditions, but percentages remained significantly higher in the CBT condition than in the active listening condition. For example, at 1-year follow-up, remission rates were 71% in the CBT condition and 40% in the active listening condition. We also examined the statistical significance of change on several measures of GAD severity. Overall, we found that both conditions led to decreases in the symptoms of GAD and associated depression. Analyses comparing both groups showed that relative to participants in the active listening condition, those in the CBT condition reported significantly lower levels of worry and intolerance of uncertainty at post-treatment. Furthermore, these between-group differences were maintained over most follow-up assessments.

In summary, the findings from this study suggest that the combination of CBT and a supervised medication taper is helpful for individuals with GAD who are long-term benzodiazepine users. First, it appears that CBT plus taper is more effective than active listening and taper in helping clients to *discontinue* their use of benzodiazepines. Second, relative to active listening, CBT leads to greater gains in terms of diagnostic remission and symptom improvement. It is noteworthy that most clients receiving CBT plus taper were able to both discontinue their use of medication and attain diagnostic remission of GAD. It may be that the 65% post-CBT remission rate is actually a conservative estimate, because some participants may have been struggling with increases in anxiety due to medication cessation. Thus, it seems that receiving a combination of CBT and supervised medication taper can be doubly beneficial for many long-term benzodiazepine users with GAD: they can rid themselves of both their medication and their GAD.

General Conclusions about Short-Term and Long-Term Effects

The general conclusions that can be drawn from the above review of our randomized clinical trials of our treatment are presented in Table 6.1.

Table 6.1 General Conclusions Based on Our Studies of Treatment Efficacy

---

Short-Term Effects

1. Most clients attain GAD remission (60 to 77%) and high end state functioning (62 to 65%) following treatment.

2. The treatment leads to statistically significant decreases (with effect sizes ranging from 3.2 to 0.90) in GAD symptoms, associated anxiety, and depression.

3. The treatment appears to be at least as efficacious as applied relaxation in improving GAD symptoms.

4. Combined with medication taper, the treatment helps most GAD clients who are long-term benzodiazepine users to cease their medication (74%) or attain GAD remission (65%).

5. Adherence is high, as very few clients (0 to 10%) drop out before all treatment modules have been covered.

Long-Term Effects

1. Treatment gains in terms of diagnostic remission, GAD symptoms, associated anxiety, and depression are maintained for up to two years after treatment termination.

2. In terms of pathological worry, further gains are made over the two years that follow treatment termination, for both individual treatment and group treatment.

3. The treatment appears to be at least as efficacious as applied relaxation at maintaining gains up to two years after treatment termination, with indication of continued improvement in pathological worry for clients receiving our treatment.

4. Combined with medication taper, the treatment leads to the maintenance of treatment gains over a one-year period (slight decrease in the percentage of clients no longer using benzodiazepines but slight increase in the percentage of clients in remission of GAD).

Short-Term Effects

Taken together, the general conclusions about the short-term effects of our CBT protocol suggest that 12 to 16 weekly sessions of treatment lead to very positive outcomes for approximately two-thirds of clients with GAD. In fact, across studies, the data are quite consistent, with remission rates ranging from 60 to 77% and high end state functioning rates ranging from 62 to 65%. Furthermore, when one considers that all analyses were carried out using the full intent-to-treat sample (with pre-treatment scores carried forward to post-treatment for noncompleters), the results are very encouraging indeed. In fact, the results appear to be superior to those reported in treatment studies using general anxiety reduction interventions. It is noteworthy that the diagnostic remission rate of 55% obtained in the applied relaxation condition of the trial comparing it to our treatment is similar to those of other studies of general anxiety reduction interventions (e.g., Öst & Breitholtz, 2000, found that 53% of GAD clients were below the GAD diagnostic threshold following applied relaxation). Based on the findings from the individual treatment studies, it could be argued that relative to a general anxiety reduction intervention such as applied relaxation, the GAD-specific treatment helps about 20% more clients attain diagnostic remission. Given that the GAD literature is replete with studies showing that different treatments are roughly equivalent, this difference in remission rates is certainly notable. However, more studies comparing treatments directly to one another are needed to gain a firmer understanding of how our treatment performs relative to other treatments for pathological worry and GAD.

It is also worth noting that treatment efficacy did not seem to be adversely affected by the gradual withdrawal of medication, in this case benzodiazepines. Not only did the treatment lead to an increment in the efficacy of a supervised medication taper procedure, it also led to diagnostic remission in 65% of GAD clients (as opposed to 20% in the active listening condition). Given that many individuals enter therapy with the hope of decreasing or ceasing their use of medication, these findings suggest that this may be an attainable goal for many clients with GAD. Considering the great number of individuals who suffer from GAD and who are long-term benzodiazepine users, the importance of offering concrete "tools" to assist them in their efforts to stop using their medication cannot be overstated.

In terms of treatment acceptability and adherence, the data show that very few clients drop out of treatment before all modules have been covered. In our four randomized controlled trials, dropout rates never exceeded 10% (with the highest rate being observed in the group treatment study). Thus, the data show that at least 90% of clients who enter therapy actually go on to complete all phases of the treatment. This suggests that the vast majority of clients perceive the treatment as being credible, acceptable, and relevant to their situation. In fact, this is exactly what clients reported on a measure of treatment credibility that we administered in every study (because the measure was not used to assess treatment efficacy, it was not systematically presented in this chapter). On a more general note, these data suggest that the treatment "makes sense" to those who suffer from GAD. In fact, the vast majority of participants mentioned that the focus on worry rather than the physiological symptoms of anxiety was helpful. As mentioned previously, given that the treatment led to important gains in terms of both pathological worry and GAD-associated symptoms, it certainly does not seem necessary to directly target the associated symptoms (for example, muscle tension).

Long-Term Effects

As evidenced from the long-term effects listed in Table 6.1, treatment gains are for the most part maintained over extended periods of time. For example, diagnostic remission rates tend to stay the same or increase over periods of one to two years. Furthermore, individual treatment and group treatment both appear to lead to further reductions in pathological worry over a two-year follow-up period. Finally, although the percentage of individuals no longer using benzodiazepines decreased from post-treatment to 1-year follow-up, there was an increase in the percentage of remitted clients over the same period of time. It is a truism that helping individuals with anxiety disorders to "get better" is much easier than helping them to "stay better." Thus, it is our position that the follow-up data are just as important as the post-treatment data when considering the treatment's impact. In terms of personal and social costs, the long-term maintenance of treatment gains and the prevention of recurrent bouts of GAD have the potential to make the greatest difference not only to those with GAD, but also to their families and the health care system in general. Considering that GAD typically has a chronic and unrelenting course, the finding that over three quarters of treated individuals are in remission 1 and 2 years after treatment is encouraging indeed.

Although it is vital that we obtain data on the long-term effects of treatment, it should be noted that follow-up assessments present certain problems. Most notably, as researchers, we are unable to properly control for the impact of participants' various life experiences during the extended follow-up phases of treatment studies. In all our studies, we systematically take note of instances where clients change their medication or receive additional therapy following treatment. However, there are many other life experiences that can impact upon the maintenance of treatment gains, many of which we are unable to properly take into account. For example, a work promotion, a new relationship, or any other significant change or transition can lead to an increase or a decrease in worry and anxiety. Thus, although the assessment of the maintenance of treatment gains is extremely important, one should keep in mind that researchers have no control over day-to-day events that may contribute to further improvement or relapse in treated individuals.

Research by Other Teams

We are very encouraged that our treatment is being implemented and tested by other clinical research teams. Colin van der Heiden and colleagues (2012) conducted a randomized controlled trial at an outpatient mental health clinic in the

Netherlands wherein clients with a primary diagnosis of GAD were randomly assigned to receive 14 sessions of our treatment or 14 sessions of metacognitive therapy, a treatment designed to modify positive and negative beliefs about worry. Both treatments were compared with a waitlist condition. Although the intolerance of uncertainty (IU)-focused treatment delivered in the trial overlapped with our treatment, it also differed in several important respects. The researchers introduced the reevaluation of positive beliefs about the usefulness of worrying at the end of treatment; they used a different cognitive exposure procedure that involved the generation of alternatives to feared outcomes after engaging in exposure; and they did not have their participants seek out uncertainty-inducing situations. Also, in this trial, one group of therapists delivered metacognitive therapy whereas another group of therapists delivered the IU-focused treatment. Unfortunately, the authors did not assess therapist characteristics and competence, making it impossible to disentangle specific treatment effects from therapist effects. In our trial comparing CBT to applied relaxation, the same therapists delivered both treatments, ensuring that therapist effects were roughly equivalent in both conditions.

Metacognitive therapy and IU-focused CBT both led to large improvements in pathological worry, symptoms of anxiety, and, interestingly, intolerance of uncertainty. Further, the majority of participants, regardless of which treatment they received, met criteria for treatment responder status. However, in general, outcomes were statistically stronger for metacognitive therapy when the two treatments were directly compared to one another. As noted earlier, the procedures of this trial were different in some notable respects from our own. The extent to which these differences in procedures (and potential differences in therapist characteristics and competence) may have contributed to the findings is unknown. However, what is clear is that more head-to-head trials will have to be conducted before any firm conclusions can be drawn regarding the efficacy of our treatment relative to others.

Readers are likely interested in knowing how our treatment performs in "real world" clinical settings where client characteristics are more variable and where delivery of treatment may be less standardized. To our knowledge, there have been no naturalistic tests of the effectiveness of our protocol as delivered in standard care. However, we are aware of settings that have incorporated our treatment either in part or in full into their CBT protocols for GAD, and these protocols have been evaluated. Torbit and Laposa (2016) examined changes in IU and worry following 12 weeks of a group CBT for GAD delivered in an outpatient anxiety disorders clinic in a tertiary care hospital in Toronto. Treatment included a mix of strategies drawn from different protocols, including ours. In one session, clients learned about the role of IU in excessive worry, and learned how to target IU by seeking out uncertainty-inducing situations. There were significant decreases in worry and intolerance of uncertainty following treatment, and changes in IU were correlated with changes in worry. Interestingly, the improvement in IU at post-treatment was comparable to that observed in our trial comparing group CBT to a wait-list control. Although we cannot know for sure, one intriguing possibility is that the single session focusing directly on IU and the confrontation of uncertainty-inducing situations may have accounted for the large change in IU.

On the basis of the data from our clinical trials, our CBT treatment targeting intolerance of uncertainty, positive beliefs about worry, negative problem orientation, and cognitive avoidance has become one of the recommended treatments in the United Kingdom (UK)'s NICE guidelines for the management of GAD. Accordingly, our treatment has been adopted by several clinics within the UK's National Health Service as part of the Improving Access to Psychological Therapies (IAPT) program (readers can learn more about this large-scale initiative at www.england.nhs.uk/mental-health/adults/iapt/). To our knowledge, there are not yet any published studies of the effectiveness of our treatment as delivered within the IAPT program, but we expect that such studies will emerge given that the outcomes of participating clients are being tracked.

Predictors of Treatment Efficacy

In the initial phases of treatment development and testing, the key question being addressed is "does the treatment work?" Once there is sufficient evidence for the efficacy of a treatment, researchers may then turn their attention to uncovering the *predictors* of treatment response, that is, the factors that make treatment more successful or less successful. There are two types of predictors that tend to be of interest to clinical researchers: pre-existing factors like life events and client characteristics, and factors related to the treatment itself. Here we discuss two predictors we have studied: (1) pre-existing cognitive style, in particular, interpretation bias; and (2) the experience of sudden gains during treatment.

Interpretation Bias

In Chapter 2, we discussed the important role of interpretation bias in excessive worry and GAD. To summarize, our research shows that people high in GAD symptoms are inclined to assume the worst when they encounter ambiguous information. Further, the way people interpret ambiguous information (that is, in a negative, neutral, or positive way) mediates the association of intolerance of uncertainty to the symptoms of GAD (Koerner & Dugas, 2008). Stated differently, cognitive vulnerability in the form of high intolerance of uncertainty makes catastrophic appraisals/interpretations of ambiguous information more likely, which in turn catalyzes worry and anxiety. Given the important role of interpretation bias in worry and GAD, we assessed the impact of these biases on the efficacy of our treatment within the context of an open trial.

Before starting treatment, clients were presented with a series of vignettes describing ambiguous scenarios (for example, "My new partner called and left a message on my answering machine, saying that we need to talk about something important"). We then examined the extent to which responses to these vignettes were associated with subsequent response to CBT. First, greater pre-treatment interpretation biases predicted greater post-treatment GAD symptoms (Donegan & Dugas, 2011), meaning that those who were more inclined to interpret ambiguous information in a negative way at the *outset* of CBT did not benefit as much from treatment. Second, change in interpretation style mediated change in GAD symptoms from pre- to post-treatment (Donegan & Dugas, 2011), meaning that those clients who were able to shift their negative interpretation style *during* treatment were more responsive to CBT. Together, these findings suggested to us that targeting interpretation style more directly during CBT may boost treatment efficacy, especially for the subgroup of clients who show a particularly strong bias to interpret ambiguity in a catastrophic way. To test this idea, we have been conducting a randomized controlled trial in which we are comparing the treatment we tested in our previous trials to a version of it that includes one additional intervention at each session called computerized cognitive bias modification (CBM).

In CBM, individuals are presented with a description of an ambiguous scenario (for example, "You hear a noise in the night") and a word that disambiguates the situation in either a threatening ("robber") or nonthreatening ("dog") way. The task is to indicate with a button press if the word and the sentence are related. When the individual associates a threatening word with an ambiguous statement, the computer provides feedback saying "You are not correct" and when the individual associates a nonthreatening word with an ambiguous statement, the computer provides feedback saying "You are correct." Each CBM session takes just a few minutes and the idea is that over many practices, individuals learn to link nonthreatening outcomes with ambiguity. Theoretically, this kind of practice should help clients access nonthreatening interpretations more readily and flexibly when they are confronted with ambiguous information, rather than jump to the worst conclusion. If this is the case, then we should expect to see that the addition of computerized cognitive bias modification boosts improvement in interpretation bias and in pathological worry.

Our trial will provide answers to questions about the value (if any) of adding CBM to CBT for GAD. However, readers should be aware that there is not enough of an evidence base at this time to recommend CBM as an intervention for any psychological disorder. Much more research is needed to determine the therapeutic potential of CBM for anxiety and related disorders before it can be considered for implementation in clinical practice.

Sudden Gains

Earlier in this chapter, we summarized the standard methods that are used in controlled trials to assess the efficacy of a psychological treatment. These typically include examining *mean* (or average) change in a primary outcome (for example, key symptoms of a disorder) from pre-treatment to post-treatment and follow-ups in a group of individuals who have received an intervention. The outcomes of each treatment completer in a trial are also examined to identify those whose symptoms no longer meet criteria for the disorder after treatment has ended. This combined approach can tell us the extent to which a treatment works. However, a limitation is that it does not tell us what is happening *during* treatment. Over the last several years, there has been growing interest in measuring session-by-session changes in cognitions, emotions, and behaviors during CBT to better understand the process of treatment, and in particular, *individual* trajectories in improvement. Researchers Tony Tang and Robert DeRubeis (1999) coined the term *sudden gains* to describe the large and unanticipated improvement in symptoms that clients sometime display in treatment, from one session to the next. It turns out that sudden gains are not a random or transient "irregularity" in the course of treatment: Tang and DeRubeis observed in clients receiving CBT for depression that sudden gains usually do not reverse once they occur, that they predict continued improvement in the later phases of treatment, and that they predict longer lasting maintenance of gains after treatment has ended.

We examined sudden gains in a sample of 59 clients who received 14 weekly sessions of our CBT for GAD protocol, and completed outcome measures before and after treatment (Deschênes & Dugas, 2013). Prior to each session, clients completed a measure of past-week worry, which were used to identify sudden gains. For a gain to be considered sudden, it had to meet three statistical criteria: (1) the decrease in worry scores from one session to the next had to be large in absolute terms; (2) worry scores had to have dropped by at least 25% relative to the previous session; and (3) the drop in worry scores had to be large in relation to fluctuations in worry in the sessions preceding and following the sudden gain. About 20% of clients showed at least one sudden gain. In these clients, the sudden gain occurred between the fifth and 12th sessions. These clients were not, at the outset, any different from those who did not experience a sudden gain. Clients who had experienced a sudden gain reported greater reductions in GAD symptoms at the post-treatment assessment than did clients who did not experience a sudden gain, and curiously, this was despite the fact that such gains reversed in about half the participants who had experienced them.

What might have explained a large sudden reduction in worry in a subset of our clients? One possibility is that these clients made important cognitive or behavioral changes in earlier sessions that boosted self-efficacy and, in turn, catalyzed change in worry, even for those who experienced a reversal in their sudden gain. More research is needed to uncover what happens in the "critical sessions" (Tang & DeRubeis, 1999) that precede a sudden gain—it may be that key treatment strategies are employed in those sessions, in which case their deepening or strengthening may improve treatment efficacy.

Behavioral Experiments for Intolerance of Uncertainty

In the last several years, we have deepened the IU component of our conceptual model and have developed a novel, single-component treatment that focuses entirely on IU. The treatment consists of three modules delivered over 12 sessions: psychoeducation and uncertainty awareness training (two sessions); behavioral experiments targeting IU, as described in Chapter 4 and Chapter 5 under Module 3 (nine sessions); and relapse prevention (final session). The major difference between this new treatment and the original treatment is that the new treatment is heavily experiential, and consists of one main strategy delivered in a protocol that is more streamlined than is typical in research studies and naturalistic clinical settings.

Why behavioral experiments? The main reason is that *experiential learning* is particularly powerful at producing deep, lasting changes in cognition, emotion, sensations, and behavior (Bennett-Levy, 2006; McManus, Van Doorn, & Yiend, 2012). Also, perhaps more than any other CBT intervention, behavioral experiments are ideally suited to shift unhelpful or dysfunctional beliefs. Given the central role of unhelpful beliefs about uncertainty in pathological worry and GAD, it made sense for us to further develop the behavioral experiments component of our CBT into a stand-alone intervention.

Readers may at this point be asking why we have decided to develop a treatment focusing entirely on IU when our CBT protocol targeting intolerance of uncertainty, positive beliefs about worry, negative problem orientation, and cognitive avoidance has already demonstrated efficacy. The main reason is that a single-component treatment may require less clinical training and may be easier to disseminate on a wider scale. Also, if clients learn one powerful strategy and practice it in a focused and intensive way, they may be more likely to stick with it during treatment, and importantly, after treatment has ended.

To determine the therapeutic potential of the behavioral experiments intervention, we delivered it to seven participants with a primary diagnosis of GAD and assessed outcomes at pre-treatment and post-treatment, and at 3-month and 6-month follow-ups (Hebert & Dugas, 2018). Recruitment and assessment procedures were largely consistent with the ones we used in our clinical trials; however, we did not include a control condition. In the early phases of developing a treatment, small-scale, uncontrolled studies are common, as they allow researchers to test therapeutic potential in a cost-efficient way, before making a decision to proceed to a more resource-intensive randomized controlled trial.

On average, we observed large, statistically significant improvements in overall GAD severity, pathological worry, GAD-associated symptoms, anxiety symptoms, depressive symptoms, and intolerance of uncertainty that were comparable in magnitude to improvements we have observed in our other trials. We also assessed changes in GAD-relevant safety behaviors using a measure that we developed for the study and found large decreases in these behaviors. Six out of seven participants achieved GAD remission and five participants maintained GAD remission into the follow-up period. The majority of participants also met criteria for moderate-to-high end state functioning at post-treatment (six participants), and at 3-month (five participants) and 6-month (six participants) follow-up. With these promising preliminary findings, we have since proceeded to a randomized controlled trial comparing the new treatment to a wait-list control condition. The trial will provide answers to important questions about whether a single-component treatment focusing entirely on behavioral experiments can achieve the same, or even better, outcomes for people with GAD.

Conclusion

In this chapter, we reviewed randomized controlled trials of our treatment conducted by our research team and by other researchers. Thus far, the findings indicate that people who complete our treatment for GAD experience large improvements in their symptoms, and that the majority of clients achieve diagnostic remission. These results have led to a growth in the implementation of our treatment in a variety of clinical settings, which is very encouraging. Having said this, about 20 to 40% of clients do not fully benefit from our treatment (or any other CBT; Covin, Ouimet, Seeds, &, Dozois 2008; Fisher, 2006; Mitte, 2005). Therefore, we remain committed to discovering ways to boost the efficacy of our treatment in an efficient and cost-effective manner. This has involved identifying client characteristics (for example, cognitive style) and intervention-related factors (for example, sudden gains) that predict treatment success, and maximizing the treatment's potential by deepening what we believe to be the most powerful strategy in the protocol— behavioral experiments targeting negative beliefs about uncertainty.

CHAPTER 7

Addressing Complicating Factors

In this, the final chapter, we will review factors that can complicate treatment and discuss ways that therapists can deal with them. It is easy to consider complicating factors exclusively from the perspective of the client. However, there are a number of characteristics that relate both to the therapist and to the context in which the treatment is offered that should not be overlooked. Thus, what follows is a discussion of complicating factors organized into four categories: client factors, motivational factors, therapist factors, and contextual factors.

Client Factors

Client-complicating factors can be divided into what the client brings to the therapy session (intra-therapeutic factors) and what the client experiences outside of therapy (extra-therapeutic events). Although extra-therapeutic events (for example, an important deadline at work or an argument with a close relative) can play an important role in treatment, they will not be discussed here because we know very little about how the myriad life events that clients with GAD experience combine and interact to influence the outcome of treatment. On the other hand, based on the empirical data and our clinical experience, we are in a position to discuss the impact of intra-therapeutic factors on the delivery, receipt, and success of treatment. Specifically, we will review the following client factors: comorbidity with other *DSM-5* disorders, comorbidity with medical conditions, pregnancy, and medication use.

Comorbidity with DSM-5 Disorders

As mentioned at the outset of this book, psychiatric comorbidity in individuals with GAD is the norm rather than the exception. In fact, epidemiological surveys have found that the majority of individuals with GAD have at least one additional *Diagnostic and Statistical Manual of Mental Disorders (DSM)* diagnosis. For example, a World Health Organization study conducted across 26 countries showed that about 80% of respondents with a lifetime diagnosis of GAD also had one or more comorbid *DSM-IV* diagnoses, most typically major depressive disorder or another anxiety disorder (Ruscio et al., 2017). Given this high rate of comorbidity, the possibility that additional diagnoses can interfere with the treatment of GAD needs to be addressed. First, we will consider comorbidity with conditions that are not personality disorders (conditions formerly referred to in the *DSM* as Axis I disorders). Then, we will consider the role of comorbidity with personality disorders (conditions formerly referred to in the *DSM* as Axis II disorders). There are two factors that limit conclusions about the impact of comorbidity on the efficacy of CBT for GAD, and likewise, the effects of CBT on comorbidity: (1) most of our knowledge comes from randomized controlled trials, which routinely exclude individuals for whom participation may be contraindicated, for example, those with a comorbid bipolar disorder, severe major depressive disorder, or substance use disorder; and (2) typically, only a subset of possible *DSM* disorders are assessed in clinical trials and in treatment settings due to constraints on time and limited resources. Personality disorders in particular may go entirely unassessed. Therefore, readers should keep these limiting factors in mind as they read the following section on comorbidity.

Although the presence of *comorbid depressive and anxiety-related disorders* coincides with a more severe form of GAD (Newman, Przeworski, Fisher, & Borkovec, 2010), a perusal of the GAD treatment literature suggests that this kind of comorbidity is not as much of a problem as was once thought. For example, there is evidence that the presence of comorbid depressive or anxiety-related disorders does not necessarily have a negative impact on treatment adherence and efficacy (e.g., Newman et al., 2010). Moreover, the successful treatment of GAD often leads to decreases in the severity of comorbid depressive and anxiety-related disorders, even when these conditions are not addressed in therapy (Borkovec, Abel, & Newman, 1995; Newman et al., 2010). In fact, one analysis of findings from a randomized controlled trial showed that those with comorbid depressive or anxiety disorders (in this case, major depressive disorder, social anxiety disorder, or specific phobia) actually showed greater improvement in their GAD symptoms following psychotherapy (cognitive or behavioral therapies, or their combination) than did those with "pure" GAD (Newman et al., 2010). Also, many of the participants no longer suffered from their comorbid diagnoses following treatment. The authors proposed a couple of explanations for these counterintuitive findings. First, given that those with comorbid diagnoses had more severe GAD at the outset, they may have had more "room for improvement" than did those without comorbidity, as reflected in greater drops in scores on outcome measures. Second, cognitive and behavioral strategies used in the treatment of GAD may have had a broad generalized effect on processes that are common across most depressive and anxiety disorders; namely, repetitive negative thinking and avoidance. Although these findings are encouraging, there nonetheless is some evidence that the presence of certain comorbid conditions, for example, panic disorder, may have a detrimental impact on the treatment of GAD (Brown & Barlow, 1992). Thus, it seems that the question of comorbidity is a complex one, and that some comorbid conditions have a greater impact on treatment efficacy than do others.

In analyzing the data from our own treatment studies, we consistently found that Axis I comorbidity did not negatively impact treatment outcome. In other words, successfully treated participants had just as many comorbid Axis I conditions as those who did not fully benefit from treatment. However, it is possible (and even probable) that each of our treatment studies did not have a sufficient sample size to allow us to properly test the hypothesis of lower efficacy in participants with this kind of comorbidity. In order to correctly address this question, we pooled the data from three completed treatment studies and reexamined the impact of Axis I comorbidity on treatment outcome (Provencher, Ladouceur, & Dugas, 2006). We found that 73% of participants had at least one comorbid Axis I condition, with the most common additional diagnoses being specific phobia, social anxiety disorder, panic disorder, and major depressive disorder. The pooled data also showed that following the treatment of GAD, there was a decrease in the number of comorbid conditions despite the fact that they were not addressed in treatment. Finally, we found that although Axis I comorbidity did not affect outcome immediately following the end of treatment, a different pattern emerged at 6-month follow-up. Specifically, follow-up outcomes were less favorable for participants with panic disorder or with multiple comorbid conditions. Thus, it appears that clients with comorbid panic disorder or with several additional conditions might receive significantly fewer benefits in the long term from the treatment described in this book.

Although it is difficult to speculate on the many ways in which the presence of comorbid depressive and anxiety-related disorders can have a negative impact following therapy (and we will not do so here), our experience with clients who have a comorbid diagnosis of panic disorder suggests that being high in *anxiety sensitivity* may interfere with the maintenance of treatment gains. Anxiety sensitivity can be assessed using a brief scale called the Anxiety Sensitivity Index (Taylor et al., 2007). Individuals who are high in anxiety sensitivity have strongly held beliefs about the dangerousness of experiencing anxiety; specifically, that it can lead to negative physical, social, or cognitive consequences. Individuals who hold these beliefs are very attuned to uncomfortable changes in their body and tend to interpret innocuous bodily sensations in a catastrophic way. Although anxiety sensitivity was once considered a risk factor for panic disorder, research has shown that it is a transdiagnostic factor (Schmidt, Zvolensky, & Maner, 2006); thus even people with other anxiety disorders, major depressive disorder, or substance use disorders can be high in anxiety sensitivity. Research has shown that individuals who are high in anxiety sensitivity have poorer outcomes following CBT for pathological anxiety than do those with moderate levels of anxiety sensitivity (Wolitzky-Taylor, Arch, Rosenfield, & Craske, 2012). We have not studied anxiety sensitivity as a moderator of outcome following our own treatment, but our clinical observations support this finding. We have found that treatment completers who are high in anxiety sensitivity sometimes fall back into the habit of trying to avoid or neutralize their worries, or return to engaging in safety behaviors, in an effort to avoid experiencing anxiety. These behaviors may lead to a resurgence of excessive worry and anxiety following treatment. Thus, for clients who are high in anxiety sensitivity, the therapist might want to spend additional time on the behavioral experiments and exposure modules of the treatment in order to help them to continue facing their occasional distressing thoughts and anxiety once therapy has ended. On a case-by-case basis, the therapist may also decide to incorporate interoceptive exposure and in vivo exposure to panic-relevant situations into their protocols, to address anxiety sensitivity more directly (see Labrecque, Dugas, Marchand, & Letarte, 2006). Finally, the therapist might consider scheduling a few booster sessions following treatment so that emerging difficulties can be dealt with before they lead to a significant deterioration in the client's state.

Another complicating factor that clients can bring to therapy relates to *personality style or the presence of comorbid personality disorders.* One study suggests that about half of people with GAD have a co-occurring personality disorder (Sanderson, Wetzler, Beck, & Betz, 1994). In fact, some researchers have suggested that GAD, especially when chronic and severe, may be the manifestation of an underlying personality disorder (Przeworski et al., 2011). Although many therapists believe that clients who have rigid and inflexible ways of relating to others benefit less from anxiety disorder treatments, the data do not provide a clear picture in the case of GAD. Some researchers suggest that the presence of personality disorders has a negligible impact on the efficacy of CBT for GAD (e.g., Dreessen, Arntz, Luttels, & Sallaerts, 1994) whereas others suggest that a comorbid personality disorder can lead to maladaptive interpersonal processes that may complicate the course and treatment of GAD (Newman, Llera, Erickson, Przeworski, & Castonguay, 2013). While there is limited research specifically on the comorbidity of GAD and *DSM* personality disorders, there is considerable research on problematic interpersonal styles, and their role in GAD and its treatment. Given that significant disturbances in interpersonal functioning typify personality disorders, research on interpersonal functioning in GAD is highly relevant and informative. Using a scale called the Inventory of Interpersonal Problems Circumplex, researchers have uncovered four distinct problematic interpersonal styles in clients with GAD: an intrusive type, an overly accommodating type, a cold/distant type, and a nonassertive type (Przeworski et al., 2011; Salzer et al., 2008). These personality styles overlap with the DSM personality disorders; for example, in a sample of people with GAD, the majority of people with a nonassertive interpersonal style also endorsed traits consistent with avoidant personality disorder (Przeworski et al., 2011).

A study showed that those who continued to report problematic interpersonal styles at the end of CBT for GAD had worse outcomes following treatment, supporting the idea that problematic interpersonal functioning can hinder successful treatment of GAD (Borkovec et al., 2002). Using sophisticated statistical methods, pretreatment personality style as a prospective predictor of response to cognitive and behavioral interventions for GAD was examined most recently (Newman, Jacobson, Erickson, & Fisher, 2017). Clients with domineering or intrusive personality styles were found to be more responsive to behavioral interventions such as applied relaxation and diaphragmatic breathing than to cognitive interventions such as cognitive reevaluation.

Taken together, research by other groups suggests that personality disorders and problematic interpersonal styles may be predictors of individual variations in response to psychotherapy. In terms of the treatment described in this book, we have yet to examine the relationship between comorbid personality disorders and treatment outcome. This is quite simply because we did not systematically assess clients for the presence of personality disorders in our previous clinical trials. However, our clinical experience has been similar to that of many other therapists. That is, we have observed that certain personality styles appear to be associated with lower treatment adherence and enactment, as well as poorer treatment outcomes. For example, we have noticed that GAD clients with elevated levels of avoidant-related beliefs often have difficulty with the problem-solving and written exposure modules of treatment. Given that both these treatment modules require clients to endure discomfort in the short term in order to make progress in the longer term, beliefs such as "I should avoid unpleasant situations at all costs" and "I cannot tolerate unpleasant feelings" can seriously interfere with treatment adherence and enactment. When working with these clients, we have found it useful to proceed at a slower pace and address the avoidant-related beliefs and low distress tolerance as they come up during therapy. Similarly, we have also found that clients with Cluster B personality features (for example, impulsive behavior in the face of distress, emotional lability, high anger) often have difficulty applying sound problem-solving principles. In cases such as these, we typically extend the problem-solving module of treatment to allow clients to "experiment" and compare impulsive and rational problem-solving approaches.

Although the actual impact of specific personality disorders on the efficacy of our GAD treatment has not been formally assessed, the aforementioned examples provide some ideas as to how certain personality features may make treatment challenging. We will continue to pay close attention to the interactions between the various personality styles of our GAD clients and their treatment outcomes.

Comorbidity with Medical Conditions

Comorbidity with medical conditions can also affect the treatment of GAD. Although, to our knowledge, there are no published data on the relationship between the presence of medical conditions and the efficacy of psychological treatments for individuals with GAD, it is clear that some medical conditions require special attention. For example, a client with a significant heart condition might require medical clearance to proceed with written exposure given the potential impact of exposure on heart rate and exertion. Having said this, we have found that in the vast majority of cases, clients with heart conditions are given the "green light" by their cardiologist to engage in exposure. Thus, our experience has been that only a small minority of cardiac patients should not employ exposure methods. Typically, these individuals have serious heart conditions that require them to avoid most forms of physical exertion. Obviously, very few individuals have such serious heart conditions.

A second medical issue that may impact the course of treatment is when a client has had a serious disease that is in remission. For GAD clients who have had a serious medical condition such as cancer, it is no surprise that cancer relapse is often a central worry theme. In such situations, the therapist may wonder if written exposure to a scenario involving cancer relapse is appropriate, both from a clinical and ethical point of view. Although we have not encountered many of these situations, we have found it useful to address them on a case-by-case basis. If the client is excessively worried about relapse, is not at high risk for relapse, and is willing to undergo exposure to mental images depicting relapse, then the use of written exposure is probably appropriate. However, if these conditions are not met, then worry about relapse may be dealt with using other strategies such as problem solving with either an instrumental or emotional focus.

Pregnancy

Readers should be aware that questions of when and how to use exposure-based strategies for pregnant clients are currently being discussed in the anxiety disorders literature, with the consensus at the moment being that more direct research addressing these questions is needed, particularly from an integrative biopsychosocial approach that takes into account the physiological changes that occur during pregnancy (Arch, Dimidjian, & Chessick, 2012).

We have found that some pregnant women are reluctant to experience the "negative thoughts" that make up their worst-case scenarios during exposure. For these women, the idea of focusing on threatening mental images during pregnancy runs counter to the notion of a harmonious pregnancy filled with positive and calming thoughts. The desire to avoid exposure to mental images of feared hypothetical scenarios may be particularly strong when the scenarios concern childbirth or the health of the child. Furthermore, many pregnant women follow preparatory classes (such as Lamaze classes) that emphasize the importance of relaxation and positive thoughts. In situations such as these, we have found it useful to again treat each client on a case-by-case basis. Although we are steadfast proponents of exposure for worries about hypothetical situations, it is our opinion that the therapist should show the utmost sensitivity to the pregnant client's wishes. Given that pregnancy is such a significant life event and that it is time-limited, we believe that it is most appropriate to forego written exposure for women who have pregnancy-related worries, but are opposed to engaging in exposure. For these women, it might be more helpful to simply encourage them to experience these worries without using neutralization or avoidance strategies, and to concentrate more on other strategies, like behavioral experiments targeting intolerance of uncertainty.

Medication Use

As mentioned previously, many individuals with GAD use some form of medication for their worry, anxiety, and associated symptoms. It is interesting to note that although the impact of medication on CBT for GAD is the subject of considerable debate, no known study has yet to systematically address this question. For some, the use of medication can enhance the efficacy of CBT because clients are better able to fully engage in treatment and develop new skills if their worry and anxiety are to some extent under control. For others, the use of medication (particularly, benzodiazepines) may reduce the short- and long-term efficacy of CBT in the following ways: (1) specific treatment interventions that involve experiential learning and confrontation of feared situations may not achieve their full effects; (2) clients may ascribe their treatment gains to their medication rather than to the psychotherapeutic interventions; or (3) medication discontinuation might bring about a relapse of GAD symptoms. In our opinion, the use of medication is most problematic when clients attribute their progress to their medication rather than to the day-to-day changes that result from their active involvement in CBT. In particular, these clients may be at risk for relapse when medication is eventually decreased or discontinued. Thus, for clients taking medication, the therapist should systematically assess attributions about progress, and address beliefs that reflect an *external locus of control* ("My progress is the result of my medication and not a consequence of my hard work"). The more that medicated clients can ascribe their progress to their own efforts, the more they will be in a position to fully benefit from CBT both in the short and long term.

In an excellent review article on the compatibility of medication and cognitive behavioral approaches to anxiety disorders, Henny Westra and Sherry Stewart (1998) concluded that medication can in fact interfere with CBT, and that the use of high potency benzodiazepines is most problematic for the success of CBT for the anxiety disorders. In particular, it appears that high-potency benzodiazepines can have a detrimental impact on CBT for anxiety because both modes of treatment are based on somewhat contradictory premises (for example, benzodiazepines aim to decrease anxiety whereas CBT aims to modify catastrophic beliefs about anxiety). Although the authors make some compelling arguments against combining benzodiazepines with CBT for the treatment of anxiety, the general issue of combination treatments for GAD awaits study in a sufficiently powered, well-controlled study.

In our clinical trials, the percentage of participants taking medication for their GAD symptoms was 35% in the initial individual treatment study (Ladouceur, Dugas, Freeston et al., 2000), 21% in the group treatment study (Dugas, Ladouceur, Léger, Freeston et al., 2003), and 55% in the CBT/applied relaxation treatment study (Dugas et al., 2010). Although none of our studies were designed to assess the impact of medication on treatment efficacy, we were able to compare outcomes for participants with and without medication in all three studies. Simply stated, medication status was unrelated to treatment outcome in each study; clients taking medication did no better or worse than clients who were not taking medication. For example, in an unpublished analysis of the data from the CBT/applied relaxation study, we found that medication status was unrelated to treatment outcome in terms of overall GAD severity, pathological worry, GAD associated symptoms, associated anxiety, and depression. It should be noted, however, that because of the limited sample size, we were unable to properly test for the impact of specific types of medication on treatment outcome. Further, because we required that participants taking medication have a stable dose (i.e., at intake, no change in dose for the past four weeks for benzodiazepines and the past 12 weeks for antidepressants), we were unable to assess the impact of medication for clients who start both medication and CBT *at the same time*. Given that this is often the case, future studies should contrast CBT alone and CBT with medication when both are initiated concurrently.

To summarize, although the impact of medication use on the efficacy of CBT for GAD is the subject of heated debate, no known study has yet to properly address this issue. It seems safe to say, however, that medication does not have a prominent effect on the treatment described in this book as preliminary analyses of the data from all treatment studies show that medication use is unrelated to short- and long-term outcomes. For now, therefore, it appears that the use of medication does not typically pose a serious threat to the treatment procedures described in this book.

Motivational Factors

Any therapist treating GAD will, at some point, have an ambivalent client who does not appear to be making much progress in treatment. A client may have many positive beliefs about worry that are resistant to change, either because they are difficult to disprove or because they are closely tied to the client's value system (e.g., "Good people worry about others"). Similarly, the client may perceive important secondary gains to having GAD such as not being asked to take on certain responsibilities at home or at work. Or, the client may not be "ready for action"; in terms of stages of change theory, most clients struggling with motivation are in the stages of contemplation (that is, aware of the problem but not committed to action) or preparation (that is, ready to take only small steps; Prochaska & Norcross, 2001).

A key factor that will be discussed here is *treatment motivation*. Like all "action-oriented" therapies, CBT requires a considerable amount of motivation on the part of the client. Given that the client is expected to actively collaborate with the therapist and carry out between-session exercises that involve considerable time and energy, it is critically important to consider the roles of *both* the client and the therapist in client motivation. Indeed, the client *and* therapist both contribute to the success or nonsuccess of the therapy endeavor, which is the reason we are not conceptualizing motivation as solely a client factor.

The general question of how motivation affects CBT outcomes has long been recognized in the anxiety disorders literature. For example, researchers have tried to understand how factors like compliance with between-session exercises relate to treatment outcome. However, systematic, theory-driven research on motivation and its role in CBT for anxiety disorders has appeared mainly in the last 15 years, largely inspired by Miller and Rollnick's (2002) seminal work on motivational interviewing, an intervention that targets ambivalence (Marker & Norton, 2018). Fortunately for readers of this book, Henny Westra and her research team at York

University in Canada have made major contributions to the understanding of client motivation in CBT for GAD. In the following paragraphs, we summarize key findings from their research.

In an initial trial, Westra and colleagues (2009) examined the extent to which four sessions of motivational interviewing ahead of a full course of CBT improved outcomes for people with GAD. One group received 14 hours of CBT (applied relaxation, cognitive interventions, and exposure) without the motivational interviewing pre-treatment whereas the other group received the same CBT protocol preceded by motivational interviewing. They found that those who received the motivational interviewing pre-treatment reported a larger reduction in pathological worry than did those who received only CBT. A closer analysis revealed that motivational interviewing appeared to benefit those who entered treatment with the most severe levels of worry. Although this particular group lost of some of their treatment gains over the 1-year follow-up, it was clear that they were still doing better than were their counterparts who had not received motivational interviewing. With these promising findings, Westra and her team (2016) proceeded to a more involved randomized controlled trial, focusing specifically on those with severe GAD. In one condition, participants received 15 weeks of CBT integrated with motivational interviewing; whereas, those in the other condition received 15 weeks of CBT alone. The CBT protocol consisted of a mix of strategies drawn from other treatments and included psychoeducation, progressive muscle relaxation, and cognitive reevaluation. Both treatments led to equivalent reductions in worry from pre-treatment to post-treatment; however, during the 1-year follow-up period, worry declines were steeper for those who had received the motivation-based CBT, suggesting that this group continued to improve. Those who received this treatment were also more likely to meet criteria for clinically significant change.

Taken together, Westra and colleagues' trials provide important evidence that actively addressing motivational processes in the treatment of GAD strengthens the outcomes of those with severe GAD. Using video recordings of treatment sessions from their clinical trials, Westra and colleagues have uncovered several important insights regarding *ambivalence* and *resistance* during CBT for GAD. Ambivalence about change refers to an "intrapsychic conflict," the essence of which is, "I want to, I don't want to" (Button, Westra, Hara, & Aviram, 2015). Resistance, on the other hand, is interpersonal and manifests as behavior that "opposes, blocks, diverts, or impedes the direction of the therapist" (Button et al., 2015). Westra and her team have studied ambivalence and resistance by observing and coding in detail the "motivational language" that clients with GAD use in treatment sessions. The key takeaways from their research are described below.

Although ambivalence and resistance are related constructs, it seems that *resistance* is the more important predictor of poorer outcome following CBT for GAD. Westra and her team found that early signs of resistance, but not ambivalence, predicted less improvement in pathological worry at the end of CBT (Button et al., 2015). In fact, early resistance accounted for 30% of the variance in outcome, which is staggering. It has been proposed that the way in which therapists manage resistance makes a difference in outcomes. For example, some therapists become less collaborative and more directive in response to client resistance, and this may contribute to ruptures in the therapeutic alliance that negatively affect treatment progress and outcome (Hara, Westra, Constantino, & Antony, 2018). Resistance in CBT as early as in the first session predicts lower compliance with between-session exercises, so this may be another pathway by which outcomes are negatively affected.

In addition, therapists may not always be aware of resistance, particularly when it is subtle. When the ratings of therapists and trained observers were compared, Westra and her team found that there was only moderate correspondence in their perceptions of clients' resistance. Moreover, the trained observers' ratings of resistance predicted homework noncompliance and post-treatment worry, whereas those of therapists did not (Hara et al., 2015). These findings emphasize the importance of training therapists to spot early signs of resistance in session (for example, by watching and discussing video recordings of treatment sessions) and suggest that detection of resistance is a trainable skill that could translate into better outcomes for CBT clients (Hara et al., 2015).

We have also examined the role of client motivation in our own clinical trials, albeit in a less detailed way. We typically assess treatment motivation and other common therapy factors (that is, client expectations vis-à-vis therapy and client perceptions of the therapist's characteristics) using standardized self-report questionnaires. In line with other treatment studies, we assess common therapy factors following the third treatment session. In our opinion, this is the most appropriate timing because it strikes a balance between clients being able to form an opinion about the treatment and the therapist, without being so far along in therapy that their opinion is unduly influenced by their progress. Overall, the findings from our treatment studies suggest that level of client motivation significantly predicts both short- and long-term outcomes. In fact, it appears that motivation is a stronger predictor of outcome than either client expectations or therapist characteristics. For example, by combining the data from our first two clinical trials, we found that although ratings of motivation, expectations, and therapist characteristics were related to each other, only treatment motivation predicted the extent of pre- to post-treatment change in pathological worry (Léger, Dugas, Langlois, & Ladouceur, 1998). Moreover, subsequent analyses of the follow-up data from the group treatment study showed that treatment motivation (again, assessed following the third therapy session) predicted overall GAD severity at 6-month and 2-year follow-ups (Dugas, Ladouceur, Léger, Langlois et al., 2003). Once more, although client expectations and therapist characteristics were related to treatment motivation, they did not predict long-term outcomes. Therefore, it appears that low treatment motivation is a considerable complicating factor for the treatment protocol described in this book. Having acknowledged the potential negative impact of low treatment motivation, we now turn our attention to the question of what can be done to increase client motivation.

For unmotivated clients who do not seem to be ambivalent about change, the therapist should consider the possibility that the treatment's rationale has not been properly presented or discussed. If this appears to be the case, the therapist should of course revisit the treatment's underlying principles and address all client questions and concerns about the logic behind the treatment procedures. The therapist may also want to reflect on relationship factors that may be contributing to the client's low motivation. For example, it may be that the therapist's "natural style" is not ideally suited to the needs of a particular client and that a slight adjustment in how the therapist relates to the client is warranted. For a client with marked dependent personality traits, for example, the therapist may want to adopt a more "nurturing" attitude in the initial stages of treatment and progressively move to a true collaboration with the client in the later stages of therapy. Thus, when unmotivated clients do not appear to be ambivalent about change, therapists should reflect on how they might be contributing to low motivation. As always, an open and nondefensive discussion about potential sources of low motivation can be very useful in helping therapists better respond to the client's needs in order to foster greater treatment motivation.

In summary, we, and others, have found that motivational processes play an important role in clients' response to CBT for GAD. Ambivalence about change is not in itself detrimental to treatment outcome; however, it can lead to client behaviors reflecting resistance. Resistance, especially when it occurs early in treatment, is a significant predictor of lower engagement in between-session exercises, and of poorer outcomes following treatment. It can also cause therapists to become less collaborative in their work with clients, which may undermine clients' sense of autonomy and self-efficacy. For this reason, it is important for therapists to attend to, and address behaviors reflecting resistance. This can be challenging to do in session, but research shows that detection of resistance is a skill that can be honed. With clients who are very high in pathological worry or who are ambivalent about addressing their GAD, integration of motivational interviewing prior to, and throughout CBT may be especially helpful. An excellent resource is Miller and Rollnick's influential book on motivation interviewing (Miller & Rollnick, 2012).

Therapist Factors

We also want to share our clinical impressions of some therapist factors that can play a role in the way clients respond to treatment. These include, but are not limited to, insensitivity to specific client needs, low treatment confidence, and the rigid use of treatment manuals.

Insensitivity to Specific Client Needs

All clients have specific needs. For example, some clients need to spend some time discussing the childhood origins of their adult worry and anxiety, whereas others need to get right down to "the business" of change. Some clients need the therapist to be directive during the first few treatment sessions, whereas others need to be involved in all treatment decisions right from the outset of therapy. Finally, some clients react well to (appropriate) therapist self-disclosure, whereas others feel uncomfortable when the therapist self discloses. These are just a few examples of the many specific needs that clients bring to therapy. Obviously, if the therapist adopts a "one size fits all" attitude, many clients will not fully benefit from treatment.

One way to think about how the therapist can adapt to each client's needs and still offer a treatment of choice for GAD (whether it be the treatment described in this book or another empirically supported treatment), is to distinguish treatment procedures from how they are presented to clients. That is, meeting a client's specific needs does not mean that the therapist does away with empirically supported procedures such as behavioral experiments and written exposure, but it might mean that these strategies are presented and carried out in a way that is "palatable" to the client. Thus, the modules of the treatment described in this book can be "wrapped" differently for each client. As a result, the examples of therapist dialogue provided in Chapter 5 should be adapted to fit not only with the therapist's clinical style, but also with the needs of each individual client.

Low Treatment Confidence

A second therapist factor that can seriously complicate the therapy enterprise is low treatment confidence. Given that clients are asked to engage in a treatment that is quite demanding in terms of time and effort, it is very important that the therapist model a high level of confidence in the treatment's rationale and procedures. For example, if during the problem-solving phase of treatment, a client applies a solution that does not lead to the desired outcome, the therapist should model a calm and confident attitude to help the client see that it is quite normal that initial problem-solving attempts are sometimes unsuccessful. In line with having a confident attitude, the therapist could point out that the ultimate goal of problem solving is not that clients solve all their problems, but rather that they acquire a "tool" that is known to be helpful for dealing with most problems. This illustrates an important point for therapists to keep in mind: being confident in treatment does not mean that one is confident that every strategy will be helpful at all times; it simply means that one is confident that the underlying principles are sound and that the strategies will be helpful in most cases.

Low treatment confidence on the part of the therapist can be particularly obstructive when a client encounters bad luck in carrying out a between-session exercise; however, it is important to stand by the principles of the treatment even when exercises do not work out exactly as planned. We suggest in fact that encountering "bad luck" while carrying out planned exercises may be an especially enlightening learning opportunity for people who are intolerant of uncertainty (and for their therapists!). One of us (MR) offers the following case example of "bad luck" in carrying out a behavioral experiment: a client who signed up to participate in a bike race needed a new bike and was struggling considerably with making this purchase. In this particular situation, the client's safety behaviors involved excessive online research into the specifications and prices of various bikes, excessive reading of reviews across multiple websites, and many return trips to bike shops without making a purchase. When asked about his concerns regarding going into a store and purchasing a new bike, the client reported fearing that he would pick the wrong bike for the race, that he would have problems with it during the race that would significantly affect his performance and ruin his experience, and that it will have been a waste of time and money. His behavioral experiment was to buy a new bike for the upcoming bike race. He was to go to his local bike shop, take a reasonable amount of time to look through the options, select one, buy it, and commit to the decision while sitting with the uncertainty about whether or not he made the best choice. At the next session, the client reported that he completed the experiment as discussed, however the actual outcome was quite negative. The client did indeed have problems with the bike while riding it during the race; there was a problem with the pedals, and he ultimately had to stop participating in the race. He then encountered issues at the bike shop when he brought it back and attempted to negotiate a repair. When discussing his coping, he felt that he had not managed the situation well; he reported that he became extremely frustrated and angry with himself when his bike did not perform as expected, and he saw this as poor coping on his part.

From the client's perspective, the experiment confirmed his fears: the bike failed to perform, he could not take part in the race, and he ended up having to pay a fee to get the (already expensive) bike repaired. This led to a discussion about the reality of facing uncertainty-inducing situations; when one invites uncertainty into their life, there is always the possibility that things will go awry. The goal is not for clients to see that negative outcomes *never* arise; rather to see just how often they do arise (infrequently), how catastrophic they *really* are (not nearly as bad as expected), and how capable they are of managing them (much more capable than anticipated). It is worth noting that this experiment was the 40th that the client had carried out in treatment, and all his other experiments had benign or positive outcomes. Thus, an important part of the post-experiment discussion involved viewing this one "failed" experiment within the broader context of 39 other successful (or at least, benign) experiments. The client concluded that if one out of every 40 experiments is negative like this one, then that is a number he can accept. The benefit of inviting uncertainty, refraining from safety behaviors, and ultimately worrying less, was more valuable to him than avoiding an occasional negative outcome.

Rigid Use of Treatment Manuals

Since the rise of the use of treatment manuals, there has been much debate about their clinical usefulness. Proponents of manualized treatments argue that they are useful for guiding therapists and clients through the different phases of specific treatment protocols, most of which have received at least some empirical support. Opponents of treatment manuals disagree with this position, and argue that the use of manuals leads to a rigid and one-size-fits-all approach to therapy that often devalues the role of common therapy factors such as therapist empathy and the therapeutic relationship. As the reader may guess, our position is closer to the former: we believe that manualized treatments *per se* are not the problem; rather, it is their improper use that can interfere with the therapist's ability to help clients benefit from treatment. Although manualized treatments can be improperly used in any number of ways, we will restrict our discussion to a common error that therapists make when using treatment manuals; namely, applying the manual in a rigid, inflexible manner.

One of the challenges faced by authors of treatment manuals (ourselves included) is to present the procedures in a way that invites their flexible use. We believe that this can best be accomplished by thoroughly discussing the theory behind the interventions, and presenting the specific procedures as *examples* of interventions that can target the underlying model components (such as intolerance of uncertainty). In this way, therapists are better able to adapt the treatment to the client's needs because they have a "theoretical blueprint" that guides them through the different phases of treatment. That is, what is most important is not the "what" (the specific treatment procedure) but the "why" (the goal of a procedure). For example, to help a client increase their tolerance for uncertainty, the therapist may use traditional cognitive reevaluation procedures to directly challenge the client's beliefs about uncertainty. Although the cognitive reevaluation of beliefs about uncertainty is not explicitly included in the treatment described in this book, it may be helpful for some clients who are initially unable to engage in behavioral experiments targeting intolerance of uncertainty due to strongly held beliefs about the dangerousness of uncertainty. Thus, therapists who have a good grasp of the principles that underlie the procedures described in a treatment manual are often able to apply the treatment in a flexible and individualized manner. Consequently, one of the most effective ways that therapists can counter the tendency to use manualized treatments in a rigid fashion is to ensure that they have a firm grasp of the theoretical underpinnings of the suggested procedures.

Another way that therapists can resist the temptation to use a manualized treatment in a nonflexible fashion is to consistently remind themselves that common therapy factors make a vital contribution to successful treatment outcomes (e.g., Asay & Lambert, 1999). For example, a number of therapist characteristics appear to be decisive in the establishment of a positive therapeutic alliance and, ultimately, positive treatment outcomes. These include having a caring and involved attitude, modeling self-confidence, unconditionally accepting the client, challenging the client when appropriate, presenting material and issues in a clear and explicit way, and being willing to self-disclose when suitable (Williams & Chambless, 1990). Returning to a point made earlier, many empirical and review articles on the treatment of GAD start out by saying that up to half of individuals with GAD do not fully benefit from treatment. These articles often go on to say that this implies that our theoretical models of GAD require further refinement, without any mention of the possibility that common therapy factors such as therapist characteristics may be contributing to the fact that many clients do not fully benefit from treatment. This is surprising given that common therapy factors, such as those mentioned above, play such a vital role in the success or nonsuccess of treatment. Thus, the fact that 25 to 50% of GAD clients do not fully benefit from different forms of CBT might be the result of specific therapy factors (i.e., a lack of refinement of GAD-specific theories and treatments), common therapy factors (i.e., client, therapist, and contextual factors), or both specific and common therapy factors. It seems reasonable to assume that a combination of both types of therapy factors ultimately plays a role in the less than optimal success rates of all GAD treatments, including the treatment described in this book. By keeping this is mind, therapists may be better able to display the positive attitudes and behaviors listed above and consequently apply the principles and procedures of manualized treatments in a flexible and personalized way.

Contextual Factors

Many contextual factors can complicate treatment delivery and interfere with successful outcomes. Here, we discuss one of the most common contextual factors that can complicate the proper delivery of any psychological treatment: namely, the restricted number of psychotherapy sessions typically covered by insurance companies and managed care organizations.

The treatment presented in this book is typically administered over 12 to 16 sessions. Given the multiple treatment modules, and our recommendation to spend considerable time on behavioral experiments targeting intolerance of uncertainty, 12 sessions is probably the minimum number of sessions required to cover all of the elements of treatment (with 14 to 16 sessions being preferable in most cases). In the current health care context, however, where fewer than 10 treatment sessions are typically covered by insurance companies and managed health care organizations, the full treatment described in this book cannot always be offered. In situations such as these, the therapist might be at a loss as to what to do. Should each treatment module be covered briefly, or should some modules be eliminated from the treatment in order to maintain the full duration of the remaining modules?

One of the strengths of our treatment protocol is that clients develop and hone a variety of skills that can be used for a broad range of anxiety-related problems. When clients become believers in these strategies, they arguably possess the most important set of skills for the prevention of further anxiety-related problems. Thus, if possible, the therapist should strive to provide the *full* treatment protocol as described in this book, to all clients with GAD. However, if this is not possible, it is best to eliminate modules and deliver the remaining ones in depth for maximum learning and consolidation. Early in our program of research, we tested two truncated versions of our treatment (Provencher, Dugas, & Ladouceur, 2004). We used a case formulation approach to identify the predominant worry type (that is, worry about ongoing problems or worry about hypothetical situations) for 18 clients with a primary diagnosis of GAD. First, we found that it was possible to reliably determine the main worry type for each client. We then proceeded to offer different scaled-down versions of the treatment to each group of participants: those who worried mainly about ongoing, real-life problems received problem-solving training whereas those who worried mainly about hypothetical situations engaged in exposure to mental imagery of feared hypothetical situations. Overall, we found that both versions of the treatment were effective, with no significant differences between the two; however, this truncated approach to the treatment of GAD did not appear to be as effective as the full treatment protocol. We have since discovered that a far more promising way to streamline our treatment is to harness the power of behavioral experiments targeting intolerance of uncertainty.

As discussed in Chapter 6, over the last several years, we have been working on a treatment that consists of one main strategy: behavioral experiments targeting intolerance of uncertainty. We believe that behavioral experiments carry the greatest potential for deep-seated and lasting changes in the cognitive, emotional, and behavioral processes underpinning GAD. We are currently testing this new treatment in a wait-list controlled randomized controlled trial. The pilot work that informed this ongoing trial suggests for the moment that the streamlined treatment produces outcomes that are similar to those we have observed with our complete treatment, suggesting that it is a promising alternative when insurance or managed care coverage limits the number of therapy sessions.

In the preceding sections, we have reviewed the main factors that can complicate the delivery, receipt, and enactment of the treatment described in this book. Although there are many other potential complicating factors, we have tried to focus on those that are most frequently encountered by therapists using our treatment protocol.

Concluding Remarks

When we set out to write a second edition of our book, we had a number of goals in mind. First, we wanted to provide therapists with up-to-date information on GAD. This seemed particularly important given the widely held assumptions that individuals with GAD are "worried well" and that the symptoms of GAD lead only to minor distress and impairment. As anyone with GAD will attest, experiencing chronic and excessive worry and anxiety on a daily basis is highly distressing and seriously interferes with one's quality of life.

A second goal of ours was to present therapists with a more elaborated *theoretical model* that can guide their clinical practice with GAD clients. In doing so, we hoped that therapists would be in a better position to conceptualize their clients' behaviors, thoughts, and emotional reactions in terms of a "theoretical blueprint" that could aid in making sense of the apparently contradictory manifestations of GAD. For example, approach behaviors such as information seeking and avoidance behaviors such as procrastination can both be seen as safety behaviors designed to reduce or avoid uncertainty, and as such ultimately serve a similar function. As readers will have noticed, we concentrate quite extensively on intolerance of uncertainty in this book, given its undeniably crucial role in pathological worry. Since writing the first edition of this book, we have learned so much more about how intolerance of uncertainty operates, and this new knowledge has influenced and shaped the way we conduct behavioral experiments with our clients with GAD. The behavioral experiments module of our treatment has evolved quite considerably, and we hope it provides clinicians with fresh ideas for ways to reduce intolerance of uncertainty and foster more balanced beliefs about uncertainty.

Our third (and perhaps primary) goal in writing this second edition was to strike a balance between presenting a clearly articulated treatment protocol that clinicians would find helpful in their everyday practice, and respecting the complex, dynamic, and idiosyncratic nature of the treatment of individuals with GAD. As discussed, many factors can complicate treatment delivery, receipt, and enactment. In most cases, the therapist can deal with the complicating factors by having a thorough understanding of the theoretical underpinnings of the treatment, the specific treatment procedures, and the common factors that underlie all forms of psychological treatments. Having said this, however, the therapy enterprise remains an extremely complex (and rewarding) endeavor that requires a great deal of knowledge, clinical judgment, and "positive attitude" on the part of the therapist. Given this state of affairs, our goal was to make available our treatment protocol to clinicians working with GAD clients, but to present it in a way that did not encourage a "cookbook" approach to treatment (the reader may have noticed that the word *technique* rarely appears in this book as we believe that it may give the impression that a given treatment procedure is not grounded in theory).

It was also our hope that this book would present the findings from our clinical trials in a way that would be "palatable" to clinicians. To accomplish this, we focused on the main findings of each study and emphasized the interpretation of the data over the presentation of the findings. Relatedly, we made every effort to present the data in a way that would help clinicians to truly feel confident about the treatment procedures. In our experience, when the therapist models self-confidence, clients stand a much better chance of fully benefiting from the treatment protocol.

On a final note, we would like to emphasize that the model and treatment described in this book continue to be works in progress. We are currently pursuing a number of lines of research that we hope will allow us to modify our theory and treatment in ways that are increasingly reflective of the clinical reality of GAD. By "following the data," we hope to be able to help more and more individuals suffering from GAD to finally break out of their worry and anxiety cycles and enjoy a greater quality of life.

References

Akiskal, H. S. (1998). Toward a definition of generalized anxiety disorder as an anxious temperament type. *Acta Psychiatrica Scandinavica, 98,* 66–73.

American Psychiatric Association. (1980). *Diagnostic and statistical manual of mental disorders* (3rd ed.). Washington, DC: American Psychiatric Association.

American Psychiatric Association. (1987). *Diagnostic and statistical manual of mental disorders* (3rd ed. Revised). Washington, DC: American Psychiatric Association.

American Psychiatric Association. (1994). *Diagnostic and statistical manual of mental disorders* (4th ed.). Washington, DC: American Psychiatric Association.

American Psychiatric Association. (2000). *Diagnostic and statistical manual of mental disorders: Text revision* (4th ed. Revised.). Washington, DC: American Psychiatric Association.

American Psychiatric Association. (2013). *Diagnostic and statistical manual of mental disorders* (5th ed.). Arlington, VA: American Psychiatric Publishing.

American Psychological Association Division 12. *Society of Clinical Psychology.* Retrieved from www.div12.org/psychological-treatments/

Anderson, K. G., Deschênes, S. S., & Dugas, M. J. (2016). Experimental manipulation of avoidable feelings of uncertainty: Effects on anger and anxiety. *Journal of Anxiety Disorders, 41,* 50–58.

Anderson, K. G., Dugas, M. J., Koerner, N., Radomsky, A. S., Savard, P., & Turcotte, J. (2012). Interpretive style and intolerance of uncertainty in individuals with anxiety disorders: A focus on generalized anxiety disorder. *Journal of Anxiety Disorders, 26,* 823–832.

Andrews, G., Hobbs, M. J., Borkovec, T. D., Beesdo, K., Craske, M. G., Heimberg, R. G., . . . Stanley, M. A. (2010). Generalized worry disorder: A review of DSM-IV generalized anxiety disorder and options for DSM-V. *Depression and Anxiety, 27,* 134–147.

Arch, J., Dimidjian, S., & Chessick, C. (2012). Are exposure-based cognitive behavioral therapies safe during pregnancy? *Archives of Women's Mental Health, 15,* 445–457.

217

Asay, T. P., & Lambert, M. J. (1999). The empirical case for the common factors in therapy: Quantitative findings. In M. A. Hubble, B. L. Duncan, & S. D. Miller (Eds.), *The heart and soul of change: What works in therapy* (pp. 23–55). Washington, DC: American Psychological Association.

Ashton, C. H. (2001). *Benzodiazepines: How they work and how to withdraw.* Newcastle upon Tyne, UK: Newcastle University.

Atkins, D. C., Bedics, J. D., McGlinchey, J. B., & Beauchaine, T. P. (2005). Assessing clinical significance: Does it matter which method we use? *Journal of Consulting and Clinical Psychology, 73*, 982–989.

Bakerman, D., Buhr, K., Koerner, N., & Dugas, M. J. (2004, November). *Exploring the link between positive beliefs about worry and worry.* Poster Presented at the Annual Convention of the Association for Advancement of Behavior Therapy, New Orleans, LA.

Barlow, D. H., Rapee, R. M., & Brown, T. A. (1992). Behavioral treatment of generalized anxiety disorder. *Behavior Therapy, 23*, 551–570.

Barlow, D. H., & Wincze, J. (1998). DSM-IV and beyond: What is generalized anxiety disorder? *Acta Psychiatrica Scandinavica, 98*, 23–29.

Barrett, J., Oxman, T. E., & Gerber, P. D. (1988). The prevalence of psychiatric disorders in primary care practice. *Archives of General Psychiatry, 45*, 1100–1106.

Beck, A. T., & Clark, D. A. (1997). An information processing model of anxiety: Automatic and strategic processes. *Behaviour Research and Therapy, 35*, 49–58.

Beck, A. T., & Emery, G. (1985). *Anxiety disorders and phobias: A cognitive perspective.* New York: Basic Books.

Beck, A. T., Epstein, N., Brown, G., & Steer, R. A. (1988). An inventory for measuring clinical anxiety: Psychometric properties. *Journal of Consulting and Clinical Psychology, 56*, 893–897.

Beck, A. T., Steer, R. A., & Brown, G. K. (1996). *Beck depression inventory manual* (2nd ed.). San Antonio, TX: Psychological Corporation.

Beekman, A. T. F., Bremmer, M. A., Deeg, D. J. H., Van Balkom, A. J. L. M., Smit, J. H., De Beurs, E., . . . van Tilburg, W. (1998). Anxiety disorders in later life: A report from the longitudinal aging study Amsterdam. *International Journal of Geriatric Psychiatry, 13*, 717–726.

Bennett-Levy, J. (2006). Therapist skills: A cognitive model of their acquisition and refinement. *Behavioural and Cognitive Psychotherapy, 34*, 57–78.

Blazer, D. G., Hughes, D., & George, L. K. (1987). Stressful life events and the onset of a generalized anxiety syndrome. *American Journal of Psychiatry, 144*, 1178–1183.

Blazer, D. G., Hughes, D., George, L. K., Schwartz, M., & Boyer, R. (1991). Generalized anxiety disorder. In L. N. Robins & D. A. Regier (Eds.), *Psychiatric disorders in America. The epidemiologic catchment area study* (pp. 180–203). New York: Free Press.

Bomyea, J., Ramsawh, H., Ball, T. M., Taylor, C. T., Paulus, M. P., Lang, A. J., & Stein, M. B. (2015). Intolerance of uncertainty as a mediator of reductions in worry in a cognitive behavioral treatment program for generalized anxiety disorder. *Journal of Anxiety Disorders, 33*, 90–94.

Borkovec, T. D. (2006). Applied relaxation and cognitive therapy for pathological worry and generalized anxiety disorder. In G. C. L. Davey & A. Wells (Eds.), *Worry and psychological disorders: Theory, assessment and treatment* (pp. 273–287). Chichester, UK: Wiley.

Borkovec, T. D., Abel, J. L., & Newman, H. (1995). Effects of psychotherapy on comorbid conditions in generalized anxiety disorder. *Journal of Consulting and Clinical Psychology, 63*, 479–483.

Borkovec, T. D., & Inz, J. (1990). The nature of worry in generalized anxiety disorder: A predominance of thought activity. *Behaviour Research and Therapy, 28*, 153–158.

Borkovec, T. D., Newman, M. G., Pincus, A. L., & Lytle, R. (2002). A component analysis of cognitive-behavioral therapy for generalized anxiety disorder and the role of interpersonal problems. *Journal of Consulting and Clinical Psychology, 70*, 288–298.

Borkovec, T. D., & Roemer, L. (1995). Perceived functions of worry among generalized anxiety disorder subjects: Distraction from more emotionally distressing topics? *Journal of Behaviour Therapy and Experimental Psychiatry, 26*, 25–30.

Brosschot, J. F., Verkuil, B., & Thayer, J. F. (2016). The default response to uncertainty and the importance of perceived safety in anxiety and stress: An evolution-theoretical perspective. *Journal of Anxiety Disorders, 41*, 22–34.

Brown, T. A., & Barlow, D. H. (1992). Comorbidity among anxiety disorders: Implications for treatment and *DSM-IV. Journal of Consulting and Clinical Psychology, 60*, 835–844.

Brown, T. A., & Barlow, D. H. (2014). *Anxiety and related disorders interview schedule for DSM-5 (ADIS-5)—adult and lifetime version: Clinical manual.* Oxford: Oxford University Press.

Brown, T. A., Barlow, D. H., & Liebowitz, M. R. (1994). The empirical basis of generalized anxiety disorder. *American Journal of Psychiatry, 151*, 1272–1280.

Brown, T. A., Chorpita, B. F., & Barlow, D. H. (1998). Structural relationships among dimensions of the *DSM—IV* anxiety and mood disorders and dimensions of negative affect, positive affect, and autonomic arousal. *Journal of Abnormal Psychology, 107*, 179–192.

Brown, T. A., Di Nardo, P. A., Lehman, C. L., & Campbell, L. A. (2001). Reliability of *DSM-IV* anxiety and mood disorders: Implications for classification of emotional disorders. *Journal of Abnormal Psychology, 110*, 49–58.

Brown, T. A., Moras, K., Zinbarg, R. E., & Barlow, D. H. (1993). Diagnostic and symptom distinguishability of generalized anxiety disorder and obsessive-compulsive disorder. *Behavior Therapy, 24*, 227–240.

Brown, T. A., O'Leary, T. A., & Barlow, D. H. (1993). Generalized anxiety disorder. In D. H. Barlow (Ed.), *Clinical handbook of psychological disorders* (pp. 137–189). New York: Guilford Press.

Buhr, K., & Dugas, M. J. (2002). The intolerance of uncertainty scale: Psychometric properties of the English version. *Behaviour Research and Therapy, 40*, 931–945.

Buhr, K., & Dugas, M. J. (2006). Investigating the construct validity of intolerance of uncertainty and its unique relationship with worry. *Journal of Anxiety Disorders, 20*, 222–236.

Buhr, K., & Dugas, M. J. (2009). The role of fear of anxiety and intolerance of uncertainty in worry: An experimental manipulation. *Behaviour Research and Therapy, 47*, 215–223.

Butler, G., & Mathews, A. (1983). Cognitive processes in anxiety. *Advances in Behaviour Research and Therapy, 5*, 51–62.

Button, M. L., Westra, H. A., Hara, K. M., & Aviram, A. (2015). Disentangling the impact of resistance and ambivalence on therapy outcomes in cognitive behavioural therapy for generalized anxiety disorder. *Cognitive Behaviour Therapy, 44*, 44–53.

Carleton, R. N. (2012). The intolerance of uncertainty construct in the context of anxiety disorders: Theoretical and practical perspectives. *Expert Review of Neurotherapeutics, 12*, 937–947.

Carleton, R. N., Norton, P. J., & Asmundson, G. J. G. (2007). Fearing the unknown: A short version of the intolerance of uncertainty scale. *Journal of Anxiety Disorders, 21*, 105–117.

Carter, R. M., Wittchen, H. U., Pfister, H., & Kessler, R. C. (2001). One-year prevalence of subthreshold and threshold *DSM-IV* generalized anxiety disorder in a nationally representative sample. *Depression and Anxiety, 13*, 78–88.

Chambless, D. L., Baker, M. J., Baucom, D. H., Beutler, L. E., Calhoun, K. S., Crits-Christoph, P., ... Woody, S. R. (1998). Update on empirically validated therapies, II. *The Clinical Psychologist, 51*, 3–15.

Clark, D. M., & Wells, A. (1995). A cognitive model of social phobia. In R. G. Heimberg, M. R. Liebowitz, D. A. Hope, & F. R. Schneier (Eds.), *Social phobia: Diagnosis, assessment, and treatment* (pp. 69–93). New York: Guilford Press.

Cole, D. A., Peeke, L. G., Martin, J. M., Truglio, R., & Seroczynski, A. D. (1998). A longitudinal look at the relation between depression and anxiety in children and adolescents. *Journal of Consulting and Clinical Psychology, 66*, 451–460.

Comer, J. S., Roy, A. K., Furr, J. M., Gotimer, K., Beidas, R. S., Dugas, M. J., & Kendall, P. C. (2009). The intolerance of uncertainty scale for children: A psychometric evaluation. *Psychological Assessment, 21*, 402–411.

Covin, R., Ouimet, A. J., Seeds, P. M., & Dozois, D. J. A. (2008). A meta-analysis of CBT for pathological worry among clients with GAD. *Journal of Anxiety Disorders, 22*, 108–166.

Cowie, J., Clementi, M. A., & Alfano, C. A. (2016). Examination of the intolerance of uncertainty construct in youth with generalized anxiety disorder. *Journal of Clinical Child and Adolescent Psychology, 47*, 1014–1022.

Crouch, T. A., Lewis, J. A., Erickson, T. M., & Newman, M. G. (2017). Prospective investigation of the contrast avoidance model of generalized anxiety and worry. *Behavior Therapy, 48*, 544–556.

Davey, G. C. L. (1994). Worrying, social problem-solving abilities, and social problem-solving confidence. *Behaviour Research and Therapy, 32*, 327–330.

Davey, G. C. L., Startup, H. M., MacDonald, C. B., Jenkins, D., & Patterson, K. (2005). The use of "as many as can" versus "feel like continuing" stop rules during worrying. *Cognitive Therapy and Research, 29*, 155–169.

Davey, G. C. L., Tallis, F., & Capuzzo, N. (1996). Beliefs about the consequences of worrying. *Cognitive Therapy and Research, 20*, 499–520.

Deschênes, S. S., & Dugas, M. J. (2013). Sudden gains in the cognitive-behavioral treatment of generalized anxiety disorder. *Cognitive Therapy and Research, 37*, 805–811.

Donegan, E., & Dugas, M. J. (2011, November). *Examining the relation between interpretation bias, IU, and symptom change during cognitive-behavioural therapy for generalized anxiety disorder.* Meeting of the Association for Behavioral and Cognitive Therapies, Toronto, ON.

Doucet, C., Ladouceur, R., Freeston, M. H., & Dugas, M. J. (1998). Thèmes d'inquiétudes et tendance à s'inquiéter chez les aînés. [Worry themes and the tendency to worry among older adults.] *Revue Canadienne du Vieillissement, 17*, 361–371.

Dreessen, L., Arntz, A., Luttels, C., & Sallaerts, S. (1994). Personality disorders do not influence the results of cognitive behavior therapies for anxiety disorders. *Comprehensive Psychiatry, 35*, 265–274.

Dugas, M. J., Brillon, P., Savard, P., Turcotte, J., Gaudet, A., Ladouceur, R., . . . Gervais, N. J. (2010). A randomized clinical trial of cognitive-behavioral therapy and applied relaxation for adults with generalized anxiety disorder. *Behavior Therapy, 41*, 46–58.

Dugas, M. J., Freeston, M. H., & Ladouceur, R. (1997). Intolerance of uncertainty and problem orientation in worry. *Cognitive Therapy and Research, 21*, 593–606.

Dugas, M. J., Freeston, M. H., Ladouceur, R., Rhéaume, J., Provencher, M., & Boisvert, J. M. (1998). Worry themes in primary GAD, secondary GAD, and other anxiety disorders. *Journal of Anxiety Disorders, 12*, 253–261.

Dugas, M. J., Freeston, M. H., Provencher, M. D., Lachance, S., Ladouceur, R., & Gosselin, P. (2001). Le Questionnaire sur l'inquiétude et l'anxiété: Validation dans des échantillons non cliniques et cliniques. [The Worry and Anxiety Questionnaire: Validation in clinical and nonclinical samples.] *Journal de Thérapie Comportementale et Cognitive, 11*, 31–36.

Dugas, M. J., Gagnon, F., Ladouceur, R., & Freeston, H. (1998). Generalized Anxiety Disorder: A preliminary test of a conceptual model. *Behaviour Research and Therapy, 36*, 215–226.

Dugas, M. J., Gosselin, P., & Ladouceur, R. (2001). Intolerance of uncertainty and worry: Investigating specificity in a nonclinical sample. *Cognitive Therapy and Research, 25,* 551–558.

Dugas, M. J., Hedayati, M., Karavidas, A., Buhr, K., Francis, K., & Phillips, N. A. (2005). Intolerance of uncertainty and information processing: Evidence of biased recall and interpretations. *Cognitive Therapy and Research, 29,* 57–70.

Dugas, M. J., Ladouceur, R., Léger, E., Freeston, M. H., Langlois, F., Provencher, M. D., & Boisvert, J. M. (2003). Group cognitive-behavioral therapy for generalized anxiety disorder: Treatment outcome and longterm follow-up. *Journal of Consulting and Clinical Psychology, 71,* 821–825.

Dugas, M. J., Langlois, F., Rhéaume, J., & Ladouceur, R. (1998, November). Intolerance of uncertainty and worry: Investigating causality. In J. Stöber (Chair), *Worry: New findings in applied and clinical research.* Symposium conducted at the Annual Convention of the Association for Advancement of Behavior Therapy, Washington, DC.

Dugas, M. J., Laugesen, N., & Bukowski, W. M. (2012). Intolerance of uncertainty, fear of anxiety, and adolescent worry. *Journal of Abnormal Child Psychology, 40,* 863–870.

Dugas, M. J., Letarte, H., Rhéaume, J., Freeston, M. H., & Ladouceur, R. (1995). Worry and problem-solving: Evidence of a specific relationship. *Cognitive Therapy and Research, 19,* 109–120.

Dugas, M. J., Marchand, A., & Ladouceur, R. (2005). Further validation of a cognitive-behavioral model of generalized anxiety disorder: Diagnostic and symptom specificity. *Journal of Anxiety Disorders, 19,* 329–343.

Dugas, M. J., Savard, P., Gaudet, A., Turcotte, J., Laugesen, N., Robichaud, M., . . . Koerner, N. (2007). Can the components of a cognitive model predict the severity of generalized anxiety disorder? *Behavior Therapy, 38,* 169–178.

Dugas, M. J., Schwartz, A., & Francis, K. (2004). Intolerance of uncertainty, worry, and depression. *Cognitive Therapy and Research, 28,* 835–842.

Dupont, R. L., Rice, D. P., Miller, L. S., Shiraki, S. S., Rowland, C. R., & Harwood, H. J. (1996). Economic costs of anxiety disorders. *Anxiety, 2,* 167–172.

D'Zurilla, T. J., & Nezu, A. M. (2006). *Problem-solving therapy: A positive approach to clinical intervention* (3rd ed.). New York: Springer Publishing.

D'Zurilla, T. J., Nezu, A. M., & Maydeu-Olivares, A. (1998). *Manual for the social problem-solving inventory* (Revised). North Tonawanda, NY: Multi-Health Systems.

Eysenck, M. W., Mogg, K., May, J., Richards, A., & Mathews, A. (1991). Bias in interpretation of ambiguous sentences related to threat in anxiety. *Journal of Abnormal Psychology, 100,* 144–150.

First, M. B., Williams, J. B. W., Karg, R. S., & Spitzer, R. L. (2016). *Structured clinical interview for DSM-5 disorders—clinician version (SCID-5-CV).* Washington, DC: American Psychiatric Association Publishing.

Fisher, P. L. (2006). The efficacy of psychological treatments for generalised anxiety disorder. In G. C. L. Davey & A. Wells (Eds.), *Worry and its psychological disorders: Theory, assessment, and treatment* (pp. 359–377). Chichester: Wiley & Sons.

Fracalanza, K., Koerner, N., & Antony, M. M. (2014). Testing a procedural variant of written imaginal exposure for generalized anxiety disorder. *Journal of Anxiety Disorders, 28,* 559–569.

Fracalanza, K., Koerner, N., McShane, K. E., Antony, M. M. (2013, July). *A qualitative investigation of reactions to uncertainty in individuals with generalized anxiety disorder.* Open Paper Presented at the World Congress of Behavioral and Cognitive Therapies, Lima, Peru.

Freeston, M. H., Rhéaume, J., Letarte, H., Dugas, M. J., & Ladouceur, R. (1994). Why do people worry? *Personality and Individual Differences, 17,* 791–802.

Frisch, M. B. (1994). *Quality of life inventory: Manual and treatment guide.* Minneapolis, MN: National Computer Systems.

Goldman, N., Dugas, M. J., Sexton, K. A., & Gervais, N. J. (2007). The impact of written exposure on worry: A preliminary investigation. *Behavior Modification, 31,* 512–538.

Gosselin, P., Ladouceur, R., Langlois, F., Freeston, M. H., Dugas, M. J., & Bertrand, J. (2003). Développement et validation d'un nouvel instrument évaluant les croyances erronées à l'égard des inquiétudes [Development and validation of a new instrument evaluating erroneous beliefs about worry.] *European Review of Applied Psychology, 53,* 199–211.

Gosselin, P., Ladouceur, R., Morin, C. M., Dugas, M. J., & Baillargeon, L. (2006). Benzodiazepine discontinuation among adults with GAD: A randomized trial of cognitive-behavioral therapy. *Journal of Consulting and Clinical Psychology, 74,* 908–919.

Gosselin, P., Ladouceur, R., & Pelletier, O. (2001). Évaluation de l'attitude d'un individu face aux différents problèmes de vie: le Questionnaire d'Attitude face aux Problèmes (QAP) [Evaluation of an individual's attitude toward daily life problems: The Negative Problem Orientation Questionnaire.] *Journal de Thérapie Comportementale et Cognitive, 15,* 141–153.

Gosselin, P., Langlois, F., Freeston, M. H., Ladouceur, R., Dugas, M. J., & Pelletier, O. (2002). Le Questionnaire d'Évitement Cognitif (QEC): Développement et validation auprès d'un échantillon d'adultes et d'adolescents. [The Cognitive Avoidance Questionnaire: Development and validation in adult and adolescent samples]. *Journal de Thérapie Comportementale et Cognitive, 12,* 24–37.

Greenberg, P. E., Sisitsky, T., Kessler, R. C., Finkelstein, S. N., Berndt, E. R., Davidson, J. R. T., . . . Fyer, A. J. (1999). The economic burden of anxiety disorders in the 1990s. *Journal of Clinical Psychiatry, 60,* 427–435.

Hara, K. M., Westra, H. A., Aviram, A., Button, M. L., Constantino, M. J., & Antony, M. M. (2015). Therapist awareness of client resistance in cognitive-behavioral therapy for generalized anxiety disorder. *Cognitive Behaviour Therapy, 44,* 162–174.

Hara, K. M., Westra, H. A., Constantino, M. J., & Antony, M. M. (2018). The impact of resistance on empathy in CBT for generalized anxiety disorder. *Psychotherapy Research, 28,* 606–615.

Hazlett-Stevens, H., & Borkovec, T. D. (2004). Interpretive cues and ambiguity in generalized anxiety disorder. *Behaviour Research and Therapy, 42,* 881–892.

Hebert, E. A., & Dugas, M. J. (2018). Behavioral experiments for intolerance of uncertainty: Challenging the unknown in the treatment of generalized anxiety disorder. *Cognitive and Behavioral Practice.* https://doi.org/10.1016/j.cbpra.2018.07.007

Hebert, E. A., Dugas, M. J., Tulloch, T. G., & Holowka, D. W. (2014). Positive beliefs about worry: A psychometric evaluation of the Why Worry-II. *Personality and Individual Differences, 56,* 3–8.

Hoehn-Saric, R., Hazlett, R. L., & McLeod, D. R. (1993). Generalized anxiety disorder with early and late onset of anxiety symptoms. *Comprehensive Psychiatry, 34,* 291–298.

Hoffman, D. L., Dukes, E. M., & Wittchen, H. U. (2008). Human and economic burden of generalized anxiety disorder. *Depression and Anxiety, 25,* 72–90.

Hoyer, J., Becker, E. S., & Roth, W. T. (2001). Characteristics of worry in GAD patients, social phobics, and controls. *Depression and Anxiety, 13,* 89–96.

Hunt, C., Issakidis, C., & Andrews, G. (2002). *DSM-IV* generalized anxiety disorder in the Australian national survey of mental health and well-being. *Psychological Medicine, 32,* 649–659.

Jacobson, N. S., & Truax, P. (1991). Clinical significance: A statistical approach to defining meaningful change in psychotherapy research. *Journal of Consulting and Clinical Psychology, 59,* 12–19.

Kennedy, B. L., & Schwab, J. J. (1997). Utilization of medical specialists by anxiety disorder patients. *Psychosomatics, 38,* 109–112.

Kessler, R. C., Berglund, P., Demler, O., Jin, R., Merikangas, K. R., & Walters E. E. (2005). Lifetime prevalence and age-of-onset distributions of DSM-IV disorders in the national comorbidity survey replication. *Archives of General Psychiatry, 62,* 593–602.

Kessler, R. C., Chiu, W. T., Demler, O., Merikangas, K. R., & Walters, E. E. (2005). Prevalence, severity, and comorbidity of 12-month DSM-IV disorders in the national comorbidity survey replication. *Archives of General Psychiatry, 62,* 617–627.

Kessler, R. C., Keller, M. B., & Wittchen, H. U. (2001). The epidemiology of generalized anxiety disorder. *Psychiatric Clinics of North America, 24,* 19–39.

Kessler, R. C., McGonagle, K. A., Zhao, S., Nelson, C. B., Hugues, M., Eshleman, S., . . . Kendler, K. S. (1994). Lifetime and 12-month prevalence of *DSM-III-R* psychiatric disorders in the United States. *Archives of General Psychiatry, 51,* 8–19.

Kessler, R. C., Walters, E. E., & Wittchen, H. U. (2004). Epidemiology. In R. G. Heimberg, C. L. Turk, & D. S. Mennin (Eds.), *Generalized anxiety disorder: Advances in research and practice* (pp. 29–50). New York: Guilford Press.

Koerner, N., & Dugas, M. J. (2008). An investigation of appraisals in individuals vulnerable to excessive worry: The role of intolerance of uncertainty. *Cognitive Therapy and Research, 32,* 619–638.

Koerner, N., Dugas, M. J., Savard, P., Gaudet, A., Turcotte, J., & Marchand, A. (2004). The economic burden of anxiety disorders in Canada. *Canadian Psychology, 45,* 191–201.

Koerner, N., Fitzpatrick, S., Fracalanza, K., & McShane, K. (2016, September). *Maladaptive self-schemas and core fears in generalized anxiety disorder.* Open Paper Presented at the meeting of the European Association for Behavioural and Cognitive Therapies, Stockholm, Sweden.

Koerner, N., Mejia, T., & Kusec, A. (2017). What's in a name? Intolerance of uncertainty, other uncertainty-relevant constructs, and their differential relations to worry and generalized anxiety disorder. *Cognitive Behaviour Therapy, 46,* 141–161.

Koerner, N., & Prusaczyk, E. (2016, September). Development and initial testing of a cognitively-enhanced written exposure procedure for Generalized Anxiety Disorder. In N. Koerner (Chair), *New developments in the cognitive-behavioural conceptualization and treatment of generalized anxiety disorder.* Symposium Presented at the Meeting of the European Association for Behavioural and Cognitive Therapies, Stockholm, Sweden.

Kraemer, H. C., Kazdin, A. E., Offord, D. R., Kessler, R. C., Jensen, P. S., & Kupfer, D. J. (1997). Coming to terms with the terms of risk. *Archives of General Psychiatry, 54,* 337–343.

Labrecque, J., Dugas, M. J., Marchand, A., & Letarte, A. (2006). Cognitive-behavioral therapy for comorbid generalized anxiety disorder and panic disorder with agoraphobia. *Behavior Modification, 30,* 383–410.

Ladouceur, R., Blais, F., Freeston, M. H., & Dugas, M. J. (1998). Problem solving and problem orientation in generalized anxiety disorder. *Journal of Anxiety Disorders, 12,* 139–152.

Ladouceur, R., Dugas, M. J., Freeston, M. H., Léger, E., Gagnon, F., & Thibodeau, N. (2000). Efficacy of a cognitive-behavioral treatment for generalized anxiety disorder: Evaluation in a controlled clinical trial. *Journal of Consulting and Clinical Psychology, 68,* 957–964.

Ladouceur, R., Dugas, M. J., Freeston, M. H., Rhéaume, J., Blais, F., Boisvert, J. M., . . . Thibodeau, N. (1999). Specificity of generalized anxiety disorder symptoms and processes. *Behavior Therapy, 30,* 191–207.

Ladouceur, R., Gosselin, P., & Dugas, M. J. (2000). Experimental manipulation of intolerance of uncertainty: A study of a theoretical model of worry. *Behaviour Research and Therapy, 38,* 933–941.

Ladouceur, R., Talbot, F., & Dugas, M. J. (1997). Behavioral expressions of intolerance of uncertainty in worry. *Behavior Modification, 21*, 355–371.

Laugesen, N., Dugas, M. J., & Bukowski, W. M. (2003). Understanding adolescent worry: The application of a cognitive model. *Journal of Abnormal Child Psychology, 31*, 55–64.

Léger, E., Dugas, M. J., Langlois, F., & Ladouceur, R. (1998, November). *Motivation, expectations and therapeutic relationship as predictors of outcome in the treatment of GAD.* Poster Session Presented at the Annual Convention of the Association for Advancement of Behavior Therapy, Washington, DC.

Logue, M. B., Thomas, A. M., Barbee, J. G., Hoehn-Saric, R., Maddock, R. J., Schwab, J., . . . Beitman, B. D. (1993). Generalized anxiety disorder patients seek evaluation for cardiological symptoms at the same frequency as patients with panic disorder. *Journal of Psychiatric Research, 27*, 55–59.

Luhmann, C. C., Ishida, K., & Hajcak, G. (2011). Intolerance of uncertainty and decisions about delayed, probabilistic rewards. *Behavior Therapy, 42*, 378–386.

Maier, W., Gansicke, M., Freyberger, H. J., Linz, M., Heun, R., & Lecrubier, Y. (2000). Generalized anxiety disorder (ICD—10) in primary care from a cross—cultural perspective: A valid diagnostic entity? *Acta Psychiatrica Scandinavica, 101*, 29–36.

Marker, I., & Norton, P. J. (2018). The efficacy of incorporating motivational interviewing to cognitive behavior therapy for anxiety disorders: A review and meta-analysis. *Clinical Psychology Review, 62*, 1–10.

Maser, J. D. (1998). Generalized anxiety disorder and its comorbidities: Disputes at the boundaries. *Acta Psychiatrica Scandinavica, 98*, 12–22.

McManus, F., Van Doorn, K., & Yiend, J. (2012). Examining the effects of thought records and behavioral experiments in instigating belief change. *Journal of Behavior Therapy and Experimental Psychiatry, 43*, 540–547.

Meeten, F., Dash, S. R., Scarlet, A. L. S., & Davey, G. C. L. (2012). Investigating the effect of intolerance of uncertainty on catastrophic worrying and mood. *Behaviour Research and Therapy, 50*, 690–698.

Mennin, D. S., Fresco, D. M., O'Toole, M. S., & Heimberg, R. G. (2018). A randomized controlled trial of emotion regulation therapy for generalized anxiety disorder with and without co-occurring depression. *Journal of Consulting and Clinical Psychology, 86*, 268–281.

Mennin, D. S., Heimberg, R. G., Turk, C. L., & Fresco, D. M. (2002). Applying an emotion regulation framework to integrative approaches to generalized anxiety disorder. *Clinical Psychology: Science and Practice, 9*, 85–90.

Mennin, D. S., Heimberg, R. G., Turk, C. L., & Fresco, D. M. (2005). Preliminary evidence for an emotion dysregulation model of generalized anxiety disorder. *Behaviour Research and Therapy, 43*, 1281–1310.

Metzger, R. L., Miller, M. L., Cohen, M., & Sofka, M., Borkovec, T. D. (1990). Worry changes decision making: The effect of negative thoughts on cognitive processing. *Journal of Clinical Psychology, 46*, 78–88.

Meyer, T. J., Miller, M. L., Metzger, R. L., & Borkovec, T. D. (1990). Development and validation of the Penn state worry questionnaire. *Behaviour Research and Therapy, 28*, 487–495.

Miller, W. R., & Rollnick, S. (2002). *Motivational interviewing: Preparing people for change* (2nd ed.). New York: Guilford Press.

Miller, W. R., & Rollnick, S. (2012). *Motivational interviewing: Helping people change* (3rd ed.). New York: Guilford Press.

Mitte, K. (2005). Meta-analysis of cognitive-behavioral treatments for generalized anxiety disorder: A comparison with pharmacotherapy. *Psychological Bulletin, 131*, 785–795.

Mogg, K., Bradley, B. P., Miller, T., & Potts, H. (1994). Interpretation of homophones related to threat: Anxiety or response bias effects? *Cognitive Therapy and Research, 18,* 461–477.

Molina, S., & Borkovec, T. D. (1994). The Penn state worry questionnaire: Psychometric properties and associated characteristics. In G. C. L. Davey & F. Tallis (Eds.), *Perspectives on theory, assessment, and treatment* (pp. 265–283). Chichester, UK: Wiley.

Newman, M. G., Jacobson, N. C., Erickson, T. M., & Fisher, A. J. (2017). Interpersonal problems predict differential response to cognitive versus behavioral treatment in a randomized controlled trial. *Behavior Therapy, 48,* 56–68.

Newman, M. G., Llera, S. J., Erickson, T. M., Przeworski, A., & Castonguay, L. G. (2013). Worry and generalized anxiety disorder: A review and theoretical synthesis of evidence on nature, etiology, mechanisms, and treatment. *Annual Review of Clinical Psychology, 9,* 275–297.

Newman, M. G., Przeworski, A., Fisher, A. J., & Borkovec, T. D. (2010). Diagnostic comorbidity in adults with generalized anxiety disorder: Impact of comorbidity on psychotherapy outcome and impact of psychotherapy on comorbid diagnoses. *Behavior Therapy, 41,* 59–72.

Nolen-Hoeksema, S. (1998). The other end of the continuum: The costs of rumination. *Psychological Inquiry, 9,* 216–219.

Olatunji, B. O., Moretz, M. W., & Zlomke, K. R. (2010). Linking cognitive avoidance and GAD symptoms: The mediating role of fear of emotion. *Behaviour Research and Therapy, 48,* 435–441.

Osmanağaoğlu, N., Creswell, C., & Dodd, H. F. (2018). Intolerance of uncertainty, anxiety, and worry in children and adolescents: A meta-analysis. *Journal of Affective Disorders, 225,* 80–90.

Öst, L. G., & Breitholtz, E. (2000). Applied relaxation vs. cognitive therapy in the treatment of generalized anxiety disorder. *Behaviour Research and Therapy, 38,* 770–790.

Ovanessian, M. M., Koerner, N., Antony, M. M., & Dugas, M. J. (2018). *A preliminary test of the therapeutic potential of written exposure with rescripting for generalized anxiety disorder.* Manuscript submitted for publication.

Paivio, A. (1991). Dual coding theory: Retrospect and current status. *Canadian Journal of Psychology, 45,* 255–287.

Pawluk, E. J., & Koerner, N. (2013). A preliminary investigation of impulsivity in generalized anxiety disorder. *Personality and Individual Differences, 54,* 732–737.

Pawluk, E. J., & Koerner, N. (2016). The relationship between negative urgency and generalized anxiety disorder symptoms: The role of intolerance of negative emotions and intolerance of uncertainty of uncertainty. *Anxiety, Stress, & Coping, 29,* 606–615.

Pepperdine, E., Lomax, C., & Freeston, M. H. (2018). Disentangling intolerance of uncertainty and threat appraisal in everyday situations. *Journal of Anxiety Disorders, 57,* 31–38.

Prochaska, J. O., & Norcross, J. C. (2001). Stages of change. *Psychotherapy, 38,* 443–448.

Provencher, M. D., Dugas, M. J., & Ladouceur, R. (2004). Efficacy of problem-solving training and cognitive exposure in the treatment of generalized anxiety disorder: A case replication series. *Cognitive and Behavioral Practice, 11,* 404–414.

Provencher, M. D., Freeston, M. H., Dugas, M. J., & Ladouceur, R. (2000). Catastrophizing assessment of worry and threat schemata among worriers. *Behavioural and Cognitive Psychotherapy, 28,* 211–224.

Provencher, M. D., Ladouceur, R., & Dugas, M. J. (2006). La comorbidité dans le trouble d'anxiété généralisée: Prévalence et évolution suite à une thérapie cognitivo-comportementale

[Comorbidity in generalized anxiety disorder: Prevalence and course after cognitive-behavioural therapy.] *Canadian Journal of Psychiatry, 51,* 91–99.

Pruzinsky, T., & Borkovec, T. D. (1990). Cognitive and personality characteristics of worriers. *Behaviour Research and Therapy, 28,* 507–512.

Przeworski, A., Newman, M. G., Pincus, A. L., Kasoff, M. B., Yamasaki, A. S., Castonguay, L. G., & Berlin, K. S. (2011). Interpersonal pathoplasticity in individuals with generalized anxiety disorder. *Journal of Abnormal Psychology, 120,* 286–298.

Rapee, R. M. (1991). Generalized anxiety disorder: A review of clinical features and theoretical concepts. *Clinical Psychology Review, 11,* 419–440.

Robichaud, M. (2005). *An in-depth examination of social problem-solving ability* (Doctoral dissertation). Retrieved from http://spectrum.library.concordia.ca/

Robichaud, M., & Dugas, M. J. (2005a). Negative problem orientation (part I): Psychometric properties of a new measure. *Behaviour Research and Therapy, 43,* 391–401.

Robichaud, M., & Dugas, M. J. (2005b). Negative problem orientation (part II): Construct validity and specificity to worry. *Behaviour Research and Therapy, 43,* 403–412.

Robichaud, M., Dugas, M. J., & Conway, M. (2003). Gender differences in worry and associated cognitive-behavioral variables. *Journal of Anxiety Disorders, 17,* 501–516.

Roemer, L., & Orsillo, S. M. (2002). Expanding our conceptualization of and treatment for generalized anxiety disorder: Integrating mindfulness/acceptance-based approaches with existing cognitive-behavioral models. *Clinical Psychology: Science and Practice, 9,* 54–68.

Roemer, L., Orsillo, S. M., & Salters-Pedneault, K. (2008). Efficacy of an acceptance-based behavior therapy for generalized anxiety disorder: Evaluation in a randomized controlled trial. *Journal of Consulting and Clinical Psychology, 76,* 1083–1089.

Roemer, L., Salters, K., Raffa, S. D., & Orsillo, S. M. (2005). Fear and avoidance of internal experiences in GAD: Preliminary tests of a conceptual model. *Cognitive Therapy and Research, 29,* 71–88.

Roy-Byrne, P. P., & Katon, W. (1997). Generalized anxiety disorder in primary care: The precursor/modifier pathway to increased healthcare utilization. *Journal of Clinical Psychiatry, 58,* 34–38.

Ruscio, A. M., Hallion, L. S., Lim, C. C. W., Aguilar-Gaxiola, S., Al-Hamzawi, A., Alonso J., . . . Scott, K. M. (2017). Cross-sectional comparison of the epidemiology of DSM-5 generalized anxiety disorder across the globe. *JAMA Psychiatry, 74,* 465–475.

Salkovskis, P. M. (1991). The importance of behaviour in the maintenance of anxiety and panic: A cognitive account. *Behavioural and Cognitive Psychotherapy, 19,* 6–19.

Salzer, S., Pincus, A. L., Hoyer, J., Kreische, R., Leichsenring, F., & Leibing, E. (2008). Interpersonal subtypes within generalized anxiety disorder. *Journal of Personality Assessment, 90,* 292–299.

Sanderson, W. C., Wetzler, S., Beck, A. T., & Betz, F. (1994). Prevalence of personality disorders among patients with anxiety disorders. *Psychiatry Research, 51,* 167–174.

Schmidt, N. B., Zvolensky, M. J., & Maner, J. K. (2006). Anxiety sensitivity: Prospective prediction of panic attacks and Axis I pathology. *Journal of Psychiatric Research, 40,* 691–699.

Sexton, K. A., & Dugas, M. J. (2008). The cognitive avoidance questionnaire: Validation of the English translation. *Journal of Anxiety Disorders, 22,* 355–370.

Sexton, K. A., & Dugas, M. J. (2009a). Defining distinct negative beliefs about uncertainty: Validating the factor structure of the intolerance of uncertainty scale. *Psychological Assessment, 21,* 176–186.

Sexton, K. A., & Dugas, M. J. (2009b). An investigation of factors associated with cognitive avoidance in worry. *Cognitive Therapy and Research, 33,* 150–162.

Shirneshan, E., Bailey, J., Relyea, G., Franklin, B. E., Solomon, D. K., & Brown, L. M. (2013). Incremental direct medical expenditures associated with anxiety disorders for the U.S. adult population: Evidence from the medical expenditure panel survey. *Journal of Anxiety Disorders, 27,* 720–727.

Sprujit-Metz, D., & Sprujit-Metz, R. (1997). Worries and health in adolescence: A latent variable approach. *Journal of Youth and Adolescence, 26,* 485–501.

Stanley, M. A., & Novy, D. M. (2000). Cognitive-behavior therapy for generalized anxiety in late life: An evaluative overview. *Journal of Anxiety Disorders, 14,* 191–207.

Stein, M. B. (2004). Public health perspectives on generalized anxiety disorder. *Journal of Clinical Psychiatry, 65,* 3–7.

Stein, M. B., & Heimberg, R. G. (2004). Well-being and life satisfaction in generalized anxiety disorder: Comparison to major depressive disorder in a community sample. *Journal of Affective Disorders, 79,* 161–166.

Stöber, J., & Borkovec, T. D. (2002). Reduced concreteness of worry in generalized anxiety disorder: Findings from a therapy study. *Cognitive Therapy and Research, 26,* 89–96.

Talbot, F., Dugas, M. J., & Ladouceur, R. (1999). Intolérance à l'incertitude et inquiétude: Effet de l'induction d'anxiété [Intolerance of uncertainty and worry: Effect of anxiety induction]. *Revue Francophone de Clinique Comportementale et Cognitive, 4,* 5–10.

Tallis, F., Eysenck, M., & Mathews, A. (1991). Elevated evidence requirements and worry. *Personality and Individual Differences, 12,* 21–27.

Tang, T. Z., & DeRubeis, R. J. (1999). Sudden gains and critical sessions in cognitive-behavioral therapy for depression. *Journal of Consulting and Clinical Psychology, 67,* 894–904.

Taylor, S., Zvolensky, M. J., Cox, B. J., Deacon, B., Heimberg, R. G., Ledley, D. R., . . . Cardenas, S. J. (2007). Robust dimensions of anxiety sensitivity: Development and initial validation of the anxiety sensitivity index-3. *Psychological Assessment, 19,* 176–188.

Thielsch, C., Andor, T., & Ehring, T. (2015). Do metacognitions and intolerance of uncertainty predict worry in everyday life? An ecological momentary assessment study. *Behavior Therapy, 46,* 532–543.

Torbit, L., & Laposa, J. M. (2016). Group CBT for GAD: The role of change in intolerance of uncertainty in treatment outcomes. *International Journal of Cognitive Therapy, 9,* 356–368.

Trope, Y., & Liberman, N. (2010). Construal-level theory of psychological distance. *Psychological Review, 117,* 440–463.

Üstün, T. B., & Sartorius, N. (Eds.). (1995). *Mental illness in general health care: An international study.* Chichester, UK: Wiley.

van der Heiden, C., Muris, P., & van der Molen, H. T. (2012). Randomized controlled trial on the effectiveness of metacognitive therapy and intolerance-of-uncertainty therapy for generalized anxiety disorder. *Behaviour Research and Therapy, 50,* 100–109.

Vasey, M. W., & Borkovec, T. D. (1992). A catastrophizing assessment of worrisome thoughts. *Cognitive Therapy and Research, 16,* 505–520.

Vrana, S. R., Cuthbert, B. N., & Lang, P. J. (1986). Fear imagery and text processing. *Psychophysiology, 23,* 247–253.

Wegner, D. M., & Zanakos, S. (1994). Chronic thought suppression. *Journal of Personality, 62,* 615–640.

Wells, A. (2006). Metacognitive therapy for worry and generalized anxiety disorder. In G. C. L. Davey & A. Wells (Eds.), *Worry and psychological disorders: Theory, assessment and treatment* (pp. 259–272). Chichester, UK: Wiley.

Wells, A., & Carter, K. (1999). Preliminary tests of a cognitive model of generalized anxiety disorder. *Behaviour Research and Therapy, 37,* 585–594.

Westra, H. A., Arkowitz, H., & Dozois, D. J. A. (2009). Adding a motivational interviewing pretreatment to cognitive behavioral therapy for generalized anxiety disorder: A preliminary randomized controlled trial. *Journal of Anxiety Disorders, 23,* 1106–1117.

Westra, H. A., Constantino, M. J., & Antony, M. M. (2016). Integrating motivational interviewing with cognitive-behavioral therapy for severe generalized anxiety disorder: An allegiance-controlled randomized clinical trial. *Journal of Consulting and Clinical Psychology, 84,* 768–782.

Westra, H. A., & Stewart, S. H. (1998). Cognitive behavioural therapy and pharmacotherapy: Complementary or contradictory approaches to the treatment of anxiety? *Clinical Psychology Review, 18,* 307–340.

Williams, J. B. W., Gibbon, M., First, M. B., Spitzer, R. L., Davies, M., Borus, J., Wittchen, H-U. (1992). The structured clinical interview for DSMIII-R (SCID): II. Multisite test-retest reliability. *Archives of General Psychiatry, 49,* 630–636.

Williams, K. E., & Chambless, D. L. (1990). The relationship between therapist characteristics and outcome of *in vivo* exposure treatment for agoraphobia. *Behavior Therapy, 21,* 111–116.

Wittchen, H. U. (2002). Generalized anxiety disorder: Prevalence, burden, and cost to society. *Depression and Anxiety, 16,* 162–171.

Wittchen, H. U., Carter, R. M., Pfister, H., Montgomery, S. A., & Kessler, R. C. (2000). Disabilities and quality of life in pure and comorbid generalized anxiety disorder and major depression in a national survey. *International Clinical Psychopharmacology, 15,* 319–328.

Wittchen, H. U., Kessler, R. C., Beesdo, K., Krause, P., Höfler, M., & Hoyer, J. (2002). Generalized anxiety and depression in primary care: Prevalence, recognition, and management. *Journal of Clinical Psychiatry, 63,* 24–34.

Wittchen, H. U., Zhao, Z., Kessler, R. C., & Eaton, W. W. (1994). DSM-III-R generalized anxiety disorder in the national comorbidity survey. *Archives of General Psychiatry, 51,* 355–364.

Wolitzky-Taylor, K. B., Arch, J. J., Rosenfield, D., & Craske, M. G. (2012). Moderators and non-specific predictors of treatment outcome for anxiety disorders: A comparison of cognitive behavioral therapy to acceptance and commitment therapy. *Journal of Consulting and Clinical Psychology, 80,* 786–799.

Woody, S., & Rachman, S. (1994). Generalized anxiety disorder as an unsuccessful search for safety. *Clinical Psychology Review, 14,* 743–753.

Yonkers, K. A., Warshaw, M. G., Massion, A. O., & Keller, M. B. (1996). Phenomenology and course of generalised anxiety disorder. *British Journal of Psychiatry, 168,* 308–313.

Zanarini, M. C., Skodol, A. E., Bender, D., Dolan, R., Sanislow, C., Schaefer, E., . . . Gunderson, J. G. (2000). The collaborative longitudinal personality disorders study: Reliability of Axis I and II diagnoses. *Journal of Personality Disorders, 14,* 291–299.

Zinbarg, R. E., Craske, M. G., & Barlow, D. H. (2006). *Mastery of your anxiety and worry* (2nd ed.). Oxford, UK: Oxford University Press.

Index

Note: Page numbers in *italics* indicate figures, in **bold** indicate tables.

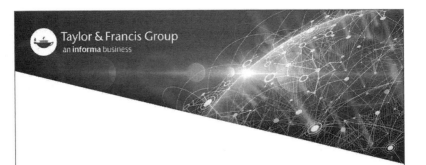